NOTES FROM INDOCHINA

on ethnic
minority cultures

edited by

Marilyn Gregerson

and

Dorothy Thomas

SIL MUSEUM OF ANTHROPOLOGY
Dallas, Texas
1980

© Summer Institute of Linguistics, Inc. 1980
Library of Congress Catalog Card Number: 78–65445
ISBN 0–88312–155–7

Cover design by Jerry Jenkins
Illustrations by David Blood and others

This title available at:

SIL Museum of Anthropology
7500 W. Camp Wisdom Road
Dallas, TX 75236

CONTENTS

MAPS

ILLUSTRATIONS

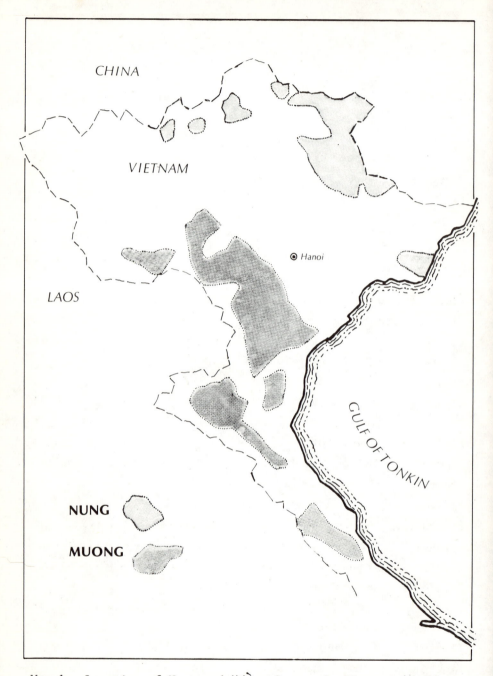

CHINA

VIETNAM

LAOS

Hanoi

GULF OF TONKIN

NUNG

MUONG

Map 1. Location of Nung and Mường Groups in Vietnam (Northern
Section.
Map 2 (opposite page). Ethnic Minorities of Vietnam (Southern
Section).

x

BRŪ

• *Quang Tri*

PACŎH

• *Hue*

PHUONG

KATU

• *Danang*

SOUTH CHINA SEA

TAKUA

JEH   CUA   • *Quang Ngai*

DUAN

KATUA

KAYONG

SEDANG   HRÊ

RENGAO

TODRAH

MONOM

HALĀNG

• *Kontum*

BAHNAR

LEGEND

Language Boundary: ·········

Language Name: BAHNAR

Place Names: *Banmethuot*

Northern Resettled Groups:

MÁN, *near Banmethuot,*

MUONG, *near Banmethuot, Tuc Trung*

WHITE TAI, *near Dalat,*

BLACK TAI, *near Dalat, Pleiku*

NUNG, *near Dalat,*

THỒ, *near Dalat, Long Khanh*

This map does not show any resettlements.

• *Pleiku*

JARAI

• *Phu Bon*

HAROI

RADE

• *Banmethuot*

• *Qui Nhon*

⊙ *Tuy Hoa*

E. MNONG

C. MNONG

N. ROGLAI

• *Nha Trang*

• *Dalat*

S. ROGLAI

CHRU

• *Phan Rang*

STIENG

W. CHAM

KOHO

S. ROGLAI

CHAM

SAIGON

CHRAU

JRO

CHRU

⊙ *Chau Doc*

W. CHAM

xi

PREFACE

This collection of articles on the minority groups of Vietnam was compiled by members of the Summer Institute of Linguistics. All the authors except one, Mr. John J. Davis, formerly of the Overseas Missionary Fellowship, are members of the SIL. Also, Mr. Davis' article is the only one from outside Vietnam (the Nyaheun are in southern Laos, west of old Kontum province in Vietnam).

The two articles on music, "Jeh Music," by Nancy Cohen, and "Rengao Vocal Music" show how prescribed the uses of music are in these closely related groups. Various types of music have specific times and uses.

The discussion of "A First Case of Historiography among the Roglai of Vietnam" by Maxwell Cobbey indicates the value of listening to in-culture interpretations of history to understand the values and motivations of that culture. "Notes on Chrau Ethnogeography" by David Thomas shows how place names have survived intact or have been changed by other languages. "Sedang Astronomy," by Wanda Jennings, also shows survivals of linguistic terms after cultural items have passed out of existence.

"Cross-Cousin Marriage and Chru Kinship Terminology" by Eugene E. Fuller shows the relationship between the Chru language and the practice of cross-cousin marriage.

The articles by Milton Barker, "House Construction among Mường Refugees," and Janice Saul, "Nung Weddings," describe aspects of life among refugees from the north who resettled in the south. Both of these groups have retained their old culture in a new environment, making only minor adaptations. In years to come it will be interesting to see if the large number of Black Tai refugees in France and Iowa can retain their culture, or if they will completely assimilate to their surrounding cultures.

Marilyn J. Gregerson's article "Notes on Rengao Law" points out the importance of good relations with all members of the community, and the mechanisms for restoring good relations after an offense has been committed. She presents eight actual cases where the law was invoked.

John J. Davis wrote "Nyaheun Medicine and Some Problems Posed to Western Medical Practice" while medical help to the Nyaheun was still a possibility for westerners. However, his critique of the problems involved shows again how important it is for those involved in culture change to be aware of the import of their activities.

The article "Mnong Lăm Texts on Sacrifice and Shamanism" presented by Evangeline Blood gives an inside view of the Mnong religious beliefs and the significance of various practices. The author was himself the son of a shaman so he knew intimately what he presented. Mrs. Blood has brought together several texts which he had written out in longhand, and in some cases she has gathered information on the same subject from several texts. Nung practices as reported in "Nung Weddings" by Janice Saul are quite different, and the Nung have professional priests.

"Death and Burial in Katu Culture" by Nancy Costello highlights the different kinds of death and the different types of burial involved. (See also Mnong Lăm, Stieng, and Cham articles in this volume.) This is common throughout the south -- the Cham are a Malayo-Polynesian group, but the Stieng and Katu, both Mon-Khmer groups isolated from the Malayo-Polynesian groups in Vietnam, have the same distinction. The Mnong texts show that for them, at least, a different spirit is involved in death from violence.

In "Aspects of Cham Culture," Doris Blood describes the life of the Hinduized Cham who stayed behind when the aristocracy fled the Vietnamese conquerors centuries ago (Lebar et al., pg. 246). Their strong matrilineal matrilocal ties have kept them distinct from the Vietnamese long after Vietnamese rule was imposed.

Lorraine Haupers' "Notes on Stieng Life" is especially interesting when compared with a description of Stieng life 100 years ago by a Catholic missionary, H. Azemar. Where they

cover the same subjects, there is surprising agreement in spite
of the fact that Père Azemar was with the Bu Deh, a different
subgroup from the Bu Lo where the Haupers worked. The major
points of difference relate to marriage customs and adoption of
a cash economy. Azemar reported little polygamy, divorce not
permitted (except perhaps for sterility), and that in cases of
adultery the woman was presumed innocent. Azemar also described
unlimited jungle; now there are extensive rubber plantations in
the area, although much jungle still remains. The Haupers say
that the Bu Deh tend to be more progressive than the Bu Lo, but
even the Bu Lo have much more dependence on a cash economy now
than the Stieng of Azemar's day.

Until the last decade or so most of the ethnographic work
in this area was done in French. For a complete bibliography
up to 1950, see:

Embree, John F. and Lillian Ota Dotson, *Bibliography of the
Peoples and Cultures of Mainland Southeast Asia,* Yale U., New
Haven, 1950. 821 pp. plus addenda of 12 pp. Covers Assam,
Burma, South China, Thailand, Laos, Cambodia, Vietnam; both
majority and minority groups.

In the past decade several books have come out in English
with good summaries of previous work:

Lebar, Frank M., Gerald C. Hickey and John K. Musgrave, *Ethnic
Groups of Mainland Southeast Asia.* HRAF Press, New Haven,
1964. 288 pp. Covers ethnic groups by families: Sino-
Tibetan, Austro-asiatic, Tai-Kadai, Malayo-Polynesian. Short
ethnographic sketches gathered from the literature. Good
bibliography, large map included.

Mole, Robert L., *The Montagnards of South Vietnam, A Study of
Nine Tribes.* Charles E. Tuttle Co., Rutland, Vermont and
Tokyo, 1970. 277 pp. Sketches of nine groups in Vietnam
from the 17th parallel south to Northern Kontum province.
Information gathered from the literature and personal corre-
spondence with observers. Maps and some illustrations.

Schrock, Joann L., et al., *Minority Groups in North Vietnam,*
U.S. Govt. Printing Office, Washington, D.C., 1972. 653 pp.
Covers the Black Tai, Laqua, Lati, Lolo, Man, Meo, Mường,

Nhang, Nung, Puok, Red Tai, Tho, White Tai. Each group is
discussed under Introduction, Background, Individual Charac-
teristics, Social Structure, Customs and Taboos, Political
Organization. Good maps for each group, some illustrations.
Information taken from the literature.
Schrock, Joann L., et al., U.S. Govt. Printing Office, Washington, D.C., 1966. 1163 pp. Similar organization to the
companion volume above. Covers the Bahnar, Bru, Cua, Halang,
Hre, Hroi, Jeh, Katu, Koho, Ma, M'nong, Muong, Raglai, Rengao,
Rhade, Sedang, Stieng, Cham, Khmer, Indian and Pakistani
ethnic groups, as well as the Hoa Hao and Cao Dai religious
groups and the Binh Xuyen political group. (The Chrau are
included under the Koho.)

There is a companion volume to this present one:
Gregerson, Marilyn, ed., *Southeast Asia*, Vol. II, no. 1,
winter 1972. 157 pp. Has articles on Chrau, Northern Roglai,
Jeh, Bru, Black Tai, Katu, Bahnar, Nung. Some photographs,
maps.

A book previously published in French is in press in an
English translation:
Condominas, Georges, *Nous avons mangé la forêt*, Paris, Mercure
de France, 1957.

The editors wish to acknowledge the valuable suggestions of
Kenneth Gregerson on the presentation of various papers
throughout the volume. Julie Blom's contribution in typing a
number of papers for the manuscript is also greatly appreciated.

                              Dorothy M. Thomas

                              Marilyn Gregerson

HOUSE CONSTRUCTION AMONG MƯỜNG REFUGEES

Milton E. Barker

The typical Mường house, as the Mường people probably built them in their native area of North Vietnam, was on pilings with bamboo walls and floor and a thatched roof, but those refugees who moved south adapted their housing to available materials and to patterns of their Vietnamese neighbors.

Perhaps the most common adaptation is that of building the house directly on the ground. This type of house is called a 'dirt house' (nhà tất) as opposed to a 'floor house' (nhà khành), which has a floor built up off the ground on pilings. Vietnamese country people also live in thatch-roofed houses with dirt floors, so perhaps this is a sign of Mường acculturation to Vietnamese. In one instance in which a Mường man was married to a Vietnamese woman, half their house had a raised bamboo floor, and the other half a dirt floor.

Some adaptations are due to the scarcity of bamboo within walking distance of the village. Wood is substituted for bamboo in certain functions. For example, corrugated aluminum is used for roofing; mud or boards for walls, floors, or windows. The only brick house with a tile roof in the village of Hòa Bình, other than the government district offices, belonged to the Vietnamese man who owned the brick kiln.

When my family and I first moved to the village of Hòa Bình, we bought a typical Mường house. We soon found several things, however, that presented problems. Much of our work in the village was research and, we thought, demanded the use of a desk. A split bamboo floor, however, is incompatible with the use of tables and chairs--the legs keep going through the floor! Further, low walls and overhanging roof reduce the amount of light in the house. My wife found herself cooking the noon meal by flashlight, and we often lit our lamp when we wanted to do paper work during the day. Our solution to these problems was to have another section added to our house which was basically Mường construction, but with some adaptations suited to our own needs.

1

We insisted that the outside walls be at least six feet high.
Our Mường contractor accomplished this by having the roof come
down only as far as the main posts, and not using any porch posts
at all. We had windows installed on all sides of the house instead of one. Our floor was of hand-sawn planks, 1-1/4 inches
thick. These rested directly on the floor beams, so our floor
was composed of only two parts instead of the usual four. Since
we had no porch posts, our main roof beams, transverse and longitudinal, served also as eave poles.

Usually a large group of men work together in erecting the
framework of a house and putting on the roof. Twenty or so
men can do that much in one day for an average-sized house.
They work in exchange for a meal which is provided by the
owner of the house. After the roof is on, the owner of the
house works alone, or with one or two helpers, to complete
the floor and walls. This requires several more days.

Alternatively, one may hire a contractor, as we did, who
in turn will hire a few men to work for him. The construction of a house takes longer this way.

Building the House. When a new house (nhà) is built, all
the materials are cut and brought to the building site first.
At the building site, post-holes (hú tô) are dug (tào), and
the posts (tô) are set into them. There are three kinds of
posts used in a typical Mường house: main posts (tô cái),
porch posts (tô hiên), and supporting posts (tô tâl). The
posts of a house employing four main posts would be arranged
as in Figure 1. Each house will have
at least four main posts which extend
high enough to support the main roof
beams. A larger house may require the
use of six or eight main posts. Each
of these posts has a hole through it
to allow the floor beam (lat or ruồng)
to pass through. The top of each main
post is left with a point entending
high enough to pass through a hole
near the end of the transverse roof
beam (khú) and hold the longitudinal
roof beam (tồn thay) in place (Figure 2). The porch posts are shorter
than the main posts, extending only
high enough to support the eave poles.

Figure 1. Typical House
Post Arrangement.

of the roof. Each of the porch posts, like the main posts,
also has a hole for the floor beams. The top of each post is
slotted to allow the
eave poles to rest
on them. The tops
of the corner porch
posts are slotted
both ways to hold
two eave poles.
The supporting posts
are shortest of all,
only high enough to
support the floor
beams. The top of
each supporting
post is slotted to allow the floor
beams to rest on it.

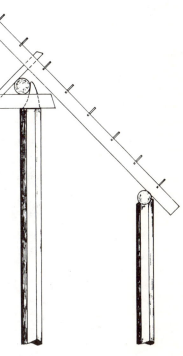

   When the posts are in place with
their tops level and lines between
them forming right angles, or as
nearly so as can be judged by the
naked eye, the floor beams are set in
place. Following that, the transverse and longitudinal roof beams are
put in place. There is one transverse
roof beam for each pair of main posts.
Each transverse roof beam has a hole
near each end through which passes the
point on the top of the main post.
The longitudinal roof beams are laid   Figure 2. Posts,
on top of the transverse roof beams   Beams, and Rafters.
just inside the points of the main
posts. The eave poles are set in place in the slots on top of
the porch posts. All of the posts, roof beams, and eave poles
are axe-hewn, generally in an octagonal shape. The posts are
approximately 8 to 12 inches in diameter, the roof beams about
6 inches in diameter, and the eave poles about 4 to 5 inches
in diameter. Sometimes, however, the transverse roof beams
may be as large or larger than the posts. Up to this point,
nothing has been nailed or tied together, but the connections
depend wholly on the use of slots and holes through which
other pieces pass. The rafters (ke) are put together so as to
form approximately a ninety degree angle at the ridge of the

roof (mái). Each rafter has a square notch near the top which
interlocks with the rafter on the other side. A wooden nail
(tenh) goes through a hole which has been put through each
rafter in the middle of these notches to hole them together.
The rafters rest on the longitudinal roof beams and are kept
from sliding down by the 'monkey shoulder' (pai voc), a piece
of wood put through a hole in the rafter and also resting on
the longitudinal roof beam. Each pair of rafters is held in
position by a long bamboo pole reaching from the peak, where
the two rafters are joined, to the ground below. The bottom
of this pole is later attached near the bottom of the next
rafter, so that it lies diagonally under the bamboo poles
which rest on the rafters. The rafters and floor beams are

Figure 3. Roof Poles.

either hand-sawn or axe-hewn in a rectangular shape about 2
1/2 to 3 inches by 5 to 6 inches. Wooden pegs are set in the
top side of each rafter at regular intervals (about 12 to 15
inches apart) to support the large bamboo poles (kheo) which
rest on the rafters.

The kheo are about 2 to 3 inches in diameter, while the
thui are about 1 to 1 1/2 inches in diameter. The thui are
small bamboo poles which are laid on top of the kheo and perpendicular to them. They extend from the ridge of the roof

to the eaves, placed about 10 to 12 inches apart. The khẹo
are tied (puộc) to the rafters, and the thui are tied to the
khẹo with bamboo strings (lạch), usually at alternate inter-
sections, as in Figure 3.

A short piece of wood is tied between two khẹo near the
ridge at each end. Another rafter rests on this and on the
end eave pole. Small wooden poles (giối), often with the
bark left on, are placed from the top of each corner post to
the top of the end rafter.

The thatch (pái) for the roof is woven (cấp) into shingles
(trenh pái) in the following manner: A large piece of bamboo
is split into strips about 2 inches wide and 4 feet long.
Each strip is left with a joint near one end and is split into
four smaller strips held together by the joint. Green grass
3 to 4 feet long is woven into these strips a little at a
time, and the end of the strip opposite the joint is tied
with a bamboo string. The shingles are then tied to the thui,
starting at the eave of the roof. They overlap one another
considerably, leaving 8 to 10 inches between the tops of suc-
cessive shingles. The thatch on the sides of the house usually extends a bit beyond that on the ends. A small opening is
left at the top of each end for smoke to get out. When the
thatch is all on, the bottom is cut off evenly all around.

When the roof is finished, the floor is put in place.
Floor beams had already been installed immediately after the
posts were set up. Large bamboo poles (cùl) are laid across
these beams perpendicular to them and with about 4 to 6 inches
between one another. The bamboo in the next layer (thả) is
smaller and is laid on top of and perpendicular to the cùl,
parallel to the floor beams. It is placed at 1 to 2 inch intervals. The top layer of flooring (khành) is made of large
bamboo which has been split and cracked open enough to lie
flat. Such strips are laid on top of the thả, perpendicular
to it and the floor beams and parallel to the cùl, as close
to one another as possible.

My language helper pointed out to me the parallelism between the four parts of the roof and the four parts of the
floor. The rafters and floor beams are both made of wood the
same size. The layers of bamboos that rest on these (cùl or
khẹo) are both of the same size. The next layers (thả or

thui) are both of the same size, but smaller than the previous ones. The parallelism breaks down between the thatch
and flooring layers, which are constructed differently.

The walls (nǎng) of the house are made of woven bamboo.
Bamboo poles are split and cracked open enough to lie flat.
These strips are then cut into lengths appropriate for weaving (tanh) a piece to fit in a certain space. Large bamboo
poles (bum), 3 to 4 inches in diameter, are laid on the floor
just outside the porch posts all around the house. Smaller
bamboo poles are tied to the outside of the porch posts all
around the house just under the lower ends of the rafters.

Notches are cut in the bum at regular intervals (3 to 4
feet apart) and directly above them in the smaller bamboo
poles. A strip of split bamboo about 2 inches wide is placed
in each pair of notches. The pre-woven sections of bamboo
wall are set in place (sometimes two thicknesses of woven
bamboo are used to make a tighter wall), and another strip of
split bamboo is placed in each pair of notches on the inside
to hold the wall in place. There are usually no inside walls,
with the exception that one corner may be enclosed by walls
4 to 5 feet high to make a room (puǒng) for changing clothes.

Windows (bóng) are generally put in only one side of the
house, and each extends the entire height of the wall (3 to
4 feet). They are framed by
small pieces of bamboo set into
the notches used to hold the
wall in place. The windows
themselves are also made of
woven bamboo like the walls.
They are supported by a bamboo pole which passes
through the bamboo forming
the outline of the window
and is tied to the eave of
the roof, thus allowing
each window to slide open
or closed. The lower 1/3
to 1/2 of each window is
usually covered by bamboo
bars (khò) to keep small
children from falling to the ground 5 to 8 feet below.

Figure 4. Typical Floor-
to-Ceiling Window.

Usually a small section at one corner of the house covered by the roof is left without a floor and is outside the house walls. The door (cua) to the house is in this section, and entrance is gained by means of a ladder-like set of steps (màn). The area on the ground under the roof is often used for pounding rice.

GLOSSARY OF MƯỜNG HOUSE CONSTRUCTION TERMS

nhà.............house

là nhà..........build a house

hú tộ...........post hole

tào.............to dig

tộ..............post

tộ cái..........main post

tộ hiên.........porch post

tộ tầl..........supporting post

lạt.............floor beam

ruồng...........another word for lat

khứ.............transverse roof beam

tòn thay........longitudinal roof beam

kẻ..............rafter

mái.............roof

tenh............nail (iron or wood)

pai vọc.........'monkey shoulder'--a piece of wood that
                passes through each rafter and rests on the
                longitudinal roof beam to hold the rafter
                from sliding down.

khẹo............layer of large bamboo that rests on the
                rafters.

thui............layer of small bamboo that rests on the
                khẹo.

puộc............to tie

lạch............a very small strip of bamboo used for tying

giôi............wooden pole used as corner rafter

pái.............thatch

cáp.............to weave (thatch)

trenh pái.......thatch 'shingle'

cùl.............layer of large bamboo that rests on the
                floor beams

thả.............layer of small bamboo that rests on the cùl

khành...........floor

nằng............wall

tanh............to weave (split bamboo)

bum.............large bamboo at base of wall

puồng...........room

bóng............window

khò.............window bars

cửa.............door

màn.............ladder-like stairs

nhà tất.........house on the ground

nhà khành.......house built off the ground

tôn.............corrugated aluminum

bán.............board, plank

ASPECTS OF CHAM CULTURE

Doris E. Blood

The Eastern Cham of South Vietnam are divided into two main groups, the Chăm and the Bani, on the basis of their religious systems. The Chăm (technically kaphiêr) are descendants of those who embraced a form of Hindu worship which probably came to the area in the 2nd century A. D. The Bani are descendants of those who followed the Moslem religion, also embraced in ancient days but after the Hindu influence.[1] Cham forms of Hindu and Moslem worship differ greatly from corresponding beliefs and practices outside the area. There is, however, a small group of the Bani, known as the Islam, which developed among the Cham who had lived in Saigon and had followed more traditional Moslem practices.

The Chăm and Bani live in separate villages, with the exception of one village in the Phan Rang area which is divided into Chăm and Bani sections. Many customs are followed by both groups, but in relation to religious practices, they are distinct. In this paper, only the Chăm, or Brahmanist, practices are described.

Cham subsistence is based upon wet-rice agriculture, social organization upon matrilocal residency and matrilineal descent. In addition to recently devised romanized alphabets, the Cham have an ancient system of writing which was introduced by 2nd-century Hindu grammarians. Some ancient script writings on bamboo are still in existence. In more recent decades, the script has been passed on by individual families in the form of handwritten texts in composition books. Women do not traditionally learn to read or write the script, though in a recent revival of interest in the script, its use was advocated for all children in elementary schools.

The Cham attach great importance to maintaining themselves as a distinct people in a world perceived to be hostile to them. This is seen in the reluctance of their daughters to marry outside the Cham community and in their desire for many children. Use of the Cham script also serves to maintain their identity (Cf. Blood, this volume).

One Cham legend tells of their last great king who lost
much of the kingdom to the Vietnamese. In the legend there
was a magic tree which was never to be cut down. But ignor-
ing established rules and practice, the king cut it down and
lost the kingdom as a result. This reminder from history
may possibly have its affect on present-day Chams who desire
to hold strictly to the rules and practices handed down to
them by their ancestors.

SETTLEMENT PATTERNS

The Cham of the eastern part of southern Vietnam live in
two main areas, Phan Rang and Phan Ri. Near Phan Rang there
are 30 villages in an area stretching from near the ocean to
the foothills. These villages range in size from a few hundred to over 2,000 inhabitants. Of the 30 villages, seven
are Bani (Moslem).

Vietnamese live on the outskirts of many Cham villages, some
with small stores to sell needed items, others probably existing as money lenders because of the Cham need for large
sums of money for funeral expenses.

Areas within villages are indicated by high fences which
surround each compound. Fences were traditionally built of
sturdy poles, some as high as ten feet. Cross poles were
tied at the three- or four-foot level. Fifty cartloads of
poles would be needed for an average compound. The height
and durability of the fence indicated to a stranger the
economic status of the family. It kept out undesirable
people and protected livestock from theft or from being
eaten by other animals. In the last decade fences made of
concrete blocks have gained in popularity, so that relative-
ly few stick fences remain. This has undoubtedly come about,
in part, because of the difficulty of going to the mountains
to get proper poles.

The maze of pathways in a village which results from the
compounds being fenced is broken by entrance passageways into
the compounds. To enter a compound one always enters to the
north. If the lane runs north and south, a passageway runs
at right angles to the lane for 15 or 20 feet and then turns
north for a few more feet before reaching the gate. Even if
the lane runs east and west, a gateway is not made directly

Figure 5. Entrance Gate to Cham Compound.

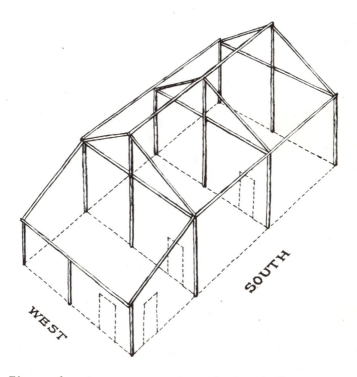

Figure 6. Arrangement of Traditional Cham House.

in the fence on the north side, but a short fenced lane leads
off to the north to make a private passageway to the gate.
The eastern gate post is said to be the male (panrong) or the
general, the western one the female (bia) or the queen.
Amulets are placed in the ground when planting the posts and
on either side of the top crossbar of the gate.

As one enters a well-established compound, the first house
on the left is the thang tông (thang means 'house'). The
entrance of this house faces east. It is the house in which
the parents live and entertain their guests. Rooms in the
house are occupied by the older children of the family.

Opposite this house and to the north is the traditional
house called thang yơ. This house is considered somewhat
sacred to the family. It is in this house that a married
couple first spend time together, entering by the west door.
It is here that people die and exit by the other door. This
house has three adjoining rooms with two exterior doors on
the west end, one on the west side, the other on the south
side. When our lone Cham friend was asked about this house,
he said, "You have never been in my thang yơ. I would not
dare invite guests there since I have a thang tông."

The thang yơ is a female structure with the twelve supporting posts representing the twelve body openings: 2 ears,
2 eyes, 2 nostrils, 1 mouth, 2 breasts, 1 navel, 1 genital
orifice and 1 rectum.

Adjacent and adjoining the thang yơ to the south is the
thang mayau. This house may provide housing for the extended
family and for guests.

Another type of house, considered to be among the four
main types but apparently not common, is the thang binai.
This house is purported to be the largest and the best and
is used for reading the script. It very probably would be a
gathering place for Cham scholars.

The kitchen house (thang ging) is also an integral part
of every compound. It is a small, mud-walled building which
is replaced as the need arises. The kitchen house serves all
the family units in the compound, but only three cooking

places are allowed in the building. A cooking place consists
of three stones placed in the packed earth to form a hearth.

Families eat together on one of the porches of the build-
ings, most commonly that of the thang mayau. A mat is spread
on an elevated wooden bed upon which the family sits. Food
is placed in the center of the mat and each person serves
himself from the main rice pot and other smaller dishes of
vegetables and meat. Guests would usually be served on the
porch of the thang tông.

In former days, a birth house was built in the middle of
the compound for the time of birth and the following days of
'lying by the fire', after which the house would be torn
down and burned. At present, since birth clinics are common
even in small towns, Cham women go to the nearest town or
the province center for the birth of their children. Puri-
fication rites may be performed after the wife returns home
in five or ten days, but the uncleanness of the birth has
taken place elsewhere so she can be secluded in the house,
possibly the thang mayau, when she returns.

The Cham calendar sets aside certain days during the
month when house building can be begun. The family calls
upon the spirits when the house is erected and also when
it enters the house to live in it. After three years, the
family employs priests to perform a ceremony designed to
make the earth clean at the site of a new house.

MARRIAGE

A fellow and a girl traditionally check their zodiacal
birth designations before considering marriage, to ensure
that the marriage will endure. In one Cham legend, a woman
had lost a number of husbands and all of her children in
death. This was attributed to her not having carefully ex-
amined how her husbands' years of birth fit with hers. Even
today, this is a factor to be considered in marriage.

According to the lunar calendar, each year is associated
with a zodiacal animal called nathăk. In a twelve-year
cycle the animals are ordered as follows: rat, water buffalo,
tiger, rabbit, dragon, serpent, horse, goat, monkey, chicken,
dog, and pig. These are the same animals as in the Chinese

cycle, though the two lunar calendars do not coincide. Five
elements called băng are included with each of the animals:
water, iron, wood, earth,and fire. As an example of the kind
of consideration made in choosing a mate, any year associated
with water would be avoided by one whose nathăk was related
to fire, since water extinguishes fire.

The girl's family makes request for marriage from the boy's
family. Girls from sixteen through twenty are marriageable
and able to ask for (pôch) a man. Men from ages eighteen
through twenty-five are marriageable. To go unmarried beyond
these ages is cause for ridicule.

A boy may get acquainted with a girl to whom he is attract-
ed by going to her compound to talk with her. He has permission to stay on the compound, but if the girl is not interested, she gives him the silent treatment and he does not pursue
the friendship. When a girl has decided on the man she wants
to marry, she tells her mother and arrangements are made between the two families. This is not to suggest that young
men and women have free choices concerning their mates.
There are still families that make marriage arrangements for
their children, even though the young people may not be acquainted. The parents may resort to sanctions to assure that
their children go through with an arranged marriage.

The girl's family chooses an intermediary, usually an
older, knowledgeable man skilled in speech, who goes to the
boy's home to ask not only his parents but the boy as well.
The young man has the privilege of declining. If there is
agreement, arrangements are made for the time of the wedding.
Possible wedding days are limited by the Cham calendar.

Both bride and groom traditionally dressed in white for
the wedding, but currently, the man wears a dark suit.

Two men are chosen to officiate at the wedding, one for
each family. These men are not of a religious order, but are
teachers (gru).[2] The official from the groom's family leads
him to the room set aside for the couple in the bride's village and turns him over to the official from her family.
There the latter official gives the exhortation:

> Best wishes for a long life. May you live till
> your hair is silver and your teeth have fallen
> out. May you always have enough to eat. Be
> united in your life together and stay close to
> each other. Work to become rich and bear many
> offspring.

The groom then takes liquor and other drinks out, presenting them to family representatives, old men, and relatives.

The bride and groom spend three days and nights in the
special room prepared for them. Traditionally it was in this
room that the couple got acquainted for the first time. They
share a tray of food, but abstain from sexual intercourse for
the three days.

The groom's family are expected to present gifts to the
couple--gifts of money, jewelry or clothes. Wealthy families
give water buffalo or gold, and a limited number of fields.

During the wedding feast, chicken, squash or any foods
mixed together are taboo. Friends of both families are invited to the two days of the wedding feast.

After the wedding, the bride and groom live in rooms set
aside for them in the compound of the girl's mother. The
couple eventually build their own house on the compound if
that has not already been done.

The wife occasionally goes to her husband's village to
visit his parents for a few days, taking a gift for her
mother-in-law, but the couple live for the most part in her
parents' village. When asked about his village, a man gives
the name of the village of his birth but adds that he married
a girl from another village.

An unmarried woman does not hold the respect of the community. If she is married, she has status in dealing with
other Cham people. If she has land through inheritance from
her mother, she needs a husband to oversee it.

Figure 7.   Traditional Cham Dress.

CHILDREN

Female children are preferred by the Cham because of the security they bring by having husbands join the family later on. Some male children are desirable also, but a very sad home is one in which all the children are males who must leave their parents, following their wives to other compounds. This pressure is so strong that a girl who has not married may enter into a liaison with a man to produce daughters, even though she may not marry him. One young woman whose husband had died, leaving her with a small boy, 'played' with a man until she had a daughter, thus providing for continued lineage for her family and security for her old age. This may not be standard practice, but neither is it necessarily condemned because a young woman is still under the protection of her mother's home and continues contributing to that household.

It is the mother's responsibility in the home to teach the girls, the father's responsibility to teach the boys. Girls were not often able to go to public school beyond the early grades until recently because of their responsibilities in caring for younger children. They are taught the rudiments of cooking, washing, carrying water, and weeding the rice fields with their mothers. They also go along with the whole family at harvest time. When a girl reaches puberty, she is introduced to the ways of revering ancestors.

Young girls often dress in trousers and overblouses as do the Vietnamese, but sometimes even very small girls wear the traditional Cham dress, which is quite distinct from the Vietnamese: a long-sleeved tunic dress reaching between mid-calf and ankle, worn over a long ankle-length underskirt. The traditional style has a V-neck with a gusset from under the arm extending clear to the hem, causing tightness in the bodice but more fullness through the waist and hips. In recent years a fitted-bodice and varieties in neckline have been borrowed from the Vietnamese. Modern underskirts are made of black or white satin, but some of the older women still wear dark, hand-woven sarong skirts under the tunic dresses. Vietnamese conical hats are worn by Cham girls and women as protection from the sun, but they protect their hair from dust and exposure by scarves which are tied about the head in several different ways.

A boy works with his father, preparing the fields for
planting rice, as well as working in the garden. He is often
responsible for trapping rats, lizards and birds, and is used
by his family to watch the water buffalo or goats. A boy
traditionally began to study the script with an older man
when he was old enough to watch the buffalo, that is at about
twelve years of age.

Boys dress as other boys do in Vietnam. Working in the
fields or teaching school, a Cham man usually cannot be distinguished from a Vietnamese in a similar occupation. Only
for special ceremonies do men wear traditional sarongs and
brocaded jackets. Boys wear local caps or hats in the sun
while their fathers may tie towels around their heads for
work in the fields. The headcloth for special occasions
often is red and is tied in a manner distinctive of the Cham.

The father is the head of the family, but he must confer
with his wife concerning matters related to land. If she is
not in agreement, he cannot act alone. The wife may also
overrule her husband in religious matters. Though she has no
standing in the Cham religious system, she may call upon a
priest and then the husband will follow along with whatever
ceremony the priest recommends in properly worshipping the
ancestors or appeasing spirits.

MULTIPLE MARRIAGE AND DIVORCE

A Cham man may take a second wife with the permission of
his first wife, who shows her willingness by going to ask
for (pôch) the new wife. The second wife is called the
'little' wife. As a general rule the two wives are not from
the same village. For this reason, the practice is not looked
upon with great favor because of the husband's need to com-
mute.

Present-day divorce among the Cham is handled in accordance
with Vietnamese government regulations. In former days, if a
couple wished to divorce, they called relatives on both sides
together to convey their intent. The paper of divorce was
written in the Cham script and the marriage was ceremonially
severed by the breaking of a chopstick.

Remarriage is possible either after the death of a partner

or after divorce. Children do not go with their father after
the death of the mother, but are reared by one of their
mother's sisters. When both parents die, if the oldest child
is a girl who is fairly mature, she will take over the property and raise the younger children.

DEATH, CREMATION, AND BURIAL

The Brahmanist Cham distinguish death from sickness and
death from accident, death in youth and death in adult years.
Death in older years brings blessing, but not so a child's
death or any death from accidents such as being killed by a
tiger, gored by a buffalo, trampled by a horse, killed by a
falling tree, or by drowning.

There are three different funeral ceremonies. Ðam jăp
brah is the ceremony performed for children up to age sixteen
and for those who die as a result of accident. Historically,
this was the ceremony for the lowest peasant or for slaves.
This is the only one of the three ceremonies where the body
is buried. The ceremony is further distinguished by not
having gongs and by fewer people participating. The body is
placed in a casket and covered with a cloth. The morning
after the ceremony, the casket is carried outside the village
by two men stripped to the waist and wearing sarongs and
head cloths. One carries a Cham bushhook, the other a high-
land bushhook. Burial may take place on certain Tuesdays or
Sundays.

Ðam prŏng 'big ceremony' (technically ðam răp chêng-hagăr)
is the desired way for a Cham person to be cremated. This
ceremony is the more auspicious and expensive, named because
of the use of gongs. Drums and gongs are beaten during the
time the priest does his work or when he puts out food and
drink for the deceased person.

Ðam sit 'small ceremony' is called technically ðam dua
urang paseh. It is a cremation ceremony similar to the ðam
prŏng but gongs are not used in this ceremony, nor are the
two standards placed at the front of the ceremonial house.

Cremations can only occur on certain Wednesdays or
Saturdays. Thus it is often necessary to wait a number of

days for the proper day. The ceremonial house (kajang) is
built and the body laid inside in its appointed position
(cf. Fig. 8). Family members keep vigil over the body until
the appropriate day arrives. The stench of the decomposing
body often becomes overwhelming, and the most auspicious
ceremonies burn an expensive incense to help alleviate this
problem.

Friends of the deceased person and his family come to pay
their respects during the two days of the actual ceremony.
Gifts of money for the deceased's family are acceptable.

There are some exceptions to immediate cremation of the
body. If a family does not have the money to pay for this
ceremony, they may bury the body. The body remains buried
for at least a year, sometimes many years, and then the bones
are dug up for the proper cremation ceremony.

On the second day of the ceremony, the body is transferred
to the cremation house (thang thôr), which is constructed like
a house with a cloth roof. Gifts for the deceased are placed
with the body. These may be clothing, towels, Cham woven
cloth and other things to enhance the person's departure.
The house is carried on the shoulders of four men by means of
two poles. The men are dressed like those who carry the body
in ɗam jăp brah described above.

The body is burned outside of the village, and afterward
nine pieces of the forehead about the size of a half-dollar
are chipped out by the priest. These bones are placed in a
small pot (klŏng) made in former times of silver, brass, or
gold, now of less expensive metal. This pot is taken home
for five worship ceremonies (padhi) which take place one
week, one month, when the year nears its end and again after
a full year. The last one is some months after that, and it
is a ceremony like that of sending someone off on a trip.
The total time is about three years. Then the pot is taken
to the burial place (kŭt) of the bones, where the bones are
removed from the pot. The skull bones of husband and wife
are not buried together, but his go to the burial place of
his parents, hers to the place of her mother's family.

The burial place is a square plot of sand inside a foundation, over which there is a flat roof. All bones are placed

here mixed together but divided by sex. The middle stone is
a marker of division with stones on either side designating
males or females. Those who have been deformed in any way
cannot be buried in the family burial place. They are buried
in a special place (kŭt lihin) for the unfortunate. The
ceremony of taking the bones to the burial place is attended
by a priest both at home and at the burial site. This final
ceremony may take place for several family members at one
time.

There is a taboo in connection with the death of father or
mother which consists of abstaining from eating chicken for
one month and from marriage of sons or daughters for a year
thereafter.

The Brahmanist priesthood is not set apart from the rest
of Cham society economically or in other aspects of everyday
life. The priests marry, have families, and work their fields.
Their distinctiveness in the society is seen in their ceremonial functions, especially in activities related to the
feast of the royal ancestors, ceremonies for the spirits of
the dead, and cremation ceremonies.

The hierarchy of the priesthood is as follows:

pô dhia (pronounced sia)--three high priests, each one
assigned to one of the royal deities. Their main duties
center on the yearly feast of the ancestors, but they are
also the ones to hand down decisions on when a proper day for
cremation would be.

ông paseh--priests who officiate at other Cham religious
ceremonies. There are perhaps fifty paseh in the Phan Rang
Cham area. The paseh together with the pô dhia are distinctive because of the clothing they wear all the time: white
sarongs, robes, and red turbans.

ông kadhăr, divided between ông kadhăr gru, the teacher,
and ông kadhăr sit, the younger--men classified as officiating musicians. The ông kadhăr is the one to chant the history of the kings at the yearly ceremony.

muk pajau--a woman responsible for caring for the wine at
religious ceremonies. In other languages of the area the
word means 'sorceress'.

ông madôn--a male musician who plays the drum.

ông ka-ing--a male dancer. These last two are also in the
Moslem (Bani) hierarchy.

Membership in the priesthood is by selection and not by
kinship relationship, except incidentally. A man advancing
through the ranks of paseh, which takes many years, is eligi-
ble for the office of pô dhia when one of the three incum-
bents dies. There does not seem to be advancement from one
position in the hierarchy to another--only the paseh are in
line for the pô dhia position. Part of the qualification for
advancement for the paseh is skill in the ancient Cham script.
The selection is made by vote in a representative body of
Cham citizens, with overtones of politics. This may be an
occasion for strife in the area. When one of the pô dhia
died in 1974, the man chosen as his successor was not pleas-
ing to one village. Fighting erupted between groups of indi-
viduals which lasted for some months.

There may be a set fee for the services of the priesthood,
but we have also heard of paseh asking for a gold ring or a
water buffalo for their services.

Fig. 8 shows the floor plan of the ceremonial hut (kajang)
for cremation. There is rigid placement of people and objects during the two or three days of ceremony before the
actual cremation. This plan is for the 'large' ceremony
(đam răp chêng-hagăr) with paseh priests and the presence of
gongs in locations 16 and 17. The people present would be of
the priesthood with the possible exception of those assigned
to locations 7, 8, 9, and 10.

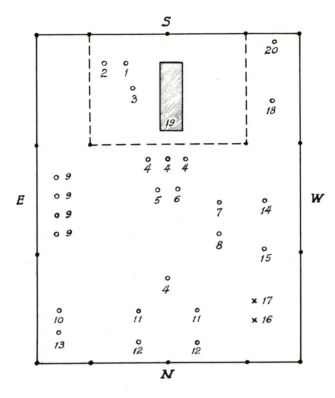

Figure 8.   Arrangement of Large Cremation Ceremony.

1) paseh pahuăk - paseh attending the body
2) paseh ralang - same
3) danok padăng ka urang matai - things set up for the dead
    person
4) thông hla - flowers
5) paseh săng - paseh who blows the conch shell
6) paseh găr - paseh who beats drum or gong
7) ragay phun - one in charge of the cremation house
8) ragay jung - another in charge of the cremation house
9) hlăk chăr - four men who carry the cremation house to
    the burning
10) pô jamửn
11) urang doh – singers
12) urang uăk kanhi - players of the 2-string turtle shell
    instrument
13) ông hăng - man with some function in the ceremony

14) muk buh - woman in charge of wine
15) urang pôk lithay - man in charge of rice
16) danok hagăr - place of the gongs
17) danok chêng - another type of gong
18) thang thôr - cremation house
19) kakung - casket or bier
20) kaya-kal ka urang matai - things to be burned with the
    body

SPIRIT WORLD

Though spirit worship does not pervade everyday life, the
times and seasons are strictly followed by the Cham.[3] As
one ceremonial dancer (muk rija) told me, "Oh, we could never
change our ways. Our ancestors passed them on to us."

An example of their strict observance of customs regarding spirits is the cremation ceremony. Two kinds of spirit
emanate from the deceased, yang and bhut. Although yang are
said to come from intelligent people and bhut from stupid
people, it is evident upon examination that bhut originate
when proper ceremonies have not taken place. Bhut are free
to go around and enter into other persons so that they die.
They bear the names of dead persons. Bhut are fearful
spirits, but can be cast out by magic. Relatives must provide for proper cremation, not only to avoid bringing the
stigma of bhut upon the deceased, but also to prevent danger
to the entire community.

Human beings have three parts: body (thap), the part of
the person which maintains life (suan), and that part which
the Cham are concerned with after death (bingŭk-yawa).

The Cham speak of suan-thap, meaning the body and its life.
They are thought of as being bound together. The suan lives
in the heart and never leaves the body except in death.
Animals also have suan.

The bingŭk-yawa lives in the body someplace and has in-
telligence. It is possible for the bingŭk-yawa to leave the
body even when a person is alive. It can come out while one
is sleeping, or if there is an accident it becomes afraid
and leaves. A person who has lost his mind has also lost

his bingŭk-yawa. When a soldier dies in battle, his bingŭk-yawa will have no place to go, and may enter a horse or a water buffalo. After death, the bingŭk-yawa watches the funeral from outside the body. It is this part of a person which goes to heaven. If a person is good, his bingŭk-yawa goes to heaven; if bad, it is taken and tied in hell. One of the reasons for the importance of cremation is that without it the bingŭk-yawa cannot go to heaven.

Considerable care is taken of the bingŭk-yawa in case of serious illness. If a person is ill and does not get well, it must be because of sin. First a ceremony of offering a chicken (ngăk manŭk) is held by the paseh of the priesthood to offer the animal to God for the release of the sin from the bingŭk-yawa (not from the thap), lest at a later time, following death, the bingŭk-yawa be punished and return to attack the children of the family with sickness and death. If offering a chicken is not successful in restoring health, offering a goat (ngăk pabe) and offering a water buffalo (ngăk kabao) follow.

Because children have a special funeral service and are not cremated, care is taken to call upon their bingŭk-yawa after death. A service of this kind would be held once a year, presided over by the woman (muk pajau) in the priestly hierarchy. This is called êu prok. The bingŭk-yawa is called and ordered not to bother other children. It is felt that because the bingŭk-yawa was acquainted with other children, it can come back to misguide and hurt them.

The cremation ceremony starts a dead person's bingŭk-yawa on its way toward becoming an ancestral spirit, one of the muk-kay. After performance of the prescribed padhi ceremonies following the cremation and extending over a period of several years when the skull bones are taken to the burial ground, the deceased becomes an ancestor spirit. From then on during the yearly feast of the ancestors this spirit is revered with others of the ancestors. It is during the time of the padhi that the Cham perform ceremonies called ngăk yang, appeasing the bingŭk-yawa lest it decide to cause trouble.

Kamlai are the bingŭk-yawa of animals and do things animals would. They cannot be seen except in the behavior of

the people whom they have entered. They make people do wrong
things. They cannot be destroyed but they can be controlled
by use of incantations, using the names of any one of the
twelve zodiacal animals. Two other spirits greatly feared
are the jin and the mala-un. The jin is not good and very
troublesome. It is like a tiger. The mala-un, the biggest
of the kamlai, is like a pig. It is related in some way to
committing incest.

Abileh are another category of spirits whose king is called
abileh Sai-tăn. He has a following of an unknown number of
abileh. Abileh Sai-tăn originated when God drank liquor and
when he slept, saliva came out of his mouth and became Sai-
tăn.

Abileh live above, in the heavens, and come down to enter
people. They too are related to animals but are intelligent.
They make people strong so that they are not afraid of anything. Their presence is known because people change in
their behavior and show signs of the strength abileh give.
They can be driven out by magic formulas of a teacher (gru).
The teacher gets a bottle of clean well water and holds a
staff and the bottle over the head of the afflicted person,
giving information about the person to the god he is invoking. He asks his god to send down magic words for casting
out the spirit. Then his god produces something supernatural
in the water. When the person washes his face and drinks the
water, the abileh becomes afraid, and the words of the magic
formula are able to cast it out.

Women and children often wear amulets around their necks
to ward off harmful spirits. The amulets are written or
drawn by one of the old scholars and then encased in material.
A very common warning to children from their mothers is a
Vietnamese borrowing qui, meaning 'evil spirit', whenever
their actions may be out of line.

There seems to be dissatisfaction among young men with
the spirit appeasement ceremonies which they see in their
villages, but if they marry Cham girls, they are caught up
in it as their life becomes embroiled in the ceremonies for
which their wives will be responsible. A decade ago, a
young man in his teens stated that he wanted to get away and

go to a progressive country. Now he is a married man living
in a Cham village with an established family. He is perhaps
somewhat disillusioned by the ceremonies for the spirits;
but as is customary, he is going along with his wife in whatever her mother has passed on to her as accepted worship of
ancestral spirits.

APPENDIX

Attending a Cham Feast for the Royal Ancestors

It was the first day of the seventh Cham lunar month (mid-September). We were invited to attend Băng Katê Yang in a Cham village in southern Vietnam by a teacher (gru) friend. Before attending the ceremony we were told that there are three places where the Cham people make offerings to the spirits of the three deceased rulers who have become lords or gods: one at the tower of King Pô Klong Girai, one at the tower of King Pô Rame and one at the substitute worship house of Queen Po Inư Nagăr. The authentic tower of this last spirit has been taken over by Vietnamese Buddhists; its substitute is some 100 kilometers away in the village of Hữu Đức or Palay Hmu Tanrăn.

Upon arrival at Palay Hmu Tanrăn, the home village of our teacher friend, we were ushered to the one-story concrete block building whose total area is perhaps 700 square feet. The main room was crowded with people and had little light and less air. It was necessary for us to watch from the hallway. A spirit of camaraderie was there. One person called to my husband. Another woman invited me to chew betel.

We saw that on the far side of this room seven Cham young women were dancing. They were dressed in white, except for the lead dancer who was wearing a colored dress. Each wore sashes around her waist and over the shoulder. They were barefoot and carried two fans each. The accompaniment to the dancing was the same as that used in other religious ceremonies, a shrill melody played on a short wind instrument accompanied by drums. The hagăr is a long wooden drum covered with skins on either end, one end beaten with a stick, the other with the hand. The other drum is flat and round.

After watching the dancing for a time, our attention was directed to the man who played a two-stringed instrument (kanhi) made from the shell of a golden turtle. He was in the company of several priests, but there did not seem to be any activity going on there. We were also shown a statue of sorts, apparently meant to represent Queen Inư Nagăr. It

was an upright pillar with a garishly painted face, wrapped
around with brightly colored cloth to represent garments.
There were no offerings in evidence, nor were people gathered
around the statue.

Later on, while outside waiting to be seated for the meal,
we noted that the women were all dressed in their best, and
probably, new dresses. Many of the Cham men were wearing the
traditional sarong topped by brightly colored brocade jackets
made in Chinese style. Turbans were also brightly colored,
most often red.

The young ladies again entertained with dancing on mats
placed outside. In addition, the Cham national assemblyman,
an elected political officer, did a similar dance with red
cloths. His motions were neither graceful nor smooth, perhaps because of his age.

Generally speaking, foreign guests were seated at a special
table or ushered to other seats. All, including the lady
foreigners, were served beer. When I declined quietly, as
did the wife of the district chief, seated nearby, they
brought me a drink made from irrigation water with ice, sugar
and pickled limes. The food was served in Vietnamese-Cham
style--large bowls of rice generously distributed down the
table, with small bowls of vegetable and meat dishes accessi-
ble to each guest without passing them. The meat served was
goat meat, prepared in four or five different ways. Salad
greens were also served, and food was eaten with chopsticks
from rice bowls.

After eating, the crowd began to disperse and we were invited to the home of the teacher to drink tea and visit with
his family.

At a later time we had opportunity to ask him more about
this ceremony of remembering the rulers. There are three
important parts to the actual worship. Ông kathăr, the man
we saw with the turtle instrument, chants a biographical
history of the gods, apparently accompanied by the kanhi.
The muk pajau, the woman participant, presents liquor and
betel to invite the spirits to partake. The pô dhia, or high
priest, says the prayers and leads the ceremonies in other

ways.   Three high priests are assigned to the three rulers,
so each presides in the place where that ruler is worshipped.
These three men hold the highest places in the Brahmanist-
related religious group.

None of these ceremonies were visible when we were there,
so the general public is invited afterwards, though apparently it would not be taboo to be there if an outsider were bold
enough to go without being invited.   In the days following
the priestly ceremonies, Cham families worship their ancestors
in their own homes in what is called băng katê muk-kay.

NOTES

[1]Maspero (LeBar, et al. 1964:245) quotes Huber as follows: "two Kufic inscriptions were found in what was southern Champa dated around 1030 A.D., and there is some indication of a Muslim community in Champa in the tenth century."

[2]Although the term gru may refer to public school teachers, it more often means older Cham men who are scholars in the script and knowledgeable of Cham customs.

[3]For information on similar beliefs of a related group, the Roglai who live west of Nha Trang, see Cobbey (1972).

REFERENCES

Aymonier, Etienne and Antoine Cabaton. 1906. *Dictionnaire Cam-Français*. Paris: Imprimerie Nationale.

Cobbey, Vurnell. 1972. "Some Northern Roglai Beliefs about the Supernatural." *Southeast Asia II* 1:125-29.

LeBar, Frank M., Gerald C. Hickey, John K. Musgrave. 1964. *Ethnic Groups of Mainland Southeast Asia*. New Haven: Human Relations Area Files Press.

Moussay, Gerard. 1971. *Dictionnaire Cam-Vietnamien-Français*. Phan Rang: Centre Culturel Cam.

THE SCRIPT AS A COHESIVE FACTOR
IN CHAM SOCIETY

Doris E. Blood

When Hindu grammarians came to the Southeast Asian penin-
sula in the 2nd century with their own writing system, they
brought with them a legacy to the Cham people of South Vietnam which is for them a vital symbol of cultural unity today.[1]

HISTORICAL CONSIDERATIONS

According to Chinese sources, Indian trade to the Malay
Archipelego brought adventurers, merchants, and warriors as
well as Hindu priests. New kingdoms arose ruled by Hindu
dynasties. The earliest, as epigraphical data would indicate,
was that in modern-day Vietnam. The kingdom of Champa was
founded in A.D. 192, and eventually extended from Binh Tuy province north to near the area of Hue. The early colonists
came from the country of the Pallavas of Kanchi in South India and brought with them the early Grantha alphabet. Their
style of writing has been found to agree with the script of
the earliest inscriptions found in Vietnam, inscriptions in
Sanskrit. Maspero (1928:40,41) states that the literary and
philosophical culture of the Cham kings was entirely Sanskrit.

The indigenous residents of the area spoke a Malayo-
Polynesian language, which the new rulers began to acquire as
well as to enrich with terms from Sanskrit which remain today.

Inscriptions in Champa were often partly in Sanskrit,
partly in Cham. The earliest extant inscription in the Cham
language is the rock-inscription of Dong-yen-chau in the province of Quang Nam. By this it has been deduced that by the
8th century the Cham script had supplanted Sanskrit and the
Cham language was in full use in the kingdom.

Lapidary script, one of the two varieties of the most
ancient script, has a script descendant known to the Cham as
Akhăr Rik.[2] The letters have peculiar shapes, and they are
complicated. Two other varieties known to some extent but
not now used are Akhăr Atuol, called the suspended character
or seal writing, and Akhăr Yôk. The latter has as its

35

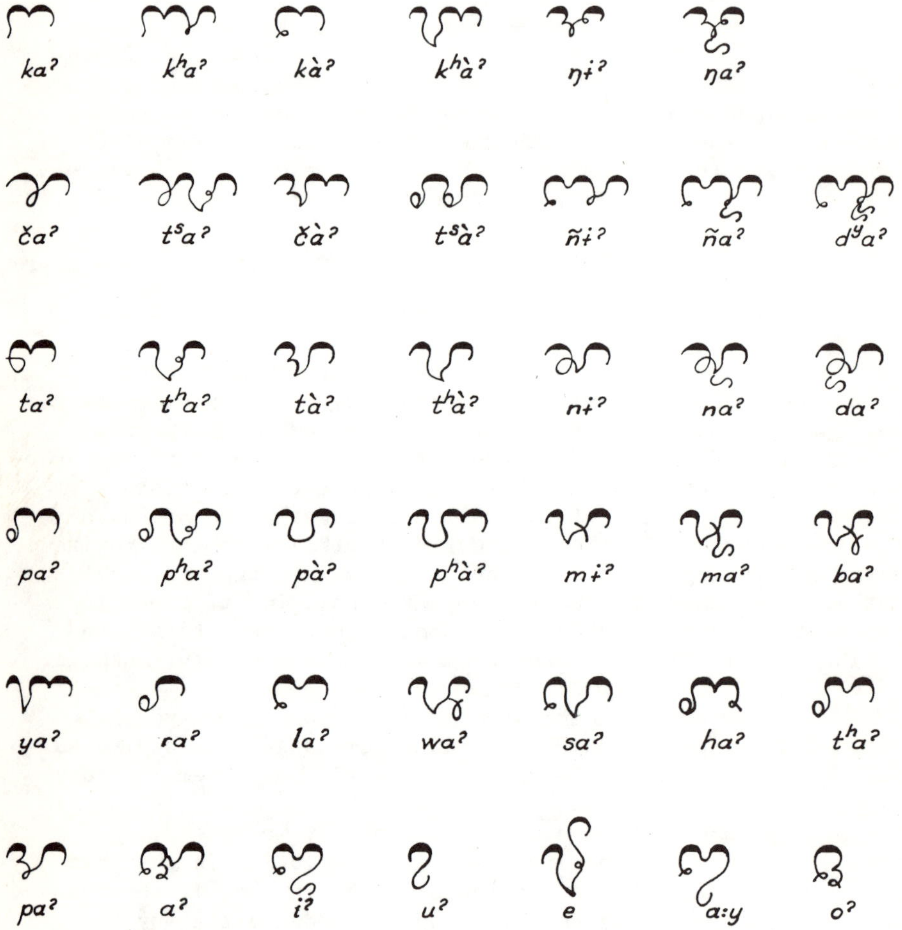

Figure 9. Main Cham Letters.

peculiarity the fact that it is written with full-sized vowel
symbols as well as consonant symbols. Akhăr Srah is the name
given to the writing which has come down to the present. Here
there are differences between the script of Vietnam and that of
the Cham in Cambodia, the latter being more angular. The
several hundred years that the Chams of Cambodia and Vietnam
have been separated have brought about language change and also
changes in the script.

THE PRESENT SHAPE OF THINGS

Almost all main letters of the script alphabet are initial
consonants, though there are also a few vowels which stand as
initials. When one recites the list of main letters of the
alphabet (as listed on the facing page), he begins with the
top row, reading from left to right. (See chart of main letters.)

For some consonant symbols there is a special convention
for its use finally. Other symbols are simply modified in
this position by a longer tail on the right side.

With the exception of nasals, each consonant letter is
considered to include an inherent a sound. The inherent
vowel sound for nasals is i; and a diacritic, called a kai
đăk, is added beneath the symbol to change this quality to a.
For the alphabet, however, these complex symbols with kai
đăk are considered to be part of the main symbol grouping, as
seen on the chart. Vowels other than the above are added by
diacritics, as are some final nasals and liquids which occur
as the second consonant of a cluster.

The following diacritics occur above a letter symbol (here
represented by ☐):

    -m   -ə-   -ŋ   -i-   -i   -ay   open
                                                                    syllables

The following diacritics occur to the left of a letter symbol:

    -o-   -a:y, -ε-   Cr-

The following diacritics occur to the left and above a letter symbol:

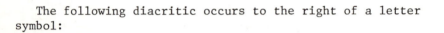

    -ɔ-   -e-

The following diacritic occurs to the right of a letter symbol:

Cy-

The following are letter-size, word-final symbols:

-h   -ŋ

This is just a brief outline of the script. A simplified listing of symbols does not adequately explain the spelling conventions of the Cham nor the exceptions to the rules.

THE SCRIPT AS A MEANS OF COMMUNICATION

We do not know to what extent the script was used during its years of development. Most manuscripts in existence to-day have to do with religious practices, myths, historical legends and epic poems. It may be that at one time judicial proceedings were recorded in the script and other matters of everyday life of Champa, but it is not now a live vehicle of communication among the Cham. A scholar may write a letter

in the script, but other men, even though they might know
the script, would choose Vietnamese by which to communicate
in writing.

The script has not been regularized as have other scripts,
such as Thai, which is used as a national language writing
system. Friendly arguments over the form of a preliminary
syllable may be heard. If used 'incorrectly', the rare form
for final ŋ, which probably had a significant function historically, may touch off strong words between script writers.
The group of scholars in France (1977:243), working from
manuscripts dating back to the 19th century, have found □
representing ə and □ representing the final ŋ, whereas
some modern script writers would distinguish the two and insist that ə is □ and ŋ is □ .

Traditionally, boys began to learn the script when they
were old enough to tend the family water buffalo, which meant
they would be around twelve years old. Teaching was done man
to boy, and a well-trained script writer would have spent
hours of rote practice, writing symbols so that they are well-
formed and in proper proportion. When my husband and I
arrived in Cham country in 1960, one out of four men was said
to know the script well. Most whom we met who knew the script
were over 40, their training probably having come in the 1930's
or before. I do not know the reason for the slacking off of
script teaching, but there were few young men learning the
script in the traditional way before the revival of interest
came.

Women do not usually learn the script. Though we had been
told of some women who could read, we never met any of them.
A revival of interest in the script in the 1970's brought
some girls into workshops to study[3], and there were girls as
well as boys in the early grades where some teachers wanted
to teach the script. Women elementary school teachers, however, showed no recognition of Cham letters nor interest in
learning them. This centuries-old division of interests
between the sexes would not be changed easily.

Many young men of today, interested in knowing the script,
do not seem to have the necessary motivation to carry on with
practice until they are proficient.   They perhaps feel that

the methods of teaching the script are outdated. After the
revival of interest, young men studying with an old scholar
asked for copies of the romanized primer to help them in
learning because it had a parallel section written in the
script. The old scholar had begun to teach the script by the
alphabet and then the twelve zodiacal animals of Cham. This
not only introduced the symbols but also the spelling formula
which is considered a part of the knowledge of the script.
The word for 'pig' pabui is spelled 'khăr băk kai kuăk kai kĭk
tut kai yăk lang kuk khăr păk, băk buăk buĭk yăk bui păk pabui'.

Those who have been investigating the script in Paris (Le
Groupe 1977:251) mention that the close similarities in forms
of some symbols have caused frequent confusion in old manuscripts. We have also heard old men read an l for a kʾ in
clearly written script. One scholar taught the script to us
by presenting similar groupings of symbols together: p ℳ
and th ℳ , kʾℳ and l ℳ , tʾℳ and p ℳ , as well as
b ℳ and w ℳ . This pedagogical device of introducing
close parallels at the same time could mean the difference
between young people continuing their study of the script or
giving up.

Another factor to consider concerning the script being a
means of communication is that the language of Cham is changing rapidly. In the decade that we were living in the area,
we noticed a distinct difference in the ability of young
people to communicate in pure Cham. As they are educated in
Vietnamese schools, they tend to borrow more and more Vietnamese on a grammatical base of the Cham language. A word
like 'book', which had heavy reference during our days of
living in a village, referring not only to real books but
school notebooks as well, was not known by some high school
girls ten years later. Some of the language of old manuscripts, such as the best-known epic poem, has become archaic
even to present-day scholars. But the loss of Cham language
has become so acute that a scholar teaching a group of young
men not only had to teach them the script forms but also had to
explain what the word meant that they were studying.

THE SCRIPT AS A SYMBOL

In spite of the fact that the script does not now stand as
a viable means of communication with the Cham, nor ever will,

it remains a highly revered symbol of their status as a
unique people.

The script is part of their religion, both Brahmanist and
Moslem. The priesthood of each division are considered to
know the script. Priests are not well respected, however, by
better educated Cham, and they probably do have an imperfect
knowledge of the script. The teachers (gru), outside of the
priesthood proper, are those who have a respected knowledge
of the script. The rare kite-flying ceremony is a case where
the script is used. Prayers written in the script are flown
by the officiating man of some religious rank. Perhaps the
most common and specialized use of the script is in the making
of amulets. Much of the extant literature is related to this.

Many homes have script portions passed down from one generation to another. Legends, poems, history and amulet formulae
make up the greater part of the corpus of script materials.
In recent decades the script has been copied into school notebooks. These manuscripts are prized highly.

There is still considerable prestige attached to knowledge
of the script, though young people do not seem to be seeking
this prestige. The newly appointed chief of district for the
Cham area, who came from another area and who was well into
Vietnamese culture, was spoken of as 'not knowing letters'.
When we asked for a teacher to help in preparing materials
for a head-start grade, the man most highly respected as a
master of the script was assigned to us. Any younger man who
had not studied the script, regardless of how quick he might
be, when considered as an informant, would be tagged as, 'he
doesn't know anything'.

Smalley (1963:14) has written, "The attachment to a writing
system may be such that educational advantages and particularly advantages for the following generation, will be scuttled
in favor of holding on to orthographic tradition from the
past." This was certainly true of innovation that was introduced in the script about 1970.

The script, of course, is fully capable of being written
to represent modern-day Cham. An innovator among the Cham
took this as his appointed task, perhaps with a view of being

venerated as the creator of the most up-to-date writing system
for his people. Where the historical spelling for 'lord' is
ᮖᮀ , he wrote it as it is pronounced today, pô ᮖᮀ . The
final r/l distinction, which at one time was contrastive, has
now become n in speech for most people, l for those who know
the script, in words which at one time ended in r.   This
scholar regularly changed the script writing to final l.
Fuming expletives of 'This is wrong' came from those who saw
it, and we soon learned that, not only would our publications
have to be diglot, but the historical r would have to be present to make any publications acceptable.

A revival of interest in the script began about 1971.
When we first became acquainted with the Cham in 1960, the
script was decidedly revered and much in evidence but not a
fighting matter. A dozen years later interest in the script
was no longer restricted to old scholars, but women, young
people and children showed interest as well.

We became aware of this after our introduction of romanized
primers in Cham to teach children in a head-start program before they began to learn Vietnamese. Fear of the romanized
form of writing centered in a concern that it would push the
script into obscurity. Some of the reaction was violent: one
group of teachers, scholars, and priests decreed that any
teacher found teaching from the new books would be relieved
of his position. Other complaints reversed usual cultural
practices of the people. One teacher remarked about his
class of five-year-olds, "They don't want to learn the new
letters, they want to learn the script", whereas children do
not make decisions of that kind. When I asked a middle-aged
woman if she would like to learn to read, she looked in dis-
dain at the primer, stating,"I only want to learn Cham letters."
So it became evident that the script was no longer just a
writing system but a lively issue throughout the society.

The more positive side of the revival of interest was that
teen-age and older Cham wanted to learn to read the script.

Because young people are today going beyond Cham village
schools into the Vietnamese educational system, the Cham
language is rapidly being lost. As a result of education
there have been broader fields of endeavor that have taken

younger generation Cham from rice cultivation into teaching, politics, and medical technician work, involving them more deeply with Vietnamese culture. So there remain to the Cham, as visible evidences of their distinctiveness as a people, the Cham towers, their religious systems and practices, and the ancient script. Of these, the script binds the people together where they may be separated by space or religion. The script belongs as much to Phan Ri Chams, who have few relics of the past, as to those in Phan Rang, who may glimpse the towers of Pô Rôme or Pô Klong Girai in the distance from most of their villages; it is just as valuable to Moslem-influenced Cham who worship Pô Aluah and bury their dead as to those of Brahmanist background who consider Pô Lingik the supreme god and cremate their dead.

Thus we see that the script acts as a cohesive device binding together the people of Champa. By 1975 it had become a symbol of their uniqueness in a hostile world that eats away at their identity.

NOTES

1. The information given here concerning the script was true until at least early 1975. I do not know the present Cham situation.

2. Cham words in this paper are spelled with the romanized alphabet in use in Cham schools in 1975.

3. Workshops in the Cham script that were held in Father Gerard Moussay's Cham Cultural Center in Phan Rang, Vietnam, and the publishing and distribution of his Cham dictionary may have been two of the factors that accelerated the revival of interest in the Cham script.

REFERENCES

Aymonier, Etienne and Antoine Cabaton. 1906. *Dictionnaire Cam-Français.* Paris: Leroux.

Diringer, David. 1949. *The Alphabet,* Vol. 1. New York: Funk and Wagnalls.

Le groupe de recherches Cam. 1977. "Essai de Translitteration Raisonnée du Cam." *BEFEO LXIV,* pp. 243-55.

Maspero, Georges. 1928. *Le Royaume du Champa.* Paris-Bruxelles: Van Oest.

Moussay, Gerard. 1971. *Dictionnaire Cam-Vietnamien-Français.* Phan Rang: Centre Culturel Cam.

Smalley, William A. 1963. *Orthography Studies.* London, England: United Bible Societies.

MNONG LĂM TEXTS ON SACRIFICE AND SHAMANISM

translated by Evangeline Blood

As the title of this paper[1] suggests, the paper consists
of a series of texts, in English translation, on two topics
of central interest to the Mnong Lăm people, namely, sacrifice and shamanism. The texts were written for me and my
husband by a Mnong Lăm boy in his late teens in 1967 and
early 1968. He later worked with me from April to December,
1974. I have translated these texts as they were originally
given to us, except that, in some cases, information on the
same subject was gathered from several texts. Parenthetical
remarks also have their sources in the original texts unless
they are just translations of the preceding words.

SACRIFICES

Sacrifice for Souls. (Pơp Bhien Lăm Mhiêng).[2] The
sacrifice for the spirit that guards the soul (yang ngăt
nhuôl), hereafter called guardian spirits, takes place at the
same time as the sacrifice to the spirits of the ancestors
(yang may yo). This is the biggest sacrifice of the Mnong
Lăm people, and is usually held in April.

On the opening day of the feast, all of the people stay in
their own village, and do not go to the woods, fields, or to
other villages. The men who are village leaders roast a male
water buffalo to make a sacrifice to their own guardian
spirits. They make a small house near the gateway to the
village, and in it they tie seven wine bottles and prepare
some buffalo meat to offer to the spirit of the earth (yang
bri teh).

Next morning, they kill another pig and again sacrifice
to the ancestors. They call on the souls of people who died
in the village long ago. At the end of this second day,
villagers are again permitted to go outside the village.

On the third day, the chief of each house sacrifices at
the door of the house unless one of the earlier sacrifices
has already been made there. So they kill a buffalo to
sacrifice to the guardian spirits at their house, as they

45

did at the opening feast. The custom in this sacrifice is
to kill a male buffalo or a male pig once every three years,
or, if the people are poor, every seven years.

These feasts take place every year. The Mnong Lăm sacrifice to many spirits to induce the spirits to help them. If
they do not sacrifice to their guardian spirits or make
smaller sacrifices to other spirits, people will still be indebted to the spirits and the spirits will become angry and
forsake them. Because they fear the spirits, they sacrifice
to the guardian spirits, the spirit of the sun (yang nar),
and the spirit of the earth (yang teh) which they call 'that
which nourishes' (yang may bă).

Sacrifices to the spirit of the earth are not held at the
place away from the village where it lives, but at the houses
or gateway of the village. Nor is any special house made for
it. The Lăm say that spirits also live with them in each of
their houses, to look after them daily.

Sacrifice after Defilement with a Corpse. When someone
picks up a corpse of a person who has died a violent death,
he is defiled. (Violent deaths include falling from a tree,
bullet wounds, falling from a vehicle, being stabbed with a
knife or spear, suicide, goring by elephant tusks, or claw-
ing by a tiger.) To cleanse himself he must make a sacrifice.

Because the spirit of violent death (yang djoh yang briêng)[3]
looks after the souls of those who have died violent deaths,
he will cause the person who touches such a corpse to meet the
same kind of death unless a sacrifice is made. With the
sacrifice, the person asks yang brieng to keep death away, to
let something good come, and also to cause the guardian
spirits of the dead person to be driven out and not enter the
person who carried the corpse.

The sacrifice is made with a goat, dog, or duck, and is
made at the edge of a river or lake, where a wine jar is set
up and the animal is roasted. The shaman sprinkles rice
wine on the water and immerses the defiled person. He also
puts his clothing in the water and lets it be washed away
with the current. Then the person drinks wine and eats dog
meat. The wine and dog meat are divided with the other

villagers present. They use just a small wine jar so that
all the wine will be drunk before they return home. From
that time the person who defiled himself no longer fears that
yang briêng will cause him a violent death.

Sacrifices for the Soul of the Rice (mhŏ yang). The Lăm
have a custom of calling on the spirit of the sky (yang trôk)
to bring rain, to help them make rice fields. In June of
every year,[4] in every village, the Lăm tie up a white rice
wine jar and roast a white chicken and a white pig. They
make a sacrifice and call on the spirit of the sky to bring
rain for making rice fields. After they call on the spirit
of the sky, they drink wine. They divide the pork with everyone, but the chicken is given only to the person who calls on
the spirit. During the sacrifice before the eating of the
meat, no one can leave the village; but afterwards, they may
all go to the woods and streams. Then they wait for the rain
to come to make their fields. They believe that if they do
not sacrifice like this, they will still get rain; but it
will come very late, causing them to be late in making their
rice fields.

Before the rice is taken out of the granary for sowing,
they take a chicken, cut its throat, and use the blood to
smear on the door of the rice granary. They feel this is
necessary so that the rice will sprout well, and they need
not fear that it will rot, die, or be diseased.

In the ninth month, when the rice is ripe but before it
is cut, they sacrifice a chicken again to insure that the
rice will be full headed. Then they harvest the rice, and
put it in the rice granary.

When summer comes, the Lăm observe the 'celebration of the
rice'. In this ceremony they sacrifice to the spirit of the
sky so that the soul of the rice will be safeguarded.

In preparation for the rice celebration ceremony, they
ferment a lot of rice wine and reserve a large quantity of
unhusked rice. Before dawn, the people of one long-house go
and take the rice stalks to the woods. They use the rice
stalks to cover the wine in jars. At seven o'clock, they
tie up the wine jars they had covered with the rice stalks
that morning.

The rice celebration takes place after rice threshing
time. People roast a pig, buffalo, or whatever they have.
After the work is finished, they prepare the meat in the
house and perform a sacrifice. They call on the spirits and
then make their way to the rice house where they smear blood
around at appropriate spots. Then it is time to return and
have the owner of the house drink wine. From then on the
evening consists only of eating, drinking and singing. This
is how the Lăm sacrifice to the spirit of the sky and the
soul of the rice.

Sacrifice for an Elephant (Tôh Yo). The Radê Lăm people
make sacrifices for their elephants, because of a mixup long
ago when their ancestors shot the special deer belonging to
the spirit of the sky instead of an elephant. From that time,
the spirit of the sky has had them sacrifice for elephants,
and elephants have to work for people. The spirit of the sky
gave them instructions for sacrificing for elephants. Because the elephant is used to help build houses, pulling logs
and trees and transporting heavy things, people must sacrifice for it.

At the first sacrifice, they roasted a pig and put out a
jar of wine. Then King Tluă Kbuă Lan called on the spirit of
the sky to give strength but also a peaceful disposition to
the elephant so that it would not attack other elephants.
After Tluă Kbuă Lan called on the spirit, he took some of the
eggs, uncooked rice, and rice wine and put them on the elephant's head.

The following personal account by a Mnong Lăm man tells
what happened at a sacrifice for an elephant in 1959:

"My family bought an elephant from a man from Laos. The
afternoon of that day the people sacrificed a pig and prayed
to the spirits. (They say the idea of calling on the soul
of the elephant is for the elephant's soul to stay with the
family.)

"At the sacrifice they set up three wine jars, one for
calling the soul of the elephant, one for serving guests,
and one for the villagers. They also had pork, blood, clothing, bananas, sugar cane, water, wine, and a dish of rice,
with a candle stuck into the bowl of rice.

"When the person finished calling the spirits, he sprinkled rice wine on the elephant's head and said:

"'Oh Pliem (the name of the elephant), you stay peacefully
in this country. We have taken you from the house of your
parents, don't go back, because they have given you to this
country. Your parents have given you to these people to look
after you.'

"After the prayer they called the buyer to feed the elephant bananas and sugar cane. After that the driver tied it
to a large tree. (Elephants need to be tied to something
large because they would uproot small trees. They can be
tied to large trees or bamboo.) Going back into the house
the driver drank rice wine and the owner of the elephant was
called to sit opposite the gongs. The person who called the
spirits took a rooster and called to the spirits again; then
the guests were fed.

"The next morning the seller of the elephant was paid.
For this elephant he was given a large gong worth 20,000
piastres and another gong worth 10,000 piastres, and also
30,000 piastres in cash. The day he was paid he left for his
village because of the belief that if he stayed too long the
guardian spirit of the elephant would stay with him.

"After the sellers left for their village, the new owners
had another sacrifice for the elephant. (The purpose of this
sacrifice is to call the soul of the elephant from its ancestors, to have it live peacefully in the elephant, and to let
the guardian spirit know that it has people caring for it.)
At this sacrifice they roasted a black pig and tied up only
one wine jar. They took pork, rice, and an egg and prepared
the sacrifice on the porch. They called on the spirits there.
After calling on the spirits they took the egg and broke it
on the head of the elephant and sprinkled wine and chanted:

"'Oh, I call you great mother spirit (Yang May To), the
one who held it in your hand, cared for, carried on the back,
molded and created this elephant, we ask all the spirits to
care for its soul. Don't let it eat roofing grass, but let
it graze in grazing grass.'

"After calling on the spirits, the driver then ate meat
and drank a lot of wine. Then he went to tie the elephant.

"From that day the people involved were under taboos for
three days. The person calling the spirits and the owners
were under the strongest taboos. They were not to go outside,
to bathe, or to smoke. The driver had to follow the following
procedures: in the morning at seven he took the elephant to
graze, but if he met someone on his way to the place where
the elephant was to be tied he was not to talk, lest he arrive
late. He also was not to look about to the right or turn to
a different place, lest later the elephant imitate him. After
letting the elephant graze he had to go back to the house
quickly.

"When he got to the house, everyone ate together. They
stayed in the house all the time they were under this taboo.
They wore the same clothes all that time. The owners of the
elephant couldn't go outside except to relieve themselves.
They could not take off their clothes nor scratch with their
fingers. If they had an itchy place they had to rub up against
a column of the house. They were not to bathe, only wash
their faces. During the time of the taboo no stranger (i.e.
non-villager) was to come into the house. If someone should
trespass, he must redo the sacrifice for the elephant. If he
doesn't have any animals to sacrifice, he must become a
slave. The people in the house with those under the taboo do
the work for them, cooking the rice, getting water, and bringing them food to eat.

"This was my grandparents' prayer for the elephant:

"'Oh elephant, I come and call you spirits of the North
and of the South. You great and small spirits, you spirits
who made mankind and everything, I will have you come and
drink wine, eat chicken liver, drink wine, eat pig liver,
drink wine, eat buffalo liver. We do service to you with
these seven jars of wine and the buffalo with a hump. So
you will look after our elephant, keep its soul healthy,
make it do its work well. We ask you again that the elephant
will live well, that all will be well, that it will be loyal,
stay in the woods to eat, stay in the large grass to get
bamboo shoots, so it can work diligently. Come and drink our
wine, oh spirit.'

"After the prayer they gave the elephant these things to
eat: bananas, sugar cane, tuberous plants, pineapple, and
breadfruit. After it finished eating, they rode the elephant
around the house. A lot of young people carrying fish traps
and nets for fishing followed the elephant. The reason is
that later on they would have the elephant wade in the water
when they went on fishing expeditions. They had the elephant
go around the house seven times. After the seventh time the
driver tied the elephant near the village. Then the villagers
ate and drank, but they were not to get drunk. (If a person
does get drunk, he is to sleep, not argue. If someone goes
against this custom, the next day he is to sacrifice a pig to
the elephant.) The next morning they were finished feasting
and the animal could be used for work."

Sacrifice for a Buffalo: Sprinkling the Buffalo (Proh puh).
Lăm villagers perform a sacrifice for the water buffalo in
the fifth month, before the rains come. Festivities begin
when towards evening they set up a large wine jar and kill a
chicken. They then syphon some wine into a bowl, and add the
blood of the chicken. Next, cutting a twig from the gun ik
plant, the head of the house and the buffalo tender go to the
buffalo pen. The head of the house chants: "Healthy, healthy
sleep, eat until full, smile and laugh, fisherman near the
edge of the water, go in peace to the rice fields. You watch
our buffaloes and pigs." Then the head of the house sprinkles wine on the back of the buffalo, and takes the gun ik
twig and dips it into the bowl of blood and wine and smears
the mixture on the head of the buffalo. Afterwards they return home, where the buffalo tender is the first one to drink
the wine used for the sacrifice.

*The Legend of the Origin of the Sacrifice for a Newborn
Child.* The story of the origin of the sacrifice for a newborn child is related as follows:

Into the ancestral family of the Tung Tang Djhang Wiêt, a
male child was once born. The spirit of King Tluă Kbuă Lan
(Kuon Mtao Tluă Kbuă Lan) said to the parents, "You bring
the child here so a sacrifice can be made for its soul." He
instructed them to set up three jars of rice wine, and roast
a bird. The spirit then put some rice in a bowl, and into
another large bowl he put a blanket, a skirt, a loincloth, a

hand of bananas, a section of sugar cane stalk, a knife, and
some blood from the bird. These items were all put out on a
mat. Above the bowl of rice, a candle was lit. Three
bottles of wine were taken from the wine jars and also put on
the mat. When they were ready, the newborn baby and its
mother sat on the mat above the wine jars.

After finishing the instructions, the spirit of the king
began to call on other spirits. This is the chant:

"Oh, our good spirits that bore us, that created us, the
one that came from the sky, from the sun. Oh, our good
spirits that held us on your lap and nursed us and chewed
our food for us, the one who makes us big, the good spirit
who gives life, makes us human beings, you take care of us,
watch over us from childhood; until we grow up and are big,
watch over us."

After praying to the spirits, he took blood from the bird
and wiped the forehead of the child and took wine and washed
the child's legs. He said, "I apply this blood to the child's
forehead as a symbol of inviting the guardian spirit into his
brain. I wash his legs with wine symbolizing that he already
has a soul."

After that, King Tluă Kbuă Lan had the mother eat a banana, sugar cane, and meat from the bird, and then drink
wine. He said, "I have the mother of the child drink wine,
eat rice, eat bananas and meat from the bird signifying that
the spirit of the sky entrusts the care of this child to its
mother. The spirit of the sky creates a person and gives him
a soul, but the work of raising, nursing, holding a child on
the lap is the daily work of the mother from birth until it
grows up."

After this, King Tluă Kbuă Lan had the people drink from
the three wine jars. He told them that the three wine jars
represented the three spirits: The spirit of the sky (Yang
Trôk), being the creator; the guardian spirits (Yang Ngăt)
Nhuôl), and the ancestral spirits (Yang May Bă). He said
that they, the members of the Tung Tang Djhang Wiet family,
would in time themselves become the ancestral spirits (Yang
May Bă).

From that time to this day, the Mnong people who follow
the customs of their ancestors remember to perform this
sacrifice for a newborn baby.

Sacrifice for the Soul of a House (Truôč Ngăt Hih). The
ancestors of the Radê Lăm people from way back had this custom:

The spirit of King Tluă Kbuă Lan came to the earth wanting
to instruct the earth people. Our ancestors (Tung Tang Djhang
Wiêt) had constructed a very long and large house. It took
them three or four years to finish the house. When the house
was finished, Tung Tang Djhang Wiêt called all the villagers
to live in this house. But the spirit of King Tluă Kbuă Lan
warned them concerning new houses. He did not let them live
there at first, so they took their belongings back to their
old houses.

The spirit of King (Kuon Mtao) Tluă Kbuă Lan said to Tung
Tang Djhang Wiêt, "Have your children roast a cow to use to
'pour' the new house, to give health to all the people living
in this house. Tie up seven wine jars."

After the king finished speaking, Tung Tang Djhang Wiêt
had his children sacrifice a cow and set out seven wine jars.
After this work was done, they called the king. Arriving in
the new house, the king had them beat the gongs and take
several bottles of wine. He poured the wine on top of the
ladder to the living room of the house, and then he called
on the spirit.

"Oh spirit of the ground, woods, creator of trees and bamboo, I call you to come and drink wine and eat the cow and
everything we give you to eat. We ask you to look after our
house, give the people living in the house good health all
the time, let them have enough food and things every day.
We ask the spirit who made the world and mankind to give us
health, not sickness, and watch over us and our children
every hour and every day."

After the king called on the spirits, he applied the blood
of the buffalo to the steps of the house at the threshhold
and the post near the communal living area. After he did
this, he said to Tung Tang Djhang Wiêt, "Do like this from

now on: before people live in a new house, make a sacrifice
for the soul of the house. If you do, you will be healthy
and not need fear Yang Briêng entering your house. But be
careful; don't call different spirits; don't call Yang
Briêng, because there is just one great spirit, the one who
made the world!" Since that time the villagers have copied
what King Tluă Kbuă Lan taught their ancestors.

Nowadays they still follow this custom, but they don't
just sacrifice to the spirit of the sky; they call on all the
spirits, the spirit of the mountain, the ground, and the sky.
They also call on the chief of evil spirits (Yang Briêng Khua
Yang Djoh).

So the Radê Lăm villagers do wrong, and do not obey the
teaching from King Tluă Kbuă Lan. The Radê Lăm do not just
worship the spirit of the sky, but they worship all the
spirits living on the earth and the sky. Because of this,
the villagers are slaves of Yang Briêng. Yang Briêng is always bad to them. Yang Briêng hates people; he is afraid
they will go back to the spirit of the sky. He does not let
them leave him. He wants people to worship him. He has
people sacrifice and call him to eat the buffalo and pig, and
drink wine. Especially he has people live in the 'fire enclosure' with him, because the spirit of the sky imprisoned
Yang Briêng in the fire enclosure. So he deceives people and
lets them do wrong. He does not want people to believe in
the spirit of the sky; he wants them to live in the fire enclosure with him.

So, in times past, the sacrifice for the house was only to
the spirit of the sky, but now Yang Briêng has them sacrifice
to him too. Nowadays they still have the house sacrifice,
because the house still has a soul, and a spirit lives in the
house.

SHAMANISM

How to Become a Shaman. The kind of person chosen by the
spirits to be a shaman is a good woman who is married and
faithful to her husband, always helping others, and always
doing sacrifices to the spirits. Since shamans (nêh jao)
are servants to the djoh spirits (yang djoh), becoming a

shaman requires appointment to that role by such spirits.
Sometimes, such a spirit reveals a divining stone to a person, indicating that that person is to become a shaman. The
old shaman instructs the new one in the chants. The old
shaman waves magic items above the head of the new shaman so
that the spirits will live in her. Taking the divining stone
with them, they sacrifice a buffalo, and the villagers feast
with the shaman. The old shaman leads the soul of the new
shaman into the village of the spirits. After the feast, the
new shaman stays in the village for seven days. On the
seventh day, they sacrifice a pig and test the new shaman.
If she passes the test, people say she has a spirit. From
that time she is able to heal people by chanting.

The Work of Diviners. A diviner, literally a 'go-between
shaman' (nêh ndrañ wat) is called when someone is sick or in
pain. She divines by using a chicken leg or by chanting.

When a shaman comes to help the sick, she uses the divining stone. The people sometimes consider her to be a malevolent spirit (čak) because she is able to see the souls of
people, and the divining stone is sometimes considered to be
her husband. The shaman looks into the stone, and then
chants with her eyes closed. She presses on the sore or
painful place. A shaman may advise a patient to sacrifice a
buffalo or a pig. The people are careful to follow such instructions, for they are afraid she will not come to help
them when they are sick again, if they disregard her advice.
Sometimes she may simply advise them not to go visiting or
to bathe too soon.

Shamans are paid with plates, dishes, rice, and sometimes
with money. It is also common for her to be paid with meat
from the animal sacrificed on behalf of the patient. The more
serious the sickness, the more the shaman is paid.

A Legend of How Two Young People Became Shamans. A long
time ago, there were a brother and sister who were orphans.
They had no house and nothing to eat.

One day, they went to a stream near Spirit Mountain to try
to catch some fish. Near the mountain, they saw a dragon
come out of a cave. The dragon was breathing fire, and when

they saw it, they were very afraid; but they did not run away,
The dragon came near to them and changed into a man. He said
to them, "I am the king of the spirits of the earth, mountain,
and water. Come to my house and I will make you my servants."

When they heard him say, "make you my servants", they were
frightened, because they didn't know what he meant. They
followed him to his village, however, in the cave at Spirit
Mountain.

Arriving at the village, they saw many spirit people working there. They saw beautiful houses, a lot of valuable
goods, and many animals. The village was very nice, and they
very much wanted to live with the spirits. They stayed there
a month, learning from the spirits. He taught them how to
become shamans and how to make sacrifices to the spirits.
They learned how to do things spirits can do--how to disappear,
how to fly, how to walk on water, as well as other things
spirits do. When the day came for them to go back to the village, the spirit gave each of them a divining stone.

Arriving at their own village, they told the people that
they had gone to the spirit village, and the spirit there had
made them shamans, so that now they were spirits also. They
told the villagers about many powerful things the spirits had
told them, but the villagers wouldn't believe them at first.
Because they wanted the people to believe them, they did many
miraculous things in front of the villagers, including dis-
appearing.

Then the villagers believed them and sacrificed to them.
Whenever anyone got sick after that, they called on these two
shamans to heal them. The shamans got very rich and powerful as healers among the Lăm. They also taught others how to
become shamans.

A Legend Concerning the Origin of Midwives, literally,
'hot water shamans' (joa dak dôh). Midwives are always women
and have no magic powers or malevolent spirits living in them.

There was once a couple who had been promised to each other
from childhood, and who were expecting a baby. According to
custom, the man went to the jungle to get a piece of sharp

bamboo to cut open his wife's abdomen to get the baby. While
in the jungle, he came across some monkeys who asked what he
was doing. He said he was coming to get the bamboo to cut
open his wife because she was expecting. The monkeys said,
"Friend, you might kill her if you cut open her stomach. We
press with our hands very gently." He said, "Would you come
to our village tomorrow morning?" The one monkey said, "We
can't come because you have dogs and crossbows always hanging in your houses. If you put these away, we can come."
He promised to go home right away and put these things away.

He hastened home in order to get there while it was still
daylight. When he got there the villagers asked him, "Why
didn't you bring the sharp bamboo?" He then told them of his
encounter with the monkeys and their advice about delivering
babies. He advised them to put away the dogs and crossbows,
lest the monkeys burn their houses.

The next day the monkeys came and were invited into the
house. They checked the stomach of the woman who was expecting the baby. They asked for hot water and pressed her stomach. When the baby was born the villagers were very happy.
They wanted the monkeys to teach them, and many women came
to learn.

After the monkeys finished teaching them, the villagers
roasted a buffalo and set out three jars of wine to serve
them. The villagers were very happy that they now knew how
to deliver babies without losing the mother.

NOTES

[1]This subgroup of the Mnong has been called variously
Lăm, Rlăm, and Rơlơm. The native author of these texts used
'Lăm'. There are approximately 4,000 Lăm people, living in
the lake district of old Darlac Province. The Mnong dialects
belong to the South Bahnaric branch of the Mon-Khmer language family.

My husband and I lived in a Mnong Lăm village from May,
1960, to May, 1962; and from June, 1962, until January, 1963,
and from October, 1966, to February, 1968, we lived in
Banmethuot and had regular contact with the Mnong Lăm. The
actual Mnong Lăm texts are available from the Dallas, Texas
office of the Summer Institute of Linguistics, Vietnam Data
Microfiche Series No. VD15-99, pages 216; 92; 84; 85; 301;
308; 213; 298; 5; 202; 199; 200; 19; 41.

[2]The Mnong Lăm spirit world includes yang (used inter-
changeably or in doublet form with brah) 'good spirits',
yang djoh 'bad spirits', čak 'malevolent spirit' (they can
possess people), čak lua 'ghost (?)', and ngăt 'souls'
(people, elephants, houses, and rice have a ngăt). The ngăt
nhuôl may be restricted to people and elephants. From these
texts a hierarchy of spirits can be deduced:

1) The main spirits (The Lăm say that originally they
called upon only these). Yang Trôk or Yang Yo Trôk 'Spirit
of the Sky', who created people, gives the soul, gives a good
disposition to elephants, and sends the rain. Yang May Bă or
Yang May Yo or Yang (Bri) Teh (Dih) 'Spirit of the ancestors'
or 'Spirit of the Earth'. (The Tung Tang Djhang Wiêt were
made the original Lam ancestors (Yang May Bă) by Kuon Mtao
Tluă Kbuă Lan.) Yang Ngăt Nhuôl 'Guardian Spirit' or Yang
Nar 'Spirit of the Sun'.

2) Lesser spirits. Kuon Mtao Tluă Kbuă Lan (Spirit or
Child ?) of the King Tluă Kbuă Lan, who taught the ancestors
how to sacrifice. Yang May To 'Great Mother Spirit', creates
elephants. Yang Djoh Yang Briêng 'Spirit of Violent Death',
keeps the souls of people who died violently.

3)   Various other yang and čak.

[3]The author associated Yang Djoh Yang Briêng with the Judeo-Christian Satan.

[4]The rainy season begins in June.

[5]Preceding most sacrifices and ceremonies, wine jars are tied to the upright poles in the part of the house reserved for visitors or, if the sacrifice is held out of doors, they are tied to a stake.

[6]See also "Notes sur le Tam Bo Mae Baap Kuon (Exchange de Sacrifices entre un Enfant et ses Père et Mère) Mnong Rlam" by Georges Condominas, *International Archives of Ethnography* 47, Pt. II, 1955.   Pp. 127-59.

[7]For a longer version of this tale, as given by the Roglai, neighbors in the high mountains to the east of the Mnong, see "The Monkey Midwife," told by A. Young, translated by Maxwell Cobbey (unpublished manuscript).

A FIRST CASE OF HISTORIOGRAPHY
AMONG THE ROGLAI

Maxwell Cobbey

This discussion looks at processes that must take place in order for a native author to produce a written history of a people who are barely emerging from illiteracy. Reports have been made on cultures that have developed, or are developing, their own written histories; but a majority of these studies seem to concern language groups that are further along in autochthonal writing than the Roglai.[1] The text discussed here, and presented in translation as the final section of this paper, was written by a Roglai man as an attempt to present the history of his people. His, as far as I am aware, is the first example of historiography among the Roglai.

BACKGROUND

The Northern Roglai have lived in scattered family units in the jungle-covered mountains west of Nha Trang, having apparently little contact with other tribal groups or with the Vietnamese nationals. Even contacts among themselves were more limited than among the tribes that live in villages. Occasionally, before the military conflict of the 1960's, trips were made by the men of a family down to the Vietnamese lowlands to sell jungle products and to buy salt, knives, and clothing for special occasions. Around 1960, some families began to leave the mountains to congregate in lowland villages because of military and political pressures that reached even the jungle areas of Viet Nam. Perhaps 15 percent of the Northern Roglai migrated to the lowlands between 1959 and 1969.

Reading and writing is a new art for the Roglai. Not many of them have been to school. Of those in the lowlands, perhaps one man in fifteen can read a little in Vietnamese, although most of them speak the market variety of Vietnamese well. Even fewer women can read.

Nothing was written in Northern Roglai itself until, in the mid 1960s, a French Catholic missionary produced religious

61

material and members of the Summer Institute of Linguistics
wrote textbooks and other reading materials. This literature had only a limited use at this time, since Roglai literacy
was just struggling to get started. A Viet-Cong program among
the Roglai who remained in the jungle included literacy in the
Roglai language, but we were unable to acertain the extent of
that program.

'Prestige' languages have been preferred for writing.
Most Roglai readers have had reading experiences only with
Vietnamese or Koho materials. Some Protestant Roglai learned
to speak Koho in order to learn more about Christianity from
the Koho people who evangelized the Roglai beginning about
1954, and some of them learned to read the New Testament in
that language. I saw almost no casual reading being done in
any language. Those who wrote letters to relatives usually
chose to use Koho if they knew it, or Vietnamese, even if
they had learned to read Roglai. Only recently have we seen
a more general trend toward the use of the Roglai language by
those who know how to read and write it.

Non-historiographical oral literature does, of course,
exist. Older men repeat legends and myths from previous
generations; everyone repeats news of recent happenings in
the life of the community; shamans repeat half-understood
prayers which have been developed and learned through the
generations; men skilled in speaking use special flowery
constructions in persuasive speech; and the most skillful
compose ballads to tell of personal adventures in hunting or
of hard times. But none of these would be 'history' as we
ordinarily think of it (Saliba 1973:285; Sturtevant 1968:
451, 456, 473; Beattie 1960:7; Wahid 1966:445). Whatever
elements of history may exist in Roglai oral literature, they
exist not so much to preserve an accurate record of the past
as to serve other functions of present society.

THE DEVELOPMENT OF A NATIVE WRITER

Mr. Y, the Roglai man whose history of the Saigon-Nha
Trang area we are now considering, is about thirty years old.
His early life was spent in the mountains. Perhaps fifteen
years ago his father took him to the lowlands. Somewhere
along the way while he was hired out to a Vietnamese family
as their carabao boy, he obtained the equivalent of perhaps
one year of schooling—enough to learn to read Vietnamese.

The rest of his reading and writing ability has been self-developed as he has served a term in the military and then later helped teach me his language. His father was for years a shaman until he left that practice to become one of the first Roglai Christians. Mr. Y showed much ability, and his limited school education was above average for a Roglai.

He wrote many stories, legends, and cultural descriptions for me during the years he helped me. A number of times I asked him to write about the days before the French came, but each time he would reply that he knew nothing of those times and said he would ask the old men about those days. Finally, a few weeks before we left Viet Nam, he surprised me by giving me this history of his area.

I'm sure that Y felt more at ease writing other papers for me about current Roglai customs and oft-repeated myths; but in spite of his experience, because he knew I wanted it, he wrote what is probably the first history of the Roglai written by a Roglai. He wrote the history with me in mind as the primary reader target rather than the Roglai, although he knew that a number of other articles that he had written for me were eventually published for the Roglai to read.

CULTURE UNPREPARED FOR HISTORY

The Roglai are not inclined to think historically, especially as this involves a sequence of events in time. The processes involved in lining up isolated events in a time frame must have been new to him, as well as some of the specific facts, which he learned from the elder men.

In the jungle, the Roglai never kept track of years or months, except to be aware when to expect rains or seasons which would affect their agriculture or food gathering. Probably none of them older than fifteen knows exactly how old he is, or the month and day of his birth. When the older ones have been required to have birth dates on their I.D. cards in recent years, they calculate, in consultation with relatives, about how many years old they are, and then at random choose a month and a day or let a Vietnamese official choose for them.

Referring to events in the past by a date is new to them and was new to Mr. Y as he wrote his history. And it was

new to him to take the isolated events of the past, as related to him by the elder men, and to arrange them together
in a consecutive framework. The Roglai had found no reason
to date events in the past. When Mr. Y did it in his history,
he was using a new tool with which he had had little experience. Consequently, what would be a glaring error to those
of us who are acquainted with the tool, was passed over by
him unnoticed. For instance, he represents the Japanese as
coming some time after 1150 (line 29) and being replaced by
the French about 1750 (line 115); but he states only "more
than fifty years" as the duration of the Japanese period
(line 56). He states that Mr. U was Ha T's age in 1920
(line 263), whereas I know Ha T to be about eleven years old
now, which would make Mr. U 66 years old at present; but I
know Mr. U to be only a couple of years older than Y, or in
his early thirties. These discrepancies were not noticed by
Y as he constructed his article in the unfamiliar field of
dated and chronologically related events.[2]

    Some important dates taken from our Western history of
Viet Nam are at variance with Y's history.[3] Certain dates
are listed here for reference with Y's dates.[4]

Y's Date	Event	Western Date
1150	Vietnamese arrive	?
	Vietnamese conquer Cham	1450
	French missionaries begin in Viet Nam	1611
	Various struggles between Vietnamese factions	1770f
	French become involved in above	1787
	Vietnamese emperor Minh Mang persecutes Catholics	1828f
	Martyrdoms and severe persecutions	1843-48

	Napoleon III declares war on Vietnamese	1857
1750 plus	Saigon captured by French	1859
	French authority established in Viet Nam	1864
after 1150	Japanese troops enter Indochina	1940
	Japanese troops occupy whole of Indochina	July, 1940
	Japan takes over Viet Nam	March 9, 1945
1750	Atom bomb	August 6, 1945
1750 plus	French return to Viet Nam	late 1945
	French defeated at Dien-Bien-Phu	May 7, 1954
	Refugees begin to leave Hanoi	August 9, 1954

Besides the actual dates, other discrepancies occur in Y's history. The Japanese are in Viet Nam before the French, and they are in Viet Nam for several generations, whereas according to Western records the Japanese followed the French (although the French then followed them in turn) and the Japanese were only in Indochina a few years between 1940 and 1945. And of course the atom bombs were dropped by the Americans rather than the French.

Agreements between Y's history and Western history should also be noted, all of which he apparently assumed I would not otherwise know:

the area was sparsely populated in earlier times (line 7),

the French arrived following the atom bomb (line 75),

they were resisted by the Vietnamese (line 78),

the tribal people in general were friendly with the
French (line 125),

there were Japanese rifles in the hands of the Vietnamese
(line 165), and

the Japanese conscripted men for the military (line 37).[5]

There are also omissions of what seem to us important
aspects of history, such as the rule of the Cham in Southern
Viet Nam, including the area of Saigon and Nha Trang. Y
only mentions this era once. This era was probably peaceful
as far as the Roglai were concerned back in their jungle
homes, so that no events from these centuries of Cham-
Vietnamese wars impressed themselves on the Roglai cultural
memory. Nor are there, as far as I know, myths developed
concerning the French or the Japanese.

Except for a single reference to the Sun God (line 204)
and a final passing reference to ancestors, there is nothing
in the account relating to the supernatural. Perhaps this
is due to the fact that Y was writing for me, a foreigner
(as evidenced by his frequent use throughout the text of the
personal form of address 'Sir').

We may ask what happened to the 'facts' between the time
they occurred and the time Y reacted his history? The two
arrivals of the French, c. 1847 and c. 1946, were coalesced
into one (or perhaps the former was completely forgotten);
educational efforts were attributed to the Japanese but those
of the French ignored; the bombing of Japan was attributed to
the French;[6] and what were probably local incidents are
magnified to national importance, such as the invitation to
drink wine with the Vietnamese (line 221) and the slaughter
that followed (line 274). Some of the facts were modified
before Y collected them from the community, others obviously
occurred as a result of his redacting, and there remains the
possibility that some elements of his history have no factual
basis.[7]

Perhaps we should regard Y's article as historical fiction
rather than pure history, but he regarded it as true history

(Cf. Hussein 1968:87; Van Sickle 1948:2:453). However, if I
had undertaken to write a Roglai history, rather than Y,
there would have been just as many problems, based on my
Western prejudices and lack of 'inside' viewpoint; the Roglai
would have needed to re-do it (Wahid 1966:448).

SOURCES

As any redactor chooses material from more than one source
and shuffles the incidents and actors together, so did Y.
Y's process of historiography falls between the techniques of
folk literature with which he was naturally familiar, and the
techniques of Western history with which he had had almost no
experience, but which he was imposing on his work. Consequently, the unconscious techniques involved in the development of folk literature should be seen in his work, with the
difference that it combines sources of fairly equal value,
whereas a myth is changed by adding elements to, or modifying
elements in, an already established corpus. In the case of
Y's work, although it is difficult to say that one element
was first and another was added later, breaking-up, and re-
attachment, and reinterpretation are all seen in his mixing
of Japanese, French and American elements.

Y's sources are both native and foreign. Some sections came
from eyewitnesses (line 272); but much came to Roglai elders by
way of non-Roglai sources of 30 or more years ago (probably
lines 30, 57, and 75). Some of the information came from Roglai
generations (lines 1 and 15).

Older Roglai sources probably did much to provide thematic
material and flavor for Y's product.

Y collected his information for his history from older
men. Over a period of several years he gave me scores of
texts on various subjects, but never one on history, other
than this one, although I requested 'history' several times.
This suggests that the information upon which he based his
historiography is not found in formal units of the standard
forms of literature. Rather, they were found as isolated
bits of information, passed on in conversation, not as a
formal myth or an epic. These conversational sections, however, were subject to the same influences that myths and
other oral literature are.

It is also probable that Y had to select between varying
accounts when he questioned the elders about former days,
but he shows almost no uncertainty in his account except in
the case of dates and he basically accepts everything that
the elders tell him. It is characteristic of the Roglai to
believe unhesitantly their own traditions, legends, and current experiences with the supernatural; but they are extremely resistant to foreign ideas that conflict with their traditions. One of my Roglai helpers refused to work on translat-
ing health materials to acquaint the people with plague and
malaria. He said that the people would not believe such
explanations for the diseases, since they already had their
own knowledge of how they occur (Cf. Van Sickle 1948: 2: 415;
Eder 1969:197).

Y also inserted, as proof of veracity, the names of people
known to me who could vouch for some of the recent events
that he recorded (lines 252 and 264). Even should a native
historian suspect that some of his history might be myth, he
would find it difficult to separate between myth and truth,
even as experienced researchers do.

All of Y's sources presumably have handled and passed on
facts in the light of their understanding of the present.
Each time an event was recounted, the influence of the audi-
ence, as well as the subconscious desires of the one speaking, kept the story within the values of the culture. In
addition to those influences, Y had special pressures in his
task of redacting and putting the history into written form
for me, his foreign employer.[8]

As Y questioned the old men about the past, the facts
presented during any one discussion typically would be judged
and corrected by those present. But Y, when alone writing
the paper, was able to chose which items to include and
which to omit. Being only a 'reporter', relieved him from
personal responsibility for the basic facts (Dundes 1968:128).

CONCLUSION

Historians have a point to make; they have a theme to
their work. The theme I see in Y's account is not a moral
one in the strict sense of right vs. wrong, as we think of

right and wrong. The emphasis is, rather, on having an advantage over one's opponent. The tribal people are represented
as having the upper hand over the Vietnamese. And this is more
important to them. The text begins with a very good relationship between the Vietnamese and the tribal people (line 27).
If a theme of injustice had been uppermost, the story could
have emphasized that the land originally had belonged to the
tribal folk, and that it was taken from them by the Vietnamese. But the first 'wrong' we might discern as having
occurred between the tribal folk and the Vietnamese is when
the tribal people hunted down the Vietnamese who, as far as
the text tells us, had been only friendly to them previously
(line 23). But this is not treated as 'wrong' in Y's history.
The implied opposite is true, in that the tribal people had
the advantage at that time, rather than the Vietnamese as is
true nowadays. This advantage is 'good' in the eyes of the
tribal culture rather than some other ideas of fairness and
justice.

There is an overt expression of hatred near the end of the
account, when the tribal people realize they can be deceived
(line 268). If this can be interpreted as 'righteous indigna-
tion', then it may indicate that it is acceptable to kill out-
right (line 157) but not to deceive.

The literature and oral traditions of a people reflect the
values that are important to them. Y's history represents
certain conditions as being true in the past. These conditions contrast markedly with present-day Roglai culture, and
hence indicate values they might wish for today. Roglai men
formerly married Vietnamese women (line 25), whereas today,
if anything, it is more likely that a Vietnamese man would
marry a Roglai woman. The Vietnamese were the ones who hid
in the jungles from their enemies (line 123) rather than the
Roglai. The Vietnamese were at the mercy of tribal people
(lines 148 and 155). Tribal soldiers always had plenty of
pay, food, clothes, and ammunition (line 142), whereas the
Vietnamese ran out of ammunition (line 177). All of these
conditions contrast sharply with those of recent times.

Oral traditions express the heartbeat of a people, since
they are retold and remodeled by the whole culture. They
are passed down through the generations, and are distributed

within each generation by many recounters, for the approval
of different audiences. On the other hand, a single piece of
literature written by a native of the culture may express the
feelings of fewer people. Nevertheless, the background of the
writer, if he be strictly a local person, is entirely within
the culture.

Where facts degenerate into obvious fiction, and where the
choice of material presented shows a prejudice, we are able
to say to the Roglai (as to peoples of any culture), "Your
feelings are showing." The keeping alive of a memory of the
past that has them on top of a present adversary reminds them
that the present is but a phase in a long process. The memory
tends to encourage and solidify for a future phase when they
may again have the advantage. It is a protest against a present situation and a means of legitimately expressing feelings
against current hardships (Dundes 1968:126; Saliba 1973:282).

THE TEXT

A Roglai History of the Saigon-Nha Trang Area

Mr. Y, 1975

1   Sir, I'm writing this paper to tell about the time
before the Vietnamese were here in the area of Saigon
and Nha Trang. Previously all around the region of
Saigon-Nha Trang here, there were only tribal people:
5   Cham, Roglai, Rade, Chrau (Tring), Koho, Cadu, Bahnar,
Sedang. In those days, it was the custom to build
houses and villages far apart, say, 50 kilometers apart.
They had the custom of making their houses and villages
with about ten or twenty families together; that was the
10   way they made their houses and villages in those days.
In those former days here in the area of Saigon-Nha
Trang, there weren't a lot of villages or people or
fields. All you could see was a lot of jungle, forests,
and trails in those days.

15   Then, suddenly, the Vietnamese appeared, coming together, bringing their children, carrying their rice
seed and other things, coming from the land of Hanoi.
They came over peaks and over the passes. They kept
coming, kept making villages, kept making more fields,
20   all the way from Hue to Danang to Saigon to our Nha
Trang here. As they met the tribal people, those Vietnamese made friends, giving food and drink, making
friends with wine and feasting in a friendly way together,
grinning from ear to ear. They gave their daughters in
25   marriage to the tribal sons, and the tribal sons in
marriage to the Vietnamese daughters. The Vietnamese
and the tribal people were in very good fellowship with
each other in those days. I'm pretty sure that was the
year 1150.

30   Then at that time suddenly and unexpectedly appeared
another race of people. The name of that race was
'Japanese', I've been told. They came to better the
conditions of the tribal people and the Vietnamese here
in our land of Saigon. Truly their soldiers and their

71

35   civilians taught the tribal people and the Vietnamese
      methods of planting corn and rice. They took all the
      young tribal and Vietnamese men into their military,
      paying them salaries. That's the way the Japanese did
      in those days. But actually, the king who ruled in
40   those days was a person of the Cham race, and all the
      Japanese soldiers there, who came to better the condi-
      tions of the tribal and Vietnamese people here in the
      land of Saigon, were really under the authority of that
      Cham king who ruled.

45   In those days, the Japanese tried to teach the trib-
      al people to read, but they didn't want to study. As
      for the Vietnamese, however, they wholeheartedly studied
      to learn reading. Then those who learned to read well,
      who were soldiers for the Japanese, became second lieu-
50   tenants, first lieutenants, captains, majors, lieutenant
      colonels, and full colonels over the soldiers. But as
      for the tribal people, they didn't know how to read.
      They only knew how to speak and discuss orally. The
      period during which the Japanese came to better the con-
55   ditions of the tribal and Vietnamese here in the land
      of Saigon was more than fifty years.

           But after that, something happened in the homeland
      of the Japanese. It was like this: The French people
      went and requested two great big bombs from the American
60   people. The Americans gave the French the bombs, and
      the French got in airplanes and dropped the bombs, ker-
      plunk, killing all the Japanese in Japan. So immediately
      the king ruling the Japanese there called for all the
      soldiers and Japanese civilians to come back home from
65   our land of Saigon-Nha Trang.

           At that time, the Japanese soldiers gave all their
      guns and cannons to the Vietnamese staying in Saigon and
      Nha Trang. Those guns, they told them, were for hunting
      meat. Then at that time airplanes came from their home-
70   land to get them. The Japanese came to Saigon and Nha
      Trang, and all the Japanese soldiers and civilians got
      in the planes and went back to their homeland. Not a
      single Japanese soldier stayed here in Saigon-Nha Trang.
      Only the tribal and Vietnamese soldiers stayed.

75   Then shortly after that, French soldiers appeared
      unexpectedly, coming in planes, ships, jeeps and tanks.
      Some came by mountain road; some came by ship. So the
      Vietnamese soldiers in Saigon waited to shoot them on
      the roads. But as for the tribal soldiers, they didn't
80   shoot at the French soldiers. All the Vietnamese sol-
      diers, and also young people, old ladies, and little
      children--some had guns, some had bushhooks, others had
      knives and sticks, some had spears, others had spoons,
      chopsticks, and kitchen utensils--going to fight the
85   French soldiers. But those French soldiers smiled and
      wondered who those people were with guns, sticks and
      knives running out striking at them. So they shot and
      killed them at once.

              And at our Nha Trang here at that time, all the
90   Vietnamese citizens living at Dien Khanh, Cam Lam, Dong
      Trang and Cam Ranh came and waited by the ocean down in
      Nha Trang, because their most important ruler in Nha
      Trang called, so that they had to come. He was a Viet-
      namese, and had a long beard from his chin to the sole
95   of his feet. He called all his soldiers, and all his
      citizens to come and wait to shoot and kill the French
      soldiers at the beach by the ocean down in Nha Trang.
      They waited there to shoot and kill the French soldiers
      for a long time, about a day. Then suddenly they saw
100   the ships coming from out in the ocean. But the Viet-
      namese soldiers there didn't aim right when they shot
      at the French soldiers, so that not a single one died.
      The French had iron vehicles. The bullets that the
      Vietnamese soldiers shot hit on the sides of the French
105   iron vehicles all right, but didn't penetrate to the
      soldiers inside. At that, the French brought their
      ships to the beach, opened the doors, and out came tanks
      and jeeps from inside the ships. Upon disembarking they
      saw the Vietnamese soldiers and the citizens there like
110   ants, like very tiny ants, spread all around, each one
      holding only a gun, a stick, or a knife. So the French
      soldiers drove their tanks and jeeps and shot the Viet-
      namese soldiers and civilians, killing hundreds of
      thousands of them here in Nha Trang, sir. I think that
115   was 1750. The dead Vietnamese soldiers and citizens
      filled the jungles. Tigers dragged them off and ate
      them, snakes ate them, all those dead bodies. So the

Vietnamese were defeated there. They weren't able to
fight against the French soldiers any more.

120   Then every one who was still alive got their stuff
together, took their children and their rice seed, and
fled over the mountains and across the ridges, looking
for a cave or a cavern to hide in, fleeing for fear of
being killed by the French. But as for the tribal peo-
125 ple, they didn't flee. When a French soldier would come
up to them, they would shake hands and laugh and talk
together. That encouraged the French soldiers. So the
commander of the French called for all the tribal people
to meet together. He picked out the outstanding and
130 able men, who knew how to speak well and who knew how to
be respectful, and he made them officials. Utung,
uccha, phuliq, ritlong, truong thong. That's how the
French named the officials among the tribal people in
those days.

135   There are the names of those that the French made
utungs: Ta-luon, Pa-ya, Ja-Vlong, Hadjah, A-Rang, Moc,
lon, A-yon, Ra-gai, Ra-bah, Neq, Pa-Hiang, Ca-Hlu, Ma-
dai, Naq, La-buh. Those were the tribal people who
were outstanding that the French made important, sir.

140   At that time, the French invited all the young men
of the tribes to become soldiers together with them.
There was money and rice, guns and bullets and clothing
for them, with all sorts of food, very plentiful. Then
the French commander commanded those tribal soldiers to
145 take their guns and go and look in the jungles and trails
and caves and caverns. If they found any Vietnamese,
men or women, infants, babies, tiny children or small
children, they were told to shoot and kill them all, cut
off their ears, and bring them back to him down in Nha
150 Trang.

       As the French commander there ordered, the tribal
soldiers immediately took their guns and ammunition and
enough rice, and went on the search immediately in the
jungle, on the trails, in the caves and caverns. They
155 shot any Vietnamese on sight, cut off their ears, and
brought them down to the French commander. Whenever

they would shoot the Vietnamese and cut off their ears
and bring them down to the French commander, he didn't
know how to praise them enough. He was so happy. They
160 had done what he wanted. So the commander provided pigs
and carabaos for the Utungs to give to those tribal soldiers to feast upon until they had all they could eat.

Whenever the tribal soldiers came to shoot and kill
the Vietnamese staying in the jungles and trails there,
165 though the Vietnamese had guns that the Japanese soldiers
had given them previously, they didn't have any ammunition to shoot the tribal soldiers who were coming to
kill them. They had used up their ammunition shooting
at the French so their guns were useless, for lack of
170 ammunition. So the tribal soldiers came and shot and
killed the Vietnamese and took their guns and ears and
brought them to the French commander. So the commander
was very happy and praised the tribal soldiers, and
trusted them completely. Whenever the tribal soldiers
175 needed more guns or ammunition the French would re-
supply them. But the Vietnamese there in the jungles
and trails, when they lacked guns or ammunition, there
was no one to give them guns and ammunition to help them.

Whenever a tribal soldier would take a Vietnamese
180 in order to cut him and kill him, the Vietnamese sometimes said, "Oh sir, take me alive and let me be your
slave." Or a girl would say, "Older brother, take me
alive, let me be your wife." But they wouldn't listen,
they went right on and killed those Vietnamese there.

185   In those days the Vietnamese who escaped alive
looked for a land to flee to, far away where they could
be hidden. Then, after a long time, more than eighty
years, those Vietnamese were very prolific out in the
jungles and trails, and became plentiful. Then they
190 would go and meet some Roglai who lived in the mountains, shake his hand and talk nicely and persuade
the Roglai to go down to Nha Trang and buy fish sauce
and salt and bring it back for them to eat together.
And they would forbid the Roglai to tell the French or
195 the Utungs that the Vietnamese were hidden in the mountains there.

In their hearts the Vietnamese were still angry
with the tribal people for killing the Vietnamese previously. Then the Vietnamese schemed together among
200 themselves to make janin wine and to call all the tribal people to come and drink the janin wine. And when
they were drunk and terribly dizzy, the Vietnamese would
stab and kill all the tribal people. That was how the
Vietnamese planned to do that year, but the Sun God
205 wouldn't let them do the killing.

The Vietnamese worked and planned together, men and
women, making a circular fence like a fort that the soldiers make. And all around at the base of that fence
they planted bamboo spikes covered with thorns. Even a
210 rat couldn't get through it. When they were finished
making the fence, they dug janin root, chopped it up and
put it in the wine jars. There weren't just a few jars
there, but from a thousand up to two or three thousand
wine jars of janin wine, so that there would be enough
215 for all the tribal people to drink. That's how the
Vietnamese thought it would be.

When they had finished putting the janin to ferment
for wine, the main ruler of the Vietnamese told his one
or two hundred representatives to go to every village
220 and every area of the tribal people and speak to the
tribal people, saying, "We come in order to invite you
brothers to come to a fellowship feast with us, so that
we won't be angry and hate each other as enemies any
more. Please wear nice skirts and new and pretty shirts
225 and new pants and come and feast. So the tribal people
were thrilled and enthusiastic; they didn't know what
to do, they were so happy. Some said, "Oh, the Vietnamese are very nice; they aren't bad to us any more."
Then those Vietnamese representatives said, "Brothers,
230 when you come to this feast, don't let one individual
stay at home in the village; every single person must
come. Your pigs and chickens, turn them all outside
and let them look for food for themselves. This feast
is going to be a long one, five days and nights, so all
235 of you come to this feast."

From this time the Vietnamese representatives
brought the invitation, there were four more days until
the appointed day when they were to have the feast of
janin wine. After that, not quite to the fourth day,
240 suddenly the word came, "Flee, brethren, the Vietnamese
are tricking us to go and drink janin now. When you get
drunk, poisoned by that janin wine, the Vietnamese will
stab and kill all of us tribal people. Flee, brothers."
Therefore the tribal people stampeded to flee, breaking
245 kettles and gourds; some carrying their children on
their backs across streams lost their children when the
carrying cloths came untied and their children floated
downstream, and they didn't care to try to swim to res-
cue them because of their fleeing from the Vietnamese.
250 What a pitiful time they had that month!

The person that tipped the tribal people off to
flee there, was named Ngeq. He was a Roglai. He had
lived with a Vietnamese family since he was small, and
the Vietnamese considered him the same as a true child
255 of theirs. So since he was with those Vietnamese he
heard of their plans to kill the tribal people; but he
had a mind to tip the tribal people off to flee in
order to escape death then.

And the Vietnamese people were very, very angry.
260 They were so mad! "Who could it be that tipped off the
tribal people to flee and escape completely like that,
and not come to the feast and drink the janin wine?" I
think that was the year 1920, sir. In that year, Mr. U
was the size of Ha T, sir. Mr. U knows about this time
265 when the Vietnamese representatives invited them to
drink the janin wine.

Then the tribal people were very angry with the
Vietnamese for deceiving them like that. So they made
bows and lots of poisoned arrows. They made knives and
270 spears. Some carried bows, some knives. Others had
spears and some had bushhooks. They went to fight those
Vietnamese. Mr. LaS and Mr. Th were among those who
went to fight then, sir.

The Vietnamese died with broken heads, spilled
275 blood, full of arrows in their bodies. Some died; some

were wounded with the arrows stuck in their bodies, and
they fled, wailing and calling on their ancestors to
help. They fled up to peaks, over the ridges, away
from the tribal people in those days.

NOTES

[1]The Moros of Mindanao, for example, have had a means of writing for hundreds of years (Saleeby 1905); all that has been recorded are codes, genealogies, and technical histories. "No Moro has yet undertaken the task of preserving in written form the literature of the people--their mythology, legends, folktales, and poetry" (Manuel 1969:18-19, quoting Datu Gumbay Piang).

The Marathas of India, already having a means of writing, began to record their history in the 16th century. "The need was felt by the Marathas to record their military exploits and political experience in writing, and this took the form of chronologies, ballads, annals, family accounts, and chronicles" (Patterson 1968:401, quoting V. G. Dighe).

When Titus Livius wrote his history of Rome, which is the oldest now extant, there were already many generations of writers of other types of historical records to set a precedent for him (Van Sickle 1948:215).

Robert van Niel has written a *Survey of Historical Source Materials in Java and Manila* in order to help historians of the region "because he believes that it is desirable, even necessary, to write indigenous history of Southeast Asian nations, localities, and institutions" (Genzor 1972:194).

[2]In the Rengao, another tribe of Viet Nam, chronology of events does not seem to be a focal point of their mythology, and informants have different ideas about when certain events took place (Gregerson 1969:249).

Even though the Moros have had a system of writing for hundreds of years, the early Moros never dated their events or documents (Saleeby 1905:53).

[3]There are other examples of local histories differing with Western ideas about the same matter. The Yaqui autochthonous historians differ with Western historians on the earlier dates of their narratives, but agree with available historical sources for the later ones (Spicer 1954:24). In Uganda, there are discrepancies between the Lugbara accounts

of the arrival of the whites and the accounts given by the
whites themselves (Middleton 1965:21). "Nyoro ideas about
the history of their relations with Europeans differ in some
respects from European ideas about the same history. It might
be said that there are two histories of these events, and if
we are to understand how present-day Nyoro think about themselves and about Europeans we shall have to know something
about them both" (Beattie 1960:7).

[4]Most of the dates in this table are found in Claude 1967:
53-65.

[5]In the 1940's, the Viet Minh "were armed with some 30,000
Japanese rifles and 2,000 machine guns--weapons picked up from
the Japanese at the time of their surrender" (Trager 1966:72).
All of these events, including sparsely populated areas becoming inhabited, occurred within the last two generations.

[6]Yaqui historians are also found to have transferred a
characteristic from one actor to another. "This spirit is
regarded, however, by the modern Yaqui historians as having
been expressed by Juan Maldonado rather than by Cajeme"
(Spicer 1954:31).

[7]"A vivid example of the need to consider the cultural
setting of historical traditions and to compare versions is
provided by Mohave Indian 'historical epics'. These were
very long, exceedingly detailed, circumstantial, sober, and
concrete accounts of Mohave migrations, cast in a form which
appears flatly historical. Yet by examining the manner in
which these tales originated--by 'dreaming'--by a comparison
of different versions, and from a few improbable or impossible
motifs contained in the tales, (Alfred L.) Kroeber concluded
that these stories were 'pseudo-history', products of imagina-
tion, literary efforts, and not in the slightest historical
by our own criteria, although they were plainly historical by
the criteria of Mohave folk history" (Sturtevant 1968:464).

[8]Dundes (1968:127) favors the recording of ethnographic
information by natives themselves in order to avoid the foreign ethnographer's ethnocentric bias, except where the native
edits the information to protect the ethnographer as they tell
their stories. "A writer judges nearly every article he writes

on the basis of what effect it will have on other people. He is always frightened lest he be misunderstood, for he knows that his words can color, mold, and determine the shape of the world and the character of its people" (Van Horn 1970:15).

REFERENCES

Alatas, Syed Hussein. 1964. *Theoretical Aspects of Southeast Asian History* 2:247-59.

Beattie, John. 1960. *Bunyoro, an African Kingdom.* Holt, Rinehart and Winston.

Clark, Lawrence. 1961. *Sayula Popoluca Texts with Grammatical Outline.* Summer Institute of Linguistics.

Claude, Edmond, et al. 1967. *Viet-Nam, Past and Present.* The Vietnamese Department of National Education and the National Commission for UNESCO.

Cobbey, Maxwell. 1975. "There Must Be a Supernatural Reason." *In Other Words* 1:2.5. Wycliffe Bible Translators.

Cowan, George H. 1965. *Some Aspects of the Lexical Structure of a Mazatec Historical Text.* Summer Institute of Linguistics.

Demetrio, Francisco. 1969a. "Towards a Classification of Bisayan Folk Beliefs and Customs." *Asian Folklore Studies* 28:27-50.
---1969b. "The Religious Dimensions of Some Philippine Folk Tales." *Asian Folklore Studies* 28:51-65.

Dozier, Edward P. 1966. *Hano, A Tewa Indian Community in Arizona.* Holt, Rinehart and Winston.

Dundes, Alan. 1968. "Oral Literature." *Introduction to Cultural Anthropology,* James A. Clifton (ed.). Houghton Mifflin Company, pp. 116-29.

Eder, Matthias. 1969. "Reality in Japanese Folktales." *Asian Folklore Studies* 28:17-26.

Genzor, Jozef. 1972. Book review in *Asian and African Studies* 8:194-95.

Gonzales, N.V.M. 1964. "Asian Literature: Some Figures in the Landscape." *Asian Studies* 2:76-81.

Gregerson, Marilyn Bergman. 1969. "Rengao Myths: A Window on the Culture." *Practical Anthropology* 16:216-27.

Herskovits, Melville J. 1945. "The Process of Cultural Change." *The Science of Man in the World Crisis,* Ralph Linton (ed.). Columbia University Press, pp. 143-70.

Howells, William. 1954. *Back of History.* Doubleday and Company.

Hussein, Ismail. 1968. "The Study of Traditional Malay Literature." *Asian Studies* 6:66-89.

Jacobs, Melville, and Bernhard J. Sterns. 1958. *General Anthropology.* Barnes and Noble.

Kosambi, D. D. 1955. "The Basis of Ancient Indian History." *Journal of the American Oriental Society* 75:226-37.

Loewen, Jacob A. 1969. "The Dynamics of Myth-Changing and Myth-Making." *Practical Anthropology* 16:170-78.

Lowie, Robert H. 1934. *An Introduction to Cultural Anthropology.* Farrar and Rinehart.

Manuel, Esperidion Arsenio. 1969. "Agyu: The Ilianon Epic of Mindanao." *UNITAS* 42, No. 2. The University of Santo Tomas, Manila.

Middleton, John. 1965. *The Lugbara of Uganda.* Holt, Rinehart and Winston.

Oswalt, Robert L. 1964. *Kashaya Texts* in *Publications in Linguistics* 36. University of California.

Patterson, L. P. Maureen. 1968. "Chitpavan Brahman Family Histories: Sources for a Study of Social Structure and

Social Change in Maharashtra." *Structure and Change in Indian Society,* Milton Singer and Bernard S. Cohen (eds.). Pp. 397-411.

Saleeby, Najeeb M. 1905. *Studies in Moro History, Law and Religion,* Department of the Interior, Ethnological Publications, Volume IV, Part 1. Bureau of Public Printing, Manila.

Saliba, John A. 1973. "Myth and Religious Man in Contemporary Anthropology." *Missiology* 1:281-93.

Spicer, Edward H. 1954. *Potam, A Yaqui Village in Sonora.* American Anthropological Association.

Sturtevant, William C. 1968. "Anthropology, History, and Ethnohistory." *Introduction to Cultural Anthropology,* James A. Clifton (ed.). Houghton Mifflin Company, pp. 450-75.

Taber, Charles R. 1969. "Why Mythology?" *Practical Anthropology* 16:145-46.

Trager, Frank N. 1966. *Why Viet Nam?* Frederik A. Praeger.

Van Horn, Marion. 1970. "Writing is Fascinating, Frustrating, Frightening." *Read, the Adult Literacy Magazine* 5:2:14-15. Port Moresby.

Van Sickle, C. E. 1948. *A Political and Cultural History of the Ancient World,* Vols. 1-2. Houghton Mifflin Company.

Wahid, Zainal Abidin Bin Abdul. 1966. "Sejarah Melayu." *Asian Studies* 4:445-51.

JEH MUSIC

Nancy Cohen

The music of the Jeh[1] encompasses both vocal and instrumental music. This paper is presented in two sections, first a study of Jeh vocal music, and then a description of Jeh musical instruments.

PART 1. VOCAL MUSIC

The Jeh divide vocal music into four distinct types: lullaby, lament, happy songs (of which there are nine), and 'foreign' songs.

The lullaby (nhen) is sung by a mother or other female relative to quiet a baby, encouraging the infant not to cry. It can be sung to a crying infant carried on the back of a woman even when harvesting rice, it being taboo to sing any other songs while harvesting.

The lament (akah) is the only song which the Jeh call a sad song. It is sung only by women. It can be sung at funerals, but Jeh insist that it is not a death 'wail'. The Jeh weep when a person dies, but they say that they do not wail. The subject matter of a lament on other occasions might have to do with reminiscing about past life in the village, activities of rice planting days, the abundance of food in pre-refugee days, or the carefree hunting and fishing of long ago. Jeh refugees dwell on these things with great sadness and longing.

The nine 'happy' tunes are called kǒdoh by the Jeh. Six of them are sung solely for entertainment: the huaĭ, the ding-ding, the ton, the tǒret, the tǒ'ngi, and the kǒdoh kǒsǎng. Two others, the si'ang and the ayaǎ, can be sung either for entertainment or for ceremonial occasions. The remaining kǒdoh tune, the bia-bia, is restricted to ceremony alone. Thus, eight of the nine kǒdoh songs can be sung at social gatherings for enjoyment while drinking wine, whereas the bia-bia is sung only in calling on the rice spirit.

85

The si'ang and the ayaă have several restrictions regarding
their usage. They can be sung only on the occasion of a feast
in the house of the host while drinking wine, or in the field
after a corn roast. It is taboo to sing these two songs at any
other time or in any other place.

The six kŏdoh songs used solely for entertainment, as well
as the lullaby and the lament, can be sung in the house alone
for enjoyment, while cooking rice, in the forest while gathering wood or vegetables, in the village, in the communal house,
or while preparing a field for planting. It is taboo for the
Jeh to sing while eating, since this would bring about an un-
favorable response from the spirits.

Both men and women sing all of the kŏdoh songs except the
ayaă, which is sung only by the men, and the bia-bia, which
is sung only by women.

A more detailed description of the nine kŏdoh songs follows.

1. The huaĭ tune is sung to report on lack of success at
hunting or gathering vegetables. A bachelor might sing it,
wondering if a certain girl wants to marry him. He uses
metaphorical language such as: "I want to buy a bracelet,
but I don't have any money." The bracelet refers to bracelets exchanged in the marriage ceremony. Or, a person could
use it in singing about his mother who has died, or who is
away from home. Only children and young adults sing the
huaĭ and the ding-ding which are said to have been borrowed
from the Sedang people, a neighboring group in Kontum Province; older people do not sing these two tunes.

2. The ding-ding is a love song and can be sung by a
young girl who is thinking about her soldier husband who has
gone on patrol for a few days. The words would go something
like this: "I love you very much; you remember me and love
me too." Children can be heard singing the ding-ding while
at play.

3. The ton is borrowed from the Halang people, also
neighbors of the Jeh. This tune can be sung in the forest
during an approaching rainstorm, using words such as: "Don't
let me get wet and cold!" Or, a girl seeing some fruit she
can't reach can sing this tune saying, "I'm hungry and want
to eat you, but I'm not able to get you. Who will climb and

pick for me?" Or, a girl seeing a man on a path far away can
also sing this tune saying, "What man is that?" It is all
right for her female companions to hear this, but not for the
man to hear.

The ton can also be used for exhortation and the text
would run something like this: "Do your work well; do it
quickly; don't take a long time doing it. Whatever you do,
do well. Talk nicely with one another; do not talk with one
another in a bad manner."

This tune has a narrow range consisting of four notes in a
minor key. It mainly centers around mi, fa, and so, dropping
down to do at phrase endings. There is frequent ornamentation
noticeable on the lower notes. The singer can whistle a
phrase of the tune in mid-song, if he wishes to do so.

4. The tŏret reveals a person's emotional or spiritual
attitudes, or can tell of a person's present situation, as
well as comparing the present with the past. In a taped recording, a Jeh refugee sings the tŏret, revealing that she
feels inferior to others and that she is afraid when someone
even speaks to her. She feels lazy and is not as steadfast
in working as she was when younger. She concludes saying she
is not strong enough to work anymore.

The tŏret is sung in a minor key. Each phrase starts on
mi, descends to do and continues back and forth between mi
and do, with occasional ornamentation on mi. Do predominates
throughout the tŏret and is always the final note of the tune.

5. The tŏ'ngi has subject matter similar to that of the
tŏret. In a taped recording of the tŏ'ngi, a Jeh refugee
sings of worshipping God with deep respect, and of speaking
only good to her husband, not bad. She is already old, she
continues, and is not able to travel far nor obtain material
possessions, whereas her guests travel long distances and
obtain many goods.

Although the texts of the tŏret and the tŏ'ngi are similar, the two tunes are distinctly different. While the tŏret
has a narrow range, the tŏ'ngi has a very wide range. It
starts on high do, progresses down to la, further down to so,

then down to <u>do</u>, on down again to <u>la</u>, <u>so</u> and <u>fa</u>, and back up
to <u>do</u>. There is ornamentation throughout the entire song.
The singer can hum a phrase of the tơ'ngi in mid-song.

6. The kơdoh kơsăng is literally a kơdoh of long ago
and is sung only by older Jeh. This song is used to sing
about being unable to reciprocate a gift, remembering loved
ones far away, or remembering the people and things of the
village and its life while being far away.

Following is a brief summary of the words of two kơdoh
kơsăng songs. The first one, sung by a grandmother to a
young man, tells about days of long ago and about a river and
a village now deserted. The second one, sung by a refugee,
apologizes to her guests for not having food to serve them.
She misses her Jeh village, now that she lives in a strange
place far from it. She is very sad, and not strong anymore
like she was when she was young.

Of all the Jeh songs, the kơdoh kơsăng is the most complex.
It is sung in a minor key using the same notes as the ton with
the addition of high <u>do</u>. Each phrase begins on high <u>do</u> and is
characterized by a highly embellished glissando as it moves
down to the lower notes, <u>so</u>, <u>fa</u>, <u>mi</u> and <u>do</u>. There is more
ornamentation in this tune than in any of the others, occur-
ring throughout the entire song, both on the downglides and
on the level notes.

Any one of four kơdoh tunes can be chosen to be sung at
the marriage ceremony--the ton, the tơret, the tơ'ngi, or
the kơdoh kơsăng. The text of the marriage song goes something like this:

Go-between: "We're going to catch a chicken,
an orphan chicken, and roast it and eat it."

Bride's mother: "I don't have an orphan
chicken."

Go-between: "Oh, yes you do!"

Bride's mother: "My child doesn't know how to
pound rice, carry wood or water, or look for
vegetables." (This is a proper response,

although every Jeh girl would know how to do
these things.)

Groom's family: "That's okay."

Groom's family: "My son doesn't know how to
weave baskets." (Again this is the right response, although very unlikely to be true.)

Bride's family: "That's okay."

Immediately after this, the young couple is brought to the
house, and the wedding ceremony proceeds.

7. Originally the si'ang was sung by a guest at a feast,
praising the host and his hospitality, and calling attention
to the tasty water buffalo meat eaten and the good wine
served. This was in the days when food was plentiful and
water buffalo were still available for sacrifice.

In a taped recording of the si'ang, sung by a refugee, she
expresses gratitude for visitors who have come a long distance
to visit her. She says she is destitute, and barely existing.
She says her visitors have many blessings and many possessions.
She doesn't get anything, things do not improve, and she is
unsuccessful.

The si'ang is in a major key, starting on a high <u>so</u>, dropping to <u>do</u>, then down to lower <u>so</u> and <u>do</u> and continues in
this lower range, with a marked beat. It ends on low <u>do</u>,
finally fading out.

8. The ayaǎ song is unique among the other kǒdoh, in that
it is lined. The leader starts the ayaǎ by saying an appropriate phrase; he then sings this phrase using the ayaǎ tune;
and finally, the entire group of men present sings this same
phrase in unison with the leader. Thus, at a feast, the host
may start the ayaǎ by saying something like "I have no water
buffalo meat to serve, no rice to give you, no wine for you
to drink," minimizing his hospitality. He then sings these
words by himself, and after this, the entire group will sing
them again along with him.

A guest may start another line, saying, "I go to look for
gold and pay it, then go home and buy a water buffalo." He
then sings the words, following which the entire group sings
them with him. The man lining the song snaps his fingers at
certain places to indicate changes of interval, phrasing, and to
to keep the group singing in unison.

The ayaǎ has a strong beat set by the leader. It is sung in
a minor key. Each phrase starts on <u>fa</u>, goes down to <u>mi</u> and to
<u>do</u>. This sequence is repeated. Then <u>do</u> is repeated three or
four times, the first two occurrences preceded by a grace note
on <u>mi</u> which slurs down to <u>do</u>. Then the entire phrase is repeated before a new line is begun. Each note, with the exception of the grace note, receives a heavy accent.

A free translation of an ayaǎ taken from a taped recording follows:

Line 1. "Oh, oh, oh, oh husband, I rest with the
newborn child in the house at Pẽng Sal, in the
house at Pẽng Sal."

Line 2. "Mother, Mother, I am a very neglected
child, I am a very neglected child."

Line 3. "Oh Father, Oh Father, you died when I
was a little child, you died when I was a
little child."

Line 4. "Mother, Mother, I am a very sad child
now, I am a very sad child now."

Line 5. "When I was still a child bringing the
pan to pan gold, slop, slop; I am the child
bringing the pan to pan gold, slop, slop."

Line 6. "Day after day I carry a pack on my back,
going off by myself; I carry a pack on my back,
going off by myself."

Line 7. "There is someone rich and able to acquire
possessions; we follow him, but we're not able
to acquire possessions; we follow him, but we're
not able to acquire possessions."

Line 8. "There is someone rich and successful, we
follow him but we're not successful anymore; we
follow him, but we're not successful anymore."

9. The bia-bia is a ceremonial song sung by the Jeh to
placate the rice spirit whose favor can give an adequate rice
harvest. It is sung by rice priestesses twice a year, once
before rice planting and once before harvest.

Each year one woman in each household is chosen to be rice
priestess for that household. She is chosen on the basis of
being successful and prosperous. During the week preceding
the ceremony, the priestess is forbidden to bathe or to eat
onions, chicken or fruit. She is the first person to plant
rice in the family field, the first to harvest the rice, the
first to put new rice in the storage granary, and the first
person to cook new rice and serve it to the others in her
household.

The rice priestess sings the bia-bia in calling on the
spirits during the time of planting and harvesting the rice
and also as she smears sacrificial blood in the proper places
in the kitchen. When performing the ceremony she must be
alone.

The words of the bia-bia are a petition for happiness,
asking that the family not be argumentative and intractable
in their relationships with one another. The rice priestess
also asks that there be sufficient rice wine and food, and
no serious sickness.

The bia-bia begins with a grace note on do, rises to mi,
descends again to do, rises to fa, descends to mi, then
finally back down to do. Do predominates in this song.
There are accented notes at certain intervals in the song on
semifinal or final falling tones from do, which appear to
mark phrase endings. This song has no ornamentation.

The bia-bia is the only tune not used by Jeh Christians because of its association with the rice spirit ceremony. They retain the si'ang and the ayaă, but use them only for entertainment, not for ceremonial purposes.

Six of the nine kŏdoh can be used in antiphonal singing, exceptions being the huaĭ, the ayaă and the bia-bia.

Jeh songs frequently use metaphorical language to convey an indirect message. These songs include the akah and all of the kŏdoh tunes except the tŏret, the si'ang and the bia-bia.

Finally, 'foreign' songs (hat[2]) usually have Vietnamese or Western tunes. Most of the 'foreign' songs are patriotic songs or church hymns, but the Jeh refer to any foreign song that they hear as hat. Patriotic songs are sung in school or in the communal house in the evening. Hymn tunes are sung in congregational singing, and children can be heard singing them at play. Children also sing the hymns in children's choir, but they do not perform any of the other Jeh songs on formal occasions.

PART II. MUSICAL INSTRUMENTS

The Jeh have eleven musical instruments. All eleven are played either inside the house or inside the communal house, but are never played outdoors.

Most Jeh instruments can be played at any time, either at a feast or when drinking wine, or just for enjoyment. Five of them, however, have restrictions regarding their usage. A wind instrument (khen) is played only at night for enjoy- ment while drinking wine and is interspersed with the sing- ing of the kŏdoh songs. The gong, a percussion instrument, was played in times past only in connection with a water buffalo feast, but it is now played at social occasions while drinking wine. The horn (dut-dut), the miniature drum (sigãl), and the small horn (koliă) are used only in connec- tion with spirit ceremonies.

A description of each of the instruments follows.

1. The large panpipe (khen) is a 12 pipe bamboo instru- ment with a wooden mouthpiece. The mouthpiece has 12

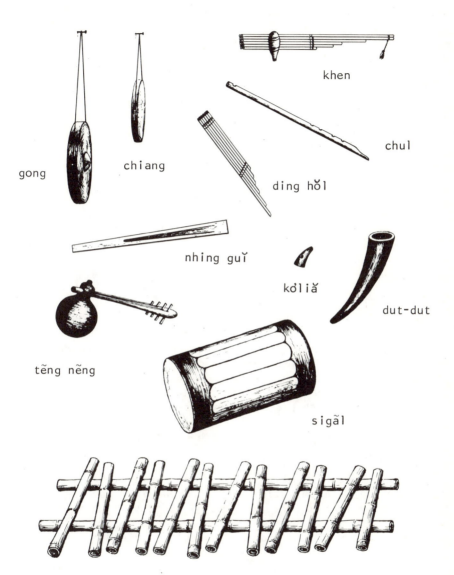

Figure 10.   Jeh Musical Instruments.

metal reeds, one for each of the pipes, which measure approximately 2 cm. in diameter and range in length from .5 to 1
meter.

2. The small panpipe (ding hŏl) is an 8 to 12 pipe bamboo
instrument, similar to the khen, but smaller and without reeds
or mouthpiece. The pipes measure approximately 1 cm. in diameter and range in length from 25 to 50 cm. It is played
by blowing the flush end of the pipes.

3. The flute (chul) is made of bamboo, approximately one
meter long and 3 cm. in diameter, and has 3 or 4 finger holes.
In one recorded melody, the flutist played three long phrases,
stopping in between each phrase to sing a kŏdoh interlude.

4. The Jeh lute (tĕng nĕng) has a hollow gourd resonator,
a bamboo neck, and 8 wire strings. Pegs are made of wood.
It is plucked with the fingers and measures about 50 cm. in
length.

On one taped recording, the player played four tunes, three
of them distinct, the fourth similar to the third. The rhythm
of the first tune was faster than the others. During the
second, third, and fourth tunes, the player beat a syncopated
rhythm on the gourd with the little finger of one hand, making
a sound like a chiang gong to accompany the tune he played
over the strings with his other fingers.

5. The large brass gong (gong) has a raised center, is
suspended by a rope from the rafters of a house, and is
beaten with a wooden stick covered on one end with cloth or
rubber. It ranges in diameter from 46 to over 100 cm. and
has sides 12 to 14 cm. wide. When played, its sound echoes
from mountain to mountain and can be heard up to a distance
of four kilometers. Some gongs are so large as to require
two men to carry them, slung on a shoulder pole between them.

6. The small brass gong (chiang) has no raised center.
It is from 36 to 46 cm. in diameter and has sides of approximately 6 cm. wide. It is played with a wooden stick or
with the fist. Usually four small gongs are played together,
three of them with the fist, while a basic rhythm is beat on
the fourth with a wooden stick. In a taped recording, two

small gongs are prominent; one is a minor third lower than
the other and is played with a syncopated beat.

    7. The large drum (sigãl) is fashioned from a hollowed-
out log. It is approximately 1 meter in length and .5 meter
in diameter. Cowhide or deerskin is stretched across both
ends as drum heads. Two people beat alternately on each end
with a wooden stick. The large drum can be heard at even
greater distances than the large gong. Many of them have
been lost, being too heavy to be carried by refugees.

    8. The horn (dut-dut) is fashioned from the horn of a
water buffalo. In former times the Jeh performed a spirit
ceremony to assure victory over their enemies. Upon returning home from this ceremony in the forest, they would blow
the horn, beat the large drum, and sound a special miniature
form of the drum to signify the completion of the ceremony.

    9. A small horn (koliă) is fashioned from the horn of a
white rhinoceros hornbill bird. It is about 15 cm. long and
is black. It has a hole at each end with a third hole in the
middle used for a mouthpiece. It is held sideways when played,
and the fingers are used at each end to modify the sound
and rhythm. This small horn may be blown only by a man and
only at a buffalo feast in conjunction with the singing of
the si'ang. It is blown first to introduce the si'ang when
sung to call on the spirits.

The preceding nine instruments are played only by men.

    10. The Jews' harp (nhing guĭ) is small, approximately
8 cm. long, and can be made of bamboo, but is more often
made of brass. Both men and women play this instrument.
One end is placed between the teeth, while the fingers of
one hand flick the free end to give rhythm and to vibrate
the tongue.

    11. The marimba (ding but) is an instrument made of bam-
boo tubes varying in length from one to two meters, or even
longer. There can be as many as twelve different tubes,
laid crossways on a wooden frame. The tubes are about 8 cm.
in diameter, each having a different tone according to its
length.

Only women play this instrument. From four to six women sit on opposite sides of the instrument, each woman responsible for three or four of the tubes, and each woman having a partner opposite her. Two partners simultaneously clap their hands next to the ends of the tube being played to sound it. Each set of two partners then takes assigned turns in order to sound each tube needed to play the melody. A strict rhythm is maintained throughout the performance.

Three instruments are not used by Jeh Christians because of their association with pagan spirits--the large horn, the special miniature form of the drum, and the small horn.

NOTES

[1]The Jeh are a Mon-Khmer speaking minority group numbering about ten thousand speakers who live in northern Kontum
Province, Vietnam, near the Laos border.

I am grateful to Jeh friends for their patient help with
this study. Thanks are due also to Marilyn Gregerson for
her helpful suggestions throughout this paper, and to Eva
Burton, Hazel Wrigglesworth and Dr. David Thomas for their
help in editing.

[2]This term is borrowed from Vietnamese hát 'sing', but
drops the high tone.

DEATH AND BURIAL IN KATU CULTURE

Nancy A. Costello

The Katu are a group of approximately 20,000 people who inhabit the mountainous jungle area west of Da Nang in Vietnam. The Katu economy is based on the cultivation of rice in swiddens using the slash and burn technique. Hunting and gathering also make a significant contribution to the Katu subsistence.

The patrilineally extended family and the patrilineal lineage system are the basis of social groupings in Katu society. The village is the largest political unit. It is governed by a loosely organized council of elders, one of whom is considered the village headman. The religious beliefs of the Katu include the recognition of a creator and his son and the belief in a large group of other spirits. Both animal and human sacrifices are offered to the spirits.

BELIEFS CONCERNING DEATH

Types of Death. The Katu believe in two kinds of death: a good death and a bad death. According to legend, long ago the spirit of the sky, the creator, decided which deaths were good, and which were bad. Good deaths are those due to old age, sickness, or sorcery. Bad deaths include accidental deaths such as drowning or falling from a tree, and any sudden or unexpected death such as homicide, childbirth, animal attack, suicide, or death from an unknown cause.

The Katu say that, at times, bad spirits (abưi) steal children at waterfalls. The spirits lure the child by putting an attractive crock at the mouth of a hole. When the child reaches the hole, he falls in and is never seen again. It is also believed that this can happen to adults, but less commonly. This is considered a bad death.

When a bad death occurs, all the pigs, chickens and dogs in the village are killed and thrown out; then the entire village moves. At the new site, houses are built with wooden statues at the doors. There are also statues at the communal house and on the trails. Their purpose is to frighten

99

away the bad spirits, and they may take a variety of forms,
Some are fashioned like human figures with huge faces, others
are squatting figures with their hands on their knees or the
head between the hands, and still others are dancing women.

To the Katu, all sicknesses are caused by the bad spirits,
who take a person's soul to the jungle; and if the soul is
not returned, the person dies. In this case, the Katu beg
for the return of the person's soul by sacrificing to the
bad spirits. A person has chills because the spirits have
put his soul in water, or a person perspires profusely because they have put his soul in the fire.

Abode of the Dead. The Katu concept of good and bad
deaths ties in with their concept of a life after death.
The soul of a person who dies a bad death is sent to the
abode of the bad spirits, called bayô. No one sacrifices to
these souls or remembers them by putting food for them as
they would do in the case of a soul of one who had died a
good death.

The soul of a person who has been killed by spearing remains with the killer. This helps the killer to succeed in
killing others as well. These spirits drink human blood
brought to them by the Katu.

The soul of a person who dies a good death remains with
the corpse in the grave until after the second burial. At
the time of this second burial, people ask the souls of those
in the grave to accept these new people and to make them
happy. Some time after the second burial (the Katu are not
sure just when), the souls go to maraaih, a place inside the
earth where the souls live like people, having houses and
fields. The Katu are aware of the existence of maraaih,
they say, because once when a man was sick, his dead grandfather took him there for one day.

After the first burial, however, a soul may return to
the village impersonating a tiger to frighten his relatives.
This results when a tiger sleeping near the grave bites the
coffin. The dead person then changes into a tiger and generally returns to his own home. In cases where this is said
to have happened, the villagers have killed the tiger before
it entered the house. One such tiger, in particular, was

known to be a dead man returning to frighten his wife, because the tiger's back was rotten like a dead person. In
another case, the villagers killed a tiger which they said
was wearing a bracelet. They assumed that it was really the
spirit of a dead woman.

A dead person becoming a tiger is not considered as
resurrection from the dead because the person has a different
body. The Katu say, however, that such a person does leave
his coffin, leaving it empty.

Resurrection from the Dead. A Katu legend states that at
the beginning of time everyone who had previously died rose
again. In this instance, people rose with improved bodies.
They were fat instead of thin. It is said that they shed
their skin like a snake and received a new body.

The legend explains that two people had a disagreement
over whether those who had died should remain dead or not.
One thought that everyone should rise again, but the other
argued that this would cause the earth to become overcrowded.
The first person told a bird to fly him around the earth to
see if there would be enough room for all the people. (He
hung onto the bird's foot as it flew.) As they were flying,
a lizard happened to see them. This lizard was of the
opinion that people should remain dead because he had climbed
a tree, and from that close proximity looked over the earth
and decided it was too crowded. After this the lizard told
everyone to bury people. Before this time people had not
died.

More recently, there have been stories telling of several
cases of people rising from the dead. One story tells of a
young man going to the grave of a close friend, to mourn.
When the young man arrived, his friend rose from his grave
and they went off to fish and catch frogs. Being afraid to
return to his home, the young man sent the food he had
caught home to his parents with his friend. Then he returned
to his grave to sleep. When his friend arrived at the young
man's home bringing the food, he told the boy's parents that
their son had sent the food. The father thought the friend
was lying, so the friend told the parents to come with him
to see that the young man was really alive, but to hide so

that their son would not be afraid. When the parents saw
their son, they rushed forward to grab him and he immediately
turned into a grasshopper.

Another story tells of a young girl who, after the death
of her boyfriend, went to his grave to mourn; but when it was
time to return home, she was afraid to go by herself. So the
young man rose and offered to take her home. He said, however, that he could not go all of the way with her. When he
turned to leave, he told her not to look back at him as he
left. But she did look back, and saw that his back was
rotted. She screamed and cried; and because she was afraid
of the young man's soul, she died of fright that night. (The
Katu feel that she died because the young man called her soul
to him.)

Another Katu story tells of a man who had died, but whose
son-in-law had not yet killed a buffalo for the second burial.
So the dead man told his son-in-law to kill a buffalo; but
since the son-in-law did not have one, he could not do this.
So he cried and cried. The bad spirits then came to him and
asked, "What do you want?" The son-in-law replied, "I want
to go to my father-in-law." When he had come to his father-
in-law in the place of the dead, his father-in-law exclaimed,
"What are you doing here?!" His son-in-law answered, "I was
afraid, because I did not have a buffalo." So the father-
in-law said, "Here, take this buffalo which you sacrificed
when I died." So his son-in-law took the buffalo. Now the
father was loaning the buffalo to him only until the next
morning. That night the son-in-law was to bring the buffalo
into the center of the village. If he did not do this, the
buffalo would turn into charcoal. Then the next morning he
was to kill the buffalo. The son-in-law returned to earth,
and his relatives were not aware that he had died (i.e.
visited the place of the dead). He told them that he now had
a buffalo, and they asked him where it was. He replied that
he would bring the buffalo to them that night. This he did,
and the next morning he killed the buffalo as instructed.

BURIAL

The Katu often make a coffin in advance and leave it in
the jungle. This way they can have a nicer looking coffin

with carving on it. Whenever a coffin has been made, it is
taboo for anyone in the village to build a house for a year,
for fear that more people might die. Coffins are made from
logs which have been split and hollowed out.

The First Burial. When a person dies, his wife and other
close relatives wash his body and put his best clothes on
him. This often consists of two or three layers of clothes.
No one touches the forehead or the knees of the corpse for
fear that this would cause them to forget the person and not
dream of him. The best cloth is then placed around the deceased and many lights are lit. The whole village then sits
and guards the corpse so that the bad spirits will not snatch
it away. They guard day and night until the burial.

Stories have been passed from generation to generation
enforcing the belief in the necessity of guarding the corpse.
One such story tells of a bad spirit named Sayiing Kruung who
long ago tried to snatch a corpse. He had a large stomach
and a great deal of body hair. The villagers were guarding
a corpse, but at the time everyone in the house was asleep
with the exception of one sick man. The sick man saw Sayiing
Kruung come to the door, so he threw some wood from the fire
at him, burning his hair. Then Sayiing Kruung ran off scream-
ing.

When someone dies, people from other villages generally
come to the funeral, unless it is the third or fourth month
(when rice is planted). These months are taboo for attending funerals. If there is a sister of the deceased who lives
in another village, she will bring a buffalo with her for a
sacrifice. This is in addition to the buffalo which her
brothers bring. She does this so that her brothers will love
her and later give their daughters as wives for her sons in
the Katu custom of cross-cousin marriages.

Several days after a person's death, a buffalo is killed,
or a pig if it was a child, and there is dancing and playing
of drums. The relatives ask the deceased to take the soul
of the buffalo with him so that he will be happy in the next
life. At this time, close relatives sing, praising the dead
person if he was a particularly good hunter or if he was
rich. The head of the buffalo is then placed on the roof of

the deceased person's house. During the following two days
when the corpse is in the house, the villagers mourn and play
drums with a slow rhythmic beat.

After the buffalo is killed, there is a feast to which
the whole family brings food. People do not take any of the
leftover food home for fear of sickness. After they have
eaten in the dead man's home, they wash their hands before
returning to their own homes.

After the first day of festivities, the body is placed in
the coffin. The dead person's belongings--his crocks, baskets, and clothes--are placed near the coffin, but they are
not taken to the grave.

Since the Katu believe that the spirits see everything as
opposite to the human world, they bury their dead in the late
afternoon so that the spirits will think it is early morning.
The spirits would not allow a person to be buried in the late
afternoon since it is so close to dark. The coffin is not
placed far beneath the earth because it will later be removed
for the second burial. Only a bowl of rice is left by the
graveside for the soul of the deceased to eat, but after this
a bowl is set out regularly at meal time until the second
burial.

The Second Burial. One or two years after the first burial, the second burial takes place. The coffin is exhumed and
taken to a grave called a ping. A ping is a large, house-like
structure in which the coffins of the dead of the whole village are placed. The ping has a hole about four meters deep
into which the coffins are piled, one on top of another and
side by side. The ping has four strong posts covered by a
roof.

Anyone from the village (even non-relatives) can be
buried in the ping provided he had a good death and the family provides a buffalo. Since the soul of the deceased is
still with the body, everything must be carefully done to
please the soul. So even if a rich person had a buffalo already available, the second burial cannot take place any
sooner than is proper. The body must first decay so that it
will not decay into other coffins in the ping.

At the second burial there are three nights of feasting and playing of gongs and drums, to which all the villagers are invited. If the deceased had killed many people, the relatives first lead a party to another village to kill. The blood is not brought back from these killings. When the party returns, the feast is held.

At this point, the coffin is taken to the ping. There may be several families taking coffins of relatives to the ping at the same time. Up to five coffins may be buried together. The coffins are placed outside the doorway to the ping. There a pig is killed, and its blood is rubbed onto a stone. This stone is then thrown down into the hole while the men call out to the souls of the people buried in the ping to receive these new people and make them happy. The buffalo head is brought to the ping with rice and alcohol for more feasting. The coffins are then placed inside the hole, side by side on top of other coffins, with no soil between. One ping may contain twenty to thirty coffins.

Burial for a Bad Death. For a bad death there is no ritual. There is no mourning, no sacrifice, and no funeral. The relatives, however, do provide a coffin. The coffin is taken far into the jungle away from any fields and trails. The relatives bury the coffin and then leave the grave as quickly as possible.

The Katu fear the soul of someone who died a bad death. When they see red in the sky at night, they believe this is the returning soul of someone who has died a bad death. They hear the soul call out and light fires outside all the houses. For six nights they stay awake.

No one wants to touch the body of a person who has died a bad death. Since no one will wear the deceased's clothes, they are thrown out.

Burying Alive. An insane person, to the Katu, is a threat to the whole village, as he might burn down a house or cause some other harm. They, therefore, bury him alive. Burying alive is also used at times as a punishment for adultery or stealing.

The villagers bury the victim in a small hole, sitting
up with his legs pushed against his chest. Enough air reaches
him so that he may exist for two weeks or more. During this
time the villagers go to the grave to listen for signs of
life. When the victim finally expires, he is left in this
same hole. There is no burial ceremony, since burying alive
is a type of bad death.

SUMMARY

The Katu belief in two types of death results in two
different sets of burial practices. Souls of people who die
of sudden, unnatural causes, are potentially harmful, but
they receive no care. Their abode is called bayô. On the
other hand, souls of people who die natural deaths due to
sickness or old age receive sacrifices, elaborate ceremonies
and feasts, food to eat, and double burials. Their final
abode is maraaih. When the Katu sacrifice, they intreat the
spirit of the sky not to let them die a bad death.

NYAHEUN MEDICINE AND SOME PROBLEMS POSED TO WESTERN MEDICAL PRACTICE

John J. Davis

Every Westerner, upon arrival in a non-literate society, is immediately confronted with the needs of the sick around him. The natural, compassionate reaction is to share with the sick some of his medical supplies and know-how. Such an act of compassion and generosity may be the right thing to do from our point of view, but by such an act one may find himself identified in the minds of the populace with their own indigenous healers.

In the medical world today, there are basically two points of view regarding such identification with the local scheme of medical practice. Some feel that an alliance should be sought with sorcerers, shamans, herb doctors, or whatever other type of healer is indigenous to the society, and that these people should be taught in the art of Western medicine as well. Another viewpoint is that Western medicine should be kept separate from any compromise which may ensue from such an alliance.

In order to make an accurate judgment as to which of the above views is best, a careful investigation into the indigenous system is necessary, for only as we understand the patterns of their medical system are we able to gauge their reactions to Western medical practice.

CAUSES OF ILLNESS

The Nyaheun believe that there is only one 'normal' cause for death, namely, progressive old age. Everything else is related to an abnormality of the spirit world which must be made right to bring about healing.

Following are some of the spirits and the symptoms of illness which the Nyaheun attribute to them:

    1. Water spirit (brah daak). Back ache, serious diarrhea, deafness, and death by drowning are attributed to the spirit of the water.

2. Mountain and forest spirit (brah nuu
kOng 'lOOng lE). All sorts of mental disorders
and loss of memory are attributed to this spirit.
It also can make one seriously ill, in a long-
term, degenerative way (not unlike the symptoms
of cancer).

3. (brah wen nyaam). This spirit deceives
people, leads them astray, and causes them to
lose their way in the forest.

4. (brah wen). Colds, coughs, headaches,
fever, and diarrhea are attributed to this
spirit.

5. (brah suuk kan ta' brah kan cat). This
is the guardian of traditional ways and customs.
A breech of custom or tradition is cause for
judgment from this spirit in the form of illness,
or failure of a crop or general bad luck.

6. Ghost (brah gyOk). Nothing more serious
than a spate of vomiting is attributed to the
'ghost'. The 'aspirin cure' for such vomiting
is to chew ginger, spitting it out around the
house, and placing some of the residue on the
head, lighting a tuft of dry grass in the fire
and filling the house with a dense cloud of
smoke.

7. Heaven and earth spirit (hla krlm kla
brEh). Very little is known of this spirit.
He is not referred to as brah, but rather as
the owner of heaven and earth. Judgment from
this spirit in the form of lightning is only
feared if the laws of the elders have been
broken.

This list is by no means exhaustive, but includes the
more commonly known spirits. One has only to hear the shaman
chanting once to know that to call on the names of all the
spirits takes study and concerted effort. The names of the

spirit of the Lao government, the spirit of USAID and the
spirit of the 'white star' (the title given the Special Forces
'Green Berets' when in Laos), have been invoked along with
the many other spirits to assure that no one is left out when
a sacrifice to set the spirit world in order is performed.
Much time and energy is taken up with the seemingly endless
round of sacrifices for illness or other reasons.

All cases of illness, with the exception of accidental
wounds received in the course of work which may be treated
immediately, must be treated by first consulting a healer.
The patient himself is never consulted as to what treatment
he prefers; everything depends upon what the diviner pre-
scribes.

HEALERS

There are three practitioners to whom the family of the
patient may turn in times of illness, plus the additional
option of seeking Western medical help. Western medicine is
often added to the others, but usually not preferred over
the indigenous system.

The Diviner. The first one consulted in the case of illness is the diviner, for it is his job to diagnose which of
the spirits has caused the illness. He receives his gift of
divination by dream or trance in the following manner. In
his dream or trance, he sees something to be measured, or he
sees a pattern of rice developing in a bowl of water. Upon
awaking he may again see the same design formed when rice is
dropped into water, or he may see the same thing he measured
(a length of bamboo, a fish net, a crossbow string, etc.)
and finds the measurements correspond. He knows, thereby,
that he is a diviner.

This healer is never remunerated, and he never goes to
the patient. An article of clothing from the patient or a
handful of polished rice which has been waved over the patient is brought to him for measurement or consideration of
the patterns which form when the rice is dropped into water.

The Shaman. A shaman receives his power from his father.
Not every son of a shaman will be a shaman, but one son will

learn the trade and inherit his father's position. Although
women shamans are very common in the neighboring Loven tribe,
women shamans are a rarity among the Nyaheun. Many would do
anything to keep from becoming a shaman, and some avoid it
for years, only to become convinced they must yield when they
fall ill and remain ill for a long time.

This type of healer goes to the patient's house and performs the prescribed ceremony for the offending spirit, and
may take in payment up to one half of the sacrificial animal.
He may then pass the meat around to others in the village in
order to insure his own future food supply, or he may sell it
as fresh meat. He usually has an assistant to help him in
the ceremony, selected from among relatives, friends, or ac-
quaintances. The main task of this assistant often is to
secure a good fee for the shaman's services, and on occasion
he is not bashful to ask for several thousands of kip.[2]
The shaman himself is never again allowed to collect cash
for his services after the initial treatment of a patient.

These men are highly respected, and the shaman is an ever-
present power at all village councils, although not the most
powerful, for there are times when others take action against
them as will be seen in a moment. While at times he may en-
joy the highest of honor, he may also suffer the gravest
suspicion.

The Sorcerer. While the diviner and the shaman are truly
indigenous to the Nyaheun, the sorcerer or sorceress has become increasingly popular in the last few years, the concept
having been borrowed from Laotian culture. Sorcerers are
reputed to have a great deal of mystical power, mostly because of their 'learned chants' and secret formulas which
they have learned from the Lao. They are called upon to undo
curses and create charms which will secure one's life from
the power of other people and of the spirits. The sorcerers
often charge very high prices for their charms and curing
rites. Largely because this type of healing is learned from
the Lao who are noted for their malevolent sorcery, the sorcerer is suspected of being able to sell curses as well as
cures.

DANGERS FOR HEALERS

Apart from illnesses caused by spirits, the Nyaheun are
nearly obsessed with fear of being poisoned. Although they
use the same terminology as the Lao for this poisoning, i.e.
'eating', they do not believe, as do the Lao and the Ngeq,
that it is a spirit which causes the death, but rather that
the cause is poison which the 'eater' has covertly placed
near the victim.

The term used for this poison (or 'medicine' or 'charm')
is nam, the same term used for Western medicine.

Death described as caused by this 'eating' is a sudden
death from no apparent cause, the symptoms being not unlike
those of cerebral malaria. If several of these deaths take
place in a short time or in a particular locale, a 'witch
hunt' begins, and the person suspected of being the 'eater'
is quietly killed. In the last year of our residence among
the Nyaheun, there were five of these executions, and additional banishments from the area. Of these, all but two were
shamans or sorcerers. The explanation given for the killings
and banishments was that 'they had eaten people'.

Any individual who has a grudge against another person
can become an eater (phi pOp or nnwOk). A dream or trance is
unnecessary, nor is it necessary to be in a certain blood-
line. All that is required is the determination to learn
what kind of poison or medicine to give the victim.

It therefore becomes apparent that any one knowledgeable
in the handling of medicines can come under suspicion of
having caused someone's death by 'eating' him.

From this we may conclude that anyone doing medical
work in such a situation would probably fare better by NOT
identifying with indigenous healers. I feel it would be
better to maintain a stand of no compromise, keeping Western
medical practices on a different level than that of indigenous healers. It would be well to be careful never to give
rise to suspicion that Western medicine might produce death.
The practitioner should cultivate a feeling of trust and
kindness, not giving the image of one who might hold a grudge

against anyone. Failure to be on the lookout for identification with the indigenous healer class might lead to being
treated as one, resulting in eviction from the area, or even
death.

My Nyaheun language teacher insisted that no foreigner
could ever be suspected of 'eating' any one, but his basis
was more that Western medicine was 'different' than that
Westerners were beyond the realm of suspicion.

At first blush it might appear that a foreign medical
worker who charged for his medicines might incur local dis-
favor since the shaman does not collect for services but
once in a patient's lifetime. The exorbitant prices charged
by his assistants, however, with much favoritism and in-
equality, is a source of great bitterness among his clients.
It therefore seems that an honest, one-price-for-everyone
system would be a welcome innovation and, in the end, gain
respect.

A diviner or a shaman is never free to refuse those who
come to him for help. He is considered to have been equipped
by the spirits for care of the sick. Likewise, once a foreigner has allowed his medical ability to be known, there is
little he can do to withdraw, for the Nyaheun would feel that
he no longer had compassion toward them--a very serious
accusation.

CROSS-COUSIN MARRIAGE AND CHRU KINSHIP TERMINOLOGY

by Eugene E. Fuller

The Chru people number about 15,000, most of whom live in Don Duong district of Tuyen Duc province, South Vietnam. They are chiefly wet rice farmers and speak an Austronesian language of the Chamic subgroup in South Vietnam-Cambodia.

The Chru are organized into clans. Clan names include: Bờju, Kờjong Prong, Tou-aneh, Touprong, Kờbàu Bờnuh, and Jờrling. Clan membership is diffuse geographically.

Chru clans are exogamous and descent is matrilineal. Property and inheritance rights are vested in the woman. When the mother dies each of the daughters receives an equal portion of the property, which may include rice fields, water buffalo and other livestock, house and chattel property. The son receives nothing and needs nothing since he marries into another family and benefits from the property of his wife and her mother.

KINSHIP TERMS

Kinship terms are used by the Chru in reference and in address. Where ego has a child, he adopts his child's position within the network of kinship relationships in addressing a kinsman. For example, female ego addresses her older brother as miă 'uncle', taking her child's point of view rather than using the term gờŭ lờkời 'woman's brother'. The terms are presented in Figure 11 as used in reference.

Second Ascending Generation and Beyond. There are just two grandparent terms, kời 'grandfather' and mò 'grandmother', which designate all male and female kinsmen, respectively, of the second ascending generation.

Chru interest focuses on the grandmother through the female line. In Chru cosmology the prominence of the grandmother is highlighted in the names for the sun and the moon. The sun is mò ia hờrời 'grandmother sun' and the moon is kời ia blàn 'grandfather moon'.

113

Figure 11.   Chru Kinship Terms.

1.	kơi	'grandfather': FF, MF; FFB, FMB, MFB, MMB.
2.	mò	'grandmother': MM, FM; MMZ, MFZ, FMZ, FFZ.
3.	ama	'father': F.
4.	wa	'father's brother': FB; MZH.
5.	me	'mother': M; MZ; FBW.
6.	miă	'mother's brother': MB; FZH; WF, HF.
7.	tơmhã	'father's sister': FZ; MBW; HM, WM.
8.	awoi	'spouse's mother': HM, WM.
9.	sơ-ai	'elder parallel sibling': for elder kinsman of male ego: B; FBS, MZS, FZD, MBD; BW; FBSW, MZSW, FZDH, MBDH; WZ; WZH;...for elder kinsman of female ego: Z; MZD, FBD, MBS, FZS; ZH; MZDH, FBDH, MBSW, FZSW; HB; HBW;...
10.	adơi	'younger parallel sibling': as in 9 above, for younger kinsman.
11.	pơsàng	'husband': H.
12.	sơdiŭ	'wife': W.
13.	gŏŭ lơkơi	'woman's (cross) brother': for female ego only: B; FBS, MZS; FZDH, MBDH.
14.	gŏŭ kơmơi	'man's (cross) sister': for male ego only: Z; FBD, MZD; FZSW, MBSW.
15.	prui	'same sex cross sibling': for male ego: FZS, MBS; ZH; FBDH, MZDH. for female ego: FZD, MBD; BW; FBSW, MZSW.
16.	anà	'child': for male ego: S,D; BS, BD; ZDH, ZSW; WZS, WZD; WBDH, WBSW. for female ego: S,D; ZS, ZD; BDH, BSW; HBS, HBD; HZDH, HZSW.
17.	kơmuan	'cross sibling's child': for male ego: ZS, ZD; BDH, BSW; WBS, WBD. for female ego: BS, BD; HBDH, HBSW; HZS, HZD.
18.	mơrtơu	'child's spouse': for male ego: DH, SW; WZDH, WZSW. for female ego: DH, SW; ZDH, ZSW.
19.	cho	'grandchild': all children of 16 and 17.
20.	chĕ	'great grandchild': all children of 19.
21.	lơnĕ	'great great grandchild': all children of 20.
22.	lơnuãi	'great great great grandchild': all children of 21.

Kinsmen more than two ascending generations from ego are
designated by modifying the grandparent terms as follows
(using the grandmother term as the model):

mò kŏ	3rd ascending generation
mò kuah	4th ascending generation
mò tɗnah rɗya	5th ascending generation
mò kŏ kùt	6th ascending generation
mò akha rɗlàng tɗlàng kɗbàu	7th ascending generation

Mò tɗnah rɗya is 'grandmother of the land', mò kŏ kùt is
'grandmother at head of the graveyard' (i.e. the first Chru
buried in that graveyard), mò akha rɗlàng tɗlàng kɗbàu is
'grandmother root of the thatching grass and the bones of the
buffalo'.

Ego would refer to any female on either side of the family
in the second through the seventh respective ascending generations with the above terms and to any male with the same respective terms, in which case kɗi 'grandfather' would be substituted for mò 'grandmother'.

First Ascending Generation. There are six terms for kinsmen of the first ascending generation, three for males and
three for females. The male terms distinguish father (ama)
from parallel uncles (wa) and cross uncles (miǎ). The female
terms class mother together with parallel aunts (me) as
opposed to cross aunts (tɗmhã). The third female term has a
very restricted usage in that only the father-in-law uses it
in reference to the mother-in-law (his wife) when speaking to
his child's spouse.

Ego's Generation. In ego's generation, an unusual type of
bifurcation is employed to distinguish 'parallel' and 'cross'
kinsmen in such a way that a man and his (real or potential),
spouse are classified together rather than apart as in many
other kinship systems.

There are two terms for so-called 'parallel' kinsmen, dis-
tinguishing relative age. The younger parallel kinsman refers
to his elder counterpart as sɗ-ai, and is referred to in turn
as adɗi. They designate siblings of the same sex as ego,
parallel cousins of the same sex as ego, and cross cousins of
the opposite sex as ego (i.e. the potential spouses of ego

and his or her same sex parallel cousins), and extend to the
spouses of all such kinsmen and to all such kinsmen of one's
own spouse.

Since the preferred spouse is chosen from among kinsmen
referred to by these two sibling terms, the terms are often
used after marriage between spouses in an affectionate sense,
although special husband (po̊sàng) and wife (so̊diŭ) terms are
also used. Either spouse may also be referred to by the
term sàng do̊nò 'household'.

Three terms are used to refer to the male and female
spouse set of which ego is not a member. Such kinsmen might
be referred to as 'cross' kinsmen, but only in the sense referred to--as of the 'other' spouse set. Two of the terms refer to kinsmen of the opposite sex, one to kinsmen of the
same sex. A female ego refers to her brother and parallel
male cousins ('parallel' in the traditional sense) as go̊ŭ
lo̊ko̊i, and she is reciprocally referred to by them as go̊ŭ
ko̊mo̊i. The spouses of all such kinsmen (being of the same
sex as ego) are referred to as prui. This last term also refers to the same-sex cross (in the traditional sense) cousins,
while their male and female spouses are referred to·, respectively, by the two opposite sex terms.

First Descending Generation. There are two terms for unmarried kinsmen of the first descending generation, and a
third which is applied to certain of these after marriage.
The term anà designates ego's own children, ego's same sex-
sibling's child, the spouse of ego's opposite-sex sibling's
child, ego's spouse's same-sex sibling's child, and the
spouse of ego's spouse's opposite-sex sibling's child. Alternately, the term ko̊muan designates ego's opposite-sex
sibling's child, the spouse of male ego's same-sex sibling's
child, ego's spouse's opposite-sex sibling's child, and the
spouse of female ego's spouse's same-sex sibling's child.
The third term mo̊rto̊u is reserved for the person who married
ego's own child, female ego's same-sex sibling's child, or
male ego's spouse's same-sex sibling's child.

All of these facts, regarding the range of reference of
terms for kinsmen of the first ascending, ego's, and first
descending generations are expressed graphically in Figures
12 and 13.

REFERENCE

Figure 12.   Kinsmen of Male Ego.

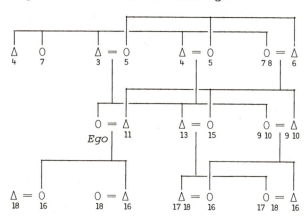

Figure 13.   Kinsmen of Female Ego.

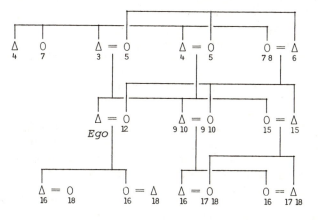

Second Descending Generation and Beyond. As in the case
of the second ascending generation, lineal and collateral
kinsmen are all classified together in the second descending
generation, in this case under the single term cho 'grandchild', which does not distinguish the sex of kinsmen.

Although seven ascending generations are distinguished by
the Chru, only five descending generations are so marked.
Like the grandchild term, the remaining three terms, listed
below, extend to all kinsmen of their respective generations.

     chě   3rd descending generation
     lǒně   4th descending generation
     lǒnuãi   5th descending generation

CHRU MARRIAGE

The Chru practice exchange marriages, the brother and sister of one family marrying the brother and sister of another
family. In such a situation each family which 'loses' a son
to another family, by exchange, also 'gains' one from that
family. Figures 12 and 13 (above) display exchange marriages
resulting in cross-cousin marriage in descending generations.
The extension of kinship terminology to affinal kin types is
entirely consistent with a preference for exchange marriage.
Although exchange marriages are desirable and do occur, they
are nevertheless rare.

Chru also prefer cross-cousin marriage. Normally, a girl's
parents (or other family member who acts as intermediary) go
to the home of the mother's brother or the father's sister to
ask for the hand of that family's son in marriage to their
daughter.

Parallel-cousin marriage is forbidden and considered incestuous, as the terminology reflects. All mother's sisters
and father's brother's wives are me 'mother' and their off-
spring socially equivalent to ego's own brothers and sisters.

Marriage within one's clan is forbidden and would be looked
upon as incestuous. The Chru consider that any such marriage
would result in a year of drought upon the entire clan.

Marriage into adjacent generations of kin is also forbidden. If a girl has no available cross cousins for marriage, she is free to seek a partner outside her kin group.
There are inter-tribal marriages where, for example, a Chru
marries a Kơho, but these are exceptions.

An account of a traditional Chru marriage follows.

Initiation. The girl's parents go to the boy's parents
and ask, "Will you give your son in marriage to our daughter?"

Betrothal. If the girl's father is brother to the boy's
mother (or if the girl's mother is sister to the boy's
father), they agree. Then there is a waiting period of one
week to fifteen days. After that the girl's parents, along
with the girl, go to make the betrothal. They usually go at
7:00 or 7:30 in the evening when it is dark because the
young people are shy.

After the girl and her parents enter the house of the boy's
parents, the host and hostess light split pitch pine to give
light to the house and offer tobacco to their guests, the
girl's parents.

Then the boy's father asks, "Why have you come this evening?" The girl's father replies, "We are not able to see or
smell and have come here because we are hungry and thirsty,"
indicating, indirectly, that they have come to request a betrothal. The girl's father continues, "We have come to ask
to hire your young buffalo, O.K.?" thus asking indirectly if
the boy is available for marriage to his daughter.

The boy's father says, "Oh, that buffalo is very inexperi-
enced. How does he know how to work?" (In speaking this way
the boy's parents indicate their willingness for the betrothal.)

The girl's parents reply, "Well, we know whether he's capable or not. We were that way. He'll learn. Generally, if
one is to speak he must practice, if he drags wood he must
tie it together, and if he wants to work he must learn."

The boy's parents say, "Ask him there." (The boy is off
to the side.)

The girl's parents turn and speak with the young man, "Oh, child, we have come here with a real desire. We've come for a drink and to ask you to care for our daughter with love and affection, even if worse comes to worst." This saying is to bind the family together.

The young man remains silent. He is shy.

The girl's parents (or the intermediary) get one of two kinds of rings or a necklace from the hand of the girl to put on the young man. The young man proceeds to argue in protest. (This is form; he doesn't want to appear too eager to marry.) Then the girl's parents or the intermediary ask on behalf of the girl that the boy take very good care of her. He is reminded that whether she is pretty or not, she can cook and even "a black pot cooks rice done," alluding to the uncomeliness of a dark complexion. "What," he is asked, "is the need of a pretty girl if she is able to prepare food? Even if she is pretty she will have to set her hand to work the rice and her foot to work the field," implying that soon enough even a pretty girl will have her comeliness affected through work.

Having said that, the ring is again put on the young man's finger (for initially he took it off in protest). The young man again resists, but to no avail. After putting the ring on the young man, his parents or the girl's father go get water to add to the wine. They carry the wine jar from its place at the head of the bed. The jar cover is removed, the water is poured in and then air is blown into the jar through a straw. Then, the straw and wine are given to the girl's parents. The father of the boy arises and puts the straw into the wine. He is urged by the girl's father to drink a bowl of the wine. After drinking a bowl he returns to his place. A helper receives the straw, siphons wine and gives it to the head of the house to offer to all the people present for the betrothal. They all drink together.

After a half hour of drinking wine, the girl's parents request a bowl of wine from the master of the house and they have their daughter come near to sip it. Then another necklace is put on the boy. The girl also rolls a cigarette, lights it and gives it to her betrothed. The boy's parents

also give their son a bowl of wine, a necklace, a ring and
direct him to give these to his betrothed. He gives the wine
to the girl and she drinks it. Then he puts the ring on her
finger and the necklace around her neck. When he puts on the
necklace all the people present say together, "Good luck, we
wish you much food and life's necessities and as many children
as the ants and termites have."

The Feast. During the evening of the betrothal the girl's
parents urge the young man to go visit their house. The boy's
parents aren't invited because if they go it may mean bad luck
for their son, although other members of his family can
attend. At the girl's parents' house wine is poured, a
chicken, pig or goat is killed and food and drink is prepared.
This is a happy time with laughing, chanting, singing and
joking. And, it is happy because a new child has come into
the family, this young man. The girl's parents bring all the
boy's family to see their house. Each person receives a
necklace or ring, but nothing is given to the young man.

An uncle (father's brother) or an older brother of the boy
speaks with him and gives him directions, warning him to be
careful how he conducts himself now so that he won't harm his
relationship with his betrothed by going after somebody else.
He is told if he listens to some bad advice and chases after
some strange girl who may be pretty, it will mean trouble for
the family. The family will wind up in debt to the girl and
her family, but the giver of the bad advice will not suffer
at all. Then they chant to the boy concerning these matters.

After the chanting, everyone returns home. The young man
being betrothed must remain in the home of his betrothed for
one week, but must not sleep with her. After one week he returns home. At that time, the girl goes to his home. There,
too, they don't have permission yet to sleep in the same bed.

The Marriage. One or two weeks later, the girl's parents
get folks together again. Then they invite many people,
especially the relatives of the boy, to come to their house.
Wine is brought out and an old man such as the girl's grandfather or her father's brother gives an invocation calling
on all the spirits he knows. A chicken is killed and cooked.
They take the chicken and wine and go into what will be the

newlyweds' room. There the old man prays again. Then the
girl's parents bring necklaces and rings for all the boy's
relatives who have come to the house.

Once again the old man prays, pours wine and gives it to
the girl. She kneels, takes the bowl of wine in both hands.
Then the old man prays that having brought this wine, they
are now trusting the spirits of the mountains and fields and
all the rest to give sufficient food and life's necessities.
The girl sips the wine.

After the girl, her betrothed receives the same service
with a prayer that having brought the wine they are trusting
all the spirits to give sufficient strength to work. The
boy sips the wine.

Now the old man separates the head, feet and wings of the
chicken and places them on a plate which he carries to the
girl's father. All the people are in the room, and the old
man divines the newlyweds' future with the head and feet and
wings of the chicken, dropping them to see how they lie. This
is to determine whether or not the boy and girl will get along,
have sufficient food, children and the necessities of life.

The old man who prays gets an old person to eat the chick-
en's head, feet and wings. Then he gathers and stores the
offering dishes, after which the people drink and get very
drunk. It is a very happy time.

After this, everybody returns home. The boy remains in
the home of his wife. They have the right to sleep together
in the same bed under the same blanket. The girl calls the
boy her husband and the boy calls the girl his wife.

The Confinement. From the day of ceremony both the newlyweds eat and remain in the house one week. They don't dare
go out of the village for fear that a bird will drop a dropping on them. If that happens they will not have good for-
tune. They may soon die or suffer poverty. At the end of
one week, on the morning of the 8th day, the girl's parents
get a chicken egg and cook it. They put it along with a
bowl of rice and a bowl of water into a pan. The pan is
placed at the head of the bed and prayer is offered to the

spirits of the house and the field.   This ends the confinement.   Now they can go out and work.

NOTE

This paper is the result of study conducted in Nha Trang,
South Vietnam, in 1971 and 1973.   The valuable technical
assistance of Marilyn Bergman Gregerson and Milton E. Barker
is gratefully acknowledged.

NOTES ON RENGAO LAW

Marilyn Gregerson

Perhaps the supreme value in Rengao[1] culture is to be on
good terms with one's fellow man. Whenever a law is broken,
the most important part of solving the case is to reinstate
friendly relations between the plaintiff and the defendant.
When 'society' is offended, one must restore friendly relations with 'all of society', which usually means one's entire
village. It is not so much some abstract sense of justice
which must be placated, but rather the more immediate rup-
tures in personal ties that must be mended. This extends in
a natural way to the need for restoring proper relationships
with supernatural beings who might also have been offended.

1. LEGAL MACHINERY

Pơkra. The Rengao have a formal institution which serves
as a mechanism for reinstating friendly relations--it is
called pơkra 'to repair or make amends'. To make amends,
the offender provides rice wine and an animal (water buffalo,
cow, goat, pig or chicken) which he kills, prepares, and
takes to the home of the offended party. There the two parties drink and eat together. The pơkra ceremony symbolizes
the fact that they are again on friendly terms and that ani-
mosity no longer exists between them.

Fines. Every offense must be satisfied by pơkra, but the
offense may also require that a fine be paid (bơhruq) to the
offended party. If a person is required to pay a fine and
does not have the wherewithal to do so, his bilateral relatives usually come to his aid.

Village Elders. Whenever an offense is committed, the
parties usually make an attempt to work out a settlement,
and then formally effect that settlement by the pơkra ceremony. If, however, they cannot come to terms, they refer the
case to the village elders. But if this course of action is
taken, the defendant can expect to have to pay for his
offense more heavily than if he had settled it 'out of court'

with the plaintiff. For one thing, he will not only have to
pдkra the plaintiff but the village elders as well.

In a single village there are typically anywhere from
three to seven men who serve as village elders; the villages
with which we were most familiar had four in each village.
A translation of the Rengao term for 'village elder' literally
means 'old one'. They are only required, however, to be 'old'
in the amount of wisdom they demonstrate. In actual years of
age, an elder may be as young as 30 years old. Ideally, he
is well-to-do; but Rengao say that since everyone is poor
nowadays, this is no longer a requirement. Two other re-
quirements are that an elder exhibit proper behavior and
that he be easy to get along with. Should an elder become
senile, he relinquishes his position, since capacity for
sound judgment is the first requirement of the post. When a
vacancy arises in the council of elders, the remaining elders
choose a replacement.

Rengao law, like law everywhere, is constantly changing
as culture changes. One informant said in discussing the
functions of the village elders:

> These elders know what the laws were from the
> olden days, so that now they can follow that
> precedent. If the laws are no longer right,
> however, they will discard them, or reform
> them so that they are in keeping with modern
> times. In every period of time, men of law
> have ruled somewhat differently. Of course,
> they never change the laws drastically; they
> must be in line with what previous elders ·have
> done.

The traditional power of the elders is unquestioned; informants say they have never heard of a case where the elders'
verdict was not carried out. In case of a fine, the elders
presumably keep in mind the total capabilities of the defendant with the aid of his bilateral relatives to pay that fine.

In only the most serious cases, such as those where
traditional law requires capital punishment, do Rengao elders
turn the culprit over to the Vietnamese government authorities.

Though the largest unit in the Rengao political system is
the village, in legal cases between parties from two villages,
the elders in the plaintiff's village are allowed to hand down
the judgment against the defendant.

Trial by Ordeal. In the event that there is doubt about
the identity of the culprit, several suspects may be asked to
submit to a trial by ordeal. They are asked to go to the
river and put their heads under the water. The one who
brings his head up first is considered the culprit, for it is
believed that a river spirit will bite the nose of the culprit if he keeps his head under water. Thus, anyone with a
guilty conscience apparently feels rather nervous about staying in the water.

The Use of Songs in Social Control. In wrongdoing of
any kind, the guilty party may be subjected to public ridicule through someone's singing about his bad behavior at a
social gathering. The singer never names the offender, but
sings of the wrongdoing in an indirect, stylized manner within his hearing. This kind of musical teasing is so humiliat-
ing that one person told me, "It makes you never again want
to do anything bad enough to have someone sing about you."

2. LEGAL OFFENSES

Homicide. Informants say that in former times, if someone were murdered, his relatives would take the murderer and
bury him alive beneath the body of the victim. And for this
there would be no revenge carried out by the murderer's relatives, since they also acknowledged that justice had been
done.

In more recent years, however, a murderer might more
likely be handed over to French or Vietnamese authorities to
be sent to prison.

> *Case 1:* About 25 years ago, a rich man
> named Yŏn stole corn from the field of a poor
> widow named Hŏwet. Yŏn had not planted any
> corn himself. The deed was discovered by
> Hŏwet who said to him, "Why did you take my
> corn? Why didn't you ask me for it?" This
> made Yŏn so angry that when Hŏwet was work-
> ing out in the field, he went out and killed

her with his machete. The village elders told
the French government officials about it, and
they arrested him and sent him to prison island.
Ydn was never heard from again.

In the following case a teen-ager killed one of his own
relatives. Probably due to his age, he was not put to death
or sent to prison, but was required to pdkra his whole village.

>   *Case 2:* One day a young unmarried man
> named Khech, about 17 years old, saw his older
> sister's son, Yech, who was about 8 years old,
> up in a fruit tree picking the fruit and
> throwing it down. Though the tree was com-
> munal property, it made the older boy angry to
> see his nephew wasting the fruit, so he shot
> the boy. The village elders required Khech's
> family to provide a buffalo, a cow and a pig as
> well as rice wine for the whole village to eat
> and drink together to make things right again.

In another, quite involved, case, a Rengao killed an
outsider:

>   *Case 3:* One day while the writer was
> teaching a literacy class of adult men in the
> school building of a Rengao resettlement vil-
> lage, the class was interrupted by the sound
> of weaponfire in the open area in front of
> the school. Gyong had just shot and killed a
> Vietnamese soldier who had caught and raped
> Gyong's wife while she was out working in her
> field. The Vietnamese soldier had been tied
> up by his superior but was in the act of
> escaping when Gyong shot him. No punishment
> was leveled against Gyong either by his own
> village or by the Vietnamese authorities.

Accidental Homicide. If a Rengao kills another person
by accident, he must pay a fine as well as whatever is specified for the pdkra ceremony.

Case 4: Yơi and Plun were two young men
who lived in the same house. Plun was the
husband of Yơi's cousin. One day while they
were out hunting together, they separated at
one point, going off in different directions.
Yơi thought he heard a deer move in the bushes,
so he shot into the thicket. His shot struck
Plun in the head and killed him. Yơi, afraid
to admit what he had done, ran back to the
village and said that the Viet Cong had killed
Plun. Plun's parents lived in another village,
but when they arrived, they pointed out that
there were no Viet Cong in the area. Finally,
Yơi broke down and confessed that he had acci-
dentally shot Plun. His family had to pơkra
four cows for a feast for both villages as
well as provide the coffin, equivalent cash of
nearly $1,000 US, and a large cow for the
family of the victim. Yơi's older brother was
well-to-do, and he was able to help Yơi put together the wealth needed to pay the fine and
pơkra.

Theft. Rengao say that when a person steals, he must return four times as much as he stole. Great distinction is
made between a person who steals a single time and an habitual thief.

A single theft offense can be taken care of by returning
the equivalent of the item stolen, plus three more of the
same item, plus whatever is needed for the pơkra ceremony.

Case 5: In September, 1969, four young
men from Plei Rơwăk shot a cow belonging to
Hyuq of Plei Jơdrơp. After shooting the animal,
they took it home and ate it. Then the four
village elders from Plei Jơdrơp, along with 30
other men from that village, marched over to
Plei Rơwăk to get compensation. When they
arrived at Plei Rơwăk, they asked the four
Plei Rơwăk elders and the four young men who
had shot and stolen the cow to come up into the
Plei Rơwak communal house. The Plei Jơdrơp elders then asked the Plei Rơwak elders to tell

them the names of the ones who had stolen the
cow. The Plei Rơwăk elders told them who they
were. The Plei Jơdrơp elders said that the
guilty ones would have to pay back one cow to
replace the stolen cow and that in addition
they would fine them three more large cows.
In final settlement of the case, they would
have to pơkra a large pig as well. The Jơdrơp
elders said they would take the four cows with
them that very day and would return the following day for the pơkra feast. The Plei
Jơdrơp elders went home to their village that
night with the four cows and returned the next
day to feast on the pig and drink wine with
the villagers in Plei Rơwăk. Good relations
were thus re-established between the two villages.

Habitual thievery is a much more serious crime than a
single isolated act and is customarily dealt with in a more
drastic way.

> *Case 6:* One young unmarried man named
> Hliam kept stealing chickens, so the elders
> of the village took him and tied him to the
> corner post of the communal house for two
> days until he promised never to steal again.
> After that he stole four valuable kettles,
> and still later he stole a motorcycle from
> a Vietnamese man. One day he was out at
> Plei Krong visiting, and the elders went to
> the American captain at the military post
> there and asked him to arrest Hliam for
> them. The captain had some men apprehend
> him and tie him up. He was then delivered
> to the district chief, who put him in jail
> where he remained for years.

Sexual Offenses. If a man discovers that his wife has
committed adultery, he calls the whole village out in front
of the communal house and accuses her lover. The interloper
has to pay the husband the equivalent of about $250 US and
provide a very large pig for the whole village to eat. One

informant told me that he knew of three or four cases   and
that in each case the defendant had to pay the same amount.

If a girl gets pregnant before she is married, she must
provide a pig, her boyfriend must provide a pig, and together they must provide a goat.[2] Then their two families
and the village elders eat the meat of the three animals together. If the man does not want to marry her, he must, in
addition, pay her the equivalent of about $85 US.

Property Damages.

> *Case 7*: Two men went out hunting one
> night with a flashlight. They saw eyes and
> thought they were those of a deer, so they
> shot it. Unfortunately, it turned out to be
> another villager's water buffalo. These inept
> hunters had to give the owner a small buffalo
> and pдkra a pig to eat with him.

Every year there are many cases of livestock getting into
fields and eating the rice. If the one who made the field
has not fenced it, he can expect no compensation. If he has
put up a fence and livestock get in anyway, the owner of the
animal must pay him rice or money, and provide a chicken and
wine for the families of the parties involved as well as the
village elders, to eat and drink after the case is settled.
If the animal only destroys a small amount of rice, it is
unnecessary to go to the elders; the two families can settle
it themselves.

Physical Injury. If a person is cutting brush and acci-
dentally cuts the leg of someone working near him, he must provide chicken and rice wine for the pдkra ceremony. This
holds true even if the injured party is his own relative.

If two children are fighting and one injures the other
so that he bleeds, the family of the child responsible for
the injury must provide a chicken and take it to the injured
party's house, where they eat the chicken and drink wine to
restore proper relations.

If a domestic animal, such as a water buffalo, gores

someone or injures him in some way, his owner must pɗkra a
chicken and wine to the injured person. The same holds true
for the owner of a dog who bites someone.

> *Case 8:* A young man was bitten by another
> villager's dog. The latter gave him the equiv-
> alent of about $4.00 US for his rather minor
> medical expenses and provided a chicken and
> wine to make amends.

Abusive Treatment. If a person uses vulgar and abusive
language in anger against another person, he must restore
friendly relations by taking a chicken and wine to the
offended party's house for the pɗkra ceremony.

If a person strikes a child, even though he may be the
parent of that child, then he must pɗkra the child chicken
and wine. Striking a child is thought to cause the spirit
of a child to leave his body, which could, in turn, cause his
death. The pɗkra ceremony apparently restores proper relations with the child's spirit so the child suffers no ill
effects.

If anyone urinates on someone else, he or his parents
must pɗkra that person wine and a chicken.[3]

Disrespect to Rice. Rice is the main staple and is vir-
tually sacred in its importance. In traditional Rengao
animism, the most important spirit, Yang Hri, was the spirit
of the rice. A person who does not show proper reverence
for rice has offended others and must restore proper relations with them. If a person takes a pot of cooked rice and
throws it down, for example, breaking the pot, then he must
pɗkra a pig to the whole village if it happens outside of
his house. If it happens inside his own house, he must pɗkra
the members of his extended family who live in that house.

There are other acts of wrongdoing, such as sorcery,
which, though condemned, are not prosecuted under Rengao law
because of the difficulty of determining guilt.

NOTES

[1]The Rengao are a group of between 10,000 and 15,000
people who live in Kontum Province, Vietnam. They
speak a language of the Mon-Khmer family, North Bahnaric sub-
grouping. Their subsistence is based on the cultivation of
rice in swiddens. Descent is bilateral and residence ambilocal (a married couple alternates residence approximately
every two years, first living with the wife's parents and
then with the husband's parents.) Houses are built on pilings and inhabited by bilaterally extended families. The
village is the largest and most significant political unit.
Traditional Rengao religion has a pantheon of spirits associated with local physical phenomena. Today the majority of
Rengao adhere to the Roman Catholic religion.

[2]This is the only offense for which a goat is required.
It is possible that this originally derived from the fact
that 'Grandmother Goat' is the mythological ancestor of the
Rengao.

[3]There is no offence if an infant urinates on the person
holding him.

RENGAO VOCAL MUSIC

Marilyn Gregerson

There is no generic term for music or singing in the Rengao[1] language. Rather, in event-oriented fashion, Rengao music designates each type of singing by a particular verb. By asking 'What has tơdra (lit. sign, tune, melody)?,' I found that various music categories could be elicited. I restrict my discussion here, however, exclusively to vocal music, which is by convention improvised and performed in solo. While group singing is unknown in traditional music, two singers may alternate in antiphonal fashion.

1. HƠNHÔNG

Hơnhông is a vocal style performed publicly by only a rel-atively few talented adults of any village. In form, hơnhông consists of an introduction followed by four phrases which are repeated again and again in a recurrent cycle. Rengao singers distinguish entire lines which are brông (resonant, lax) from those that are brŏng (clear, tense). This parallels a linguistic contrast in Rengao in which every word is phonologically either brông (pronounced with an expanded pharynx) or brŏng (pronounced with a constricted pharynx). An informant's reaction to my attempt to play a hơnhông melody on an organ was that it just wasn't possible, 'the notes weren't there', which I took to mean that the intervals are not those of the Western scale.

Hơnhông singing is appropriate in a variety of contexts, which I summarize below under the headings Social occasions, Soliloquy, and Instruction of children.

SOCIAL OCCASIONS

The verb ŭ 'to celebrate' literally means 'to drink'. The drinking of rice wine is considered indispensable to any kind of social gathering. It is, therefore, around the wine jars that people hơnhông on a social occasion. The language used in the hơnhông is poetic and metaphorical, almost never direct. Very often one celebrant will call another over to

135

the wine jar and sing a song to him. He can use the hơnhồng
in a number of ways, including just singing for entertainment
or as a way of conversing. Two or more people often hơnhồng
back and forth on some topic. Some conventional contexts
for such 'musical conversation' are:

A *Marriage Arrangement*. The go-between (or either parent) of a young girl or bachelor may call over a prospective
mate for their child and sing to him using a metaphor such
as "yesterday I saw a Vietnamese leading a water buffalo,
and I wanted to trade my gongs for the water buffalo, but I
didn't know if he would think that my gongs were good
enough." The young person would then know that he was really
saying, "I would like you to marry my child, but I don't
know if you want to." Another version of the same topic is
"I wanted to chop a tree to make a canoe, but I wasn't strong
enough to do so." The listener again knows that he is pro-
posing marriage for his child.

A *Marriage Proposal*. Either a girl or a young bachelor
can initiate a proposal by calling the prospective mate over
to the wine jar and singing to him or her. The formula calls
for the singer to belittle himself or herself and say that
the other one probably didn't want him, all in metaphorical
language. I was told that a visitor once started singing a
song to a beautiful girl, but upon learning she was married,
switched to saying she was very ugly, and probably lazy
too, and that he didn't want her.

Social Control. If a villager is guilty of wrongdoing,
one of the adults or perhaps one of the influential elders
of the village will sing a song indicting the wrongdoer. If
the person who is accused of wrongdoing knows how to hơnhồng
well, he may sing back and defend himself; but if he is
young and unskilled in the art, he is not likely to dare to
make a response. Often the accused will be embarrassed and
leave the house. It is not even necessary, however, for the
culprit to be present at the time. Nor are names ever mentioned; the singer simply tells about what the culprit did
in an indirect manner. Informants felt that this was a very
effective form of social control, for it is the height of
embarrassment to be publicly 'sung down' in this way.

Repayment of Debts. The Rengao borrow money and livestock from each other and these debts sometimes become a topic of the hơnhông. Sometimes the debtor sings about his inability to pay, or the creditor can hơnhông about the debts others owe him.

In Drunkenness. When someone gets drunk, people do not take his singing seriously and a person is permitted liberties that ordinarily he would not dare take. One of the most vulgar things that one Rengao can say to another is, "You sleep with your mother." If a person is sober and says such a thing, he is expected to provide an animal for a ceremony of reconciliation in which he asks the other person for forgiveness and eats and drinks with him. But if he is drunk, others are expected not to take such statements seriously. If he sings love songs to somebody else's wife, the woman's husband is expected not to take normal offense.

SOLILOQUY

When a person is out in the jungle or out watching the fields, he may also sing in musical soliloquy using the hơnhông style. One can sing both happy and sad themes in this style, the difference being conveyed not by the musical form, but simply by the linguistic content. A bachelor out watching the fields sings about a girl far away. A man sings about sad things like not having a family, the suffering brought by war, that people don't like him, that he is poor or has other troubles. He can also sing about good things like success in hunting or a good rice crop.

INSTRUCTION OF CHILDREN

In response to my inquiry as to whether there were any songs used to teach children, one well-known singer gave me two songs of instruction to children--one especially for a small child and another for 'a child old enough to tend cows.' These songs tell the child how to act properly, how to have good attitudes, to work hard, and to be a good person. An informant from another area, however, said he had never heard anyone in his village sing such a song, and didn't know how a child could understand such poetic language.

2. CHỚCHE

Chớche covers two types of singing which have the same usage as the hờnhông type, but it is done according either to the way singers of the Jarai tribe hờnhông or in the fashion of the Halang tribal hờnhông. Rengao singers copy these two styles, those nearer the borders of Halang terri- tory more likely acquiring the Halang style, and those nearer the Jarai, the Jarai style. In an exchange such as the marriage proposal, or in a social control usage, one person can hờnhông and the one who responds can chớche, depending upon which type he does best. One informant referred to the Jarai chớche style as being like Rengao tense phonological register (brŏng).

3. 'NHOY

'Nhoy is a type of singing ordinarily done by young un- married people. Girls use this style much more often than boys. Some examples of its uses have been described to me as follows:

One might sing the praises of a beautiful girl or hand- some young man who has caught one's eye.

One might equally sing demeaningly about a homely girl with a big stomach and dark skin. The object of such deri- sion has no recourse, unless she can successfully sing a rejoinder.

One could sing of a girl who is conceited over assumed beauty, to poke fun and embarrass her.

If a girl and a bachelor are seen conversing together, someone may compose songs to tease them about each other.

4. LÔNG

Lông means 'to cajole' or 'to lull a child to sleep' and designates improvised singing used for lullabies.

5. HỞRI

Hởri is a ballad type of singing which the Rengao say originated with the neighboring Bahnar. It typically narrates a story or legend. In this vocal type, one sings a phrase and then, in falsetto voice, adds a string of rhymes with a falling intonation. The Rengao rhyme formula usually consists of four words; the first two words alliterate and the second and third words rhyme. In this hởri type of singing (as well as in storytelling) the performer's success is rated partially on his ability to put together strings of rhymes in rapid succession. One tape-recorded sample of the hởri that I have collected is the story of Gyông, a legendary Rengao giant renowned for his bravery.

6. RỞNGÊ

Rởngê is another way of singing legends. The Rengao say it is an old style, no longer in common usage. One informant said there was now only one person in his village who was able to rởngê.

7. HAT

Hat from the Vietnamese hát 'to sing' is a type of singing which some Rengao say came to them from the Bahnar, but others consider it to be a result of French influence. This type of singing differs from others in that each word is sung on a single note rather than glided through a range of pitches. Hat songs, unlike other Rengao types, are not improvised but are learned and conventionalized. My colleague Wanda Jennings, hearing the examples of the hat type, felt that it was of a Western mode and that the timing was similar to Palestrina. Two examples that I have recorded of this type of singing are:

A ballad about an old woman who discovers she has nothing to eat with her rice. She feels that she won't be able to swallow the rice unless she has something to eat with it. Taking her fish trap and a basket to put the fish in, she goes down to the river to catch some fish. Sung with humorous detail, this song never fails to amuse Rengao listeners.

A song about the Christian God creating heaven and earth. Western Christian hymns in general are designated as hat.

8. HMOI

Hmoi is a death wail. In a taped example we have of this
type the singer keeps repeating, "O, mĭ" 'Oh, Mother' in a
variety of pitches and glides, illustrating an expression of
mourning that might be sung upon the death of a loved one.
The melody is very distinctive, unlike any of the other types
of singing. Wanda Jennings wrote the following comments on
this type after listening to my recording:

> I would call this a tetratonic scale because it
> appears there are only four tonal frequencies of
> progressions. The minor second is used more than
> all other intervals put together. Major third is
> next, then unison, then perfect fifth. It is al-
> most constant dissonance. The C seems to be the
> tonic note, which means there is an extremely fre-
> quent occurrence of the leading tone (B) demand-
> ing resolution. This accounts for the feeling of
> tension (personal communication).

The hmoi type does not call upon spirits. It is merely a
lament for the departed. In fact, informants told me that
they had never heard any songs of any type directed to the
spirits or about the spirits. Thus, I conclude that vocal
music probably did not have a religious usage until the introduction of Christian hymns.

9. CHƠCHẬP

Chơchập is a type of humming that women do to the accompaniment of gongs. No words are uttered in this rather
syncopated style of music.

NOTES

[1]The Rengao are an ethnic minority numbering between 10,000
and 15,000 whose traditional territory is in Kontum province
in the highlands of Vietnam. They speak a Mon-Khmer language
of the North Bahnaric subgroup. Subsistence consists pri-
marily of the cultivation of rice in swiddens. The settlement pattern includes a 'communal house' in the center of
each village which is used as a men's meeting house and as
bachelor sleeping quarters. All houses are built on pilings
and family residences are occupied by bilaterally extended
families. Descent is bilateral and residence ambilocal, the
couple alternating every two years between the home of the
husband's family and that of the wife's family. Politically,
the highest unit is the village, which was traditionally
governed by a group of male elders, who also prosecute legal
cases. The traditional religious system includes belief in
an impersonal high god creator and in numerous geographically
located spirits as well as those with specialized spheres of
influence.

NOTES ON STIENG LIFE

Lorraine Haupers

This paper[1] is a general sketch of some aspects of Stieng
life. The Stieng people are a highlander group of Viet Nam,
located along the Vietnamese-Cambodian border in Phước Long
Province. About 10,000 Stiengs were resettled in Lâm Đồng
Province in 1973 due to war activity. Several thousand
Stieng people are also believed to live across the border in
Cambodia (Le Bar et al. 1964:157). The Stiengs divide themselves into two major groups: buld 'the people above' (upstream)
and budêh 'the people below' (downstream).

The Stieng language is a member of the Mon-Khmer family.
It is subcategorized as South Bahnaric in the scheme of Viet
Nam minority languages. Stieng is not tonal as is Vietnamese
and does not exhibit the interesting vowel register phonemes
of many other Mon-Khmer languages. It does, however, have
the features of contrastive long and short vowels as well as
long and short initial consonants. In addition, extensive
use of semantic pairing, onomatopoeic forms, and internal
rhyming make Stieng a colorful and fascinating language.

Many Stieng men speak enough Vietnamese to care for
government business and converse in the marketplace. Very
few were able to read or write either their mother tongue or
Vietnamese, however, at the beginning of our residence among
them. As time progressed some were becoming literate.

The people are small in stature, but stockier than the
Vietnamese. Their skin is light brown and their hair black,
usually straight. Occasionally, a Stieng has slightly curly
hair. Stiengs have noses that are smaller than Euroamericans
and broader than Vietnamese.

They are a friendly, nonagressive people. The women tend
to be very shy, especially when men are present. The Stiengs
have a refreshing 'live and let live' attitude which allows
an outsider to make an easy adjustment to their culture.

143

TECHNOLOGY

Dress. Men traditionally have worn hand-woven loincloths, but in recent years have found short pants cheaper. A hand-woven loincloth is expensive because thread is purchased from Vietnamese and because it takes a woman many days of weaving. For feasts and special ceremonies, a Stieng man will wear a special ceremonial loincloth three or four yards long and at least a foot wide, with front and back flaps of an intricately woven design of red, white and yellow.

In recent years, especially since 1963, many hundreds of Stieng men have served in the local militia and therefore wear army uniforms of one kind or another. Those that do not actively serve are very glad to receive cast-off military shirts as they are sturdy and warm. It is not uncommon to see a man wearing some sort of a loincloth in combination with a rather long army shirt.

Men and women are accustomed to going barefoot everywhere, so are often victims of injuries, sores, ulcers, and snake-bite. If a man has money to spare, he may buy a pair of lightweight tennis shoes.

At home in the village, women and girls often wear only small loincloths. If it is cool, or if they are going to the market, they wear wraparound black satin sarongs bordered at the waist with a red band. In the past, they wore hand-woven sarongs as those in the most remote areas still do. These are much more durable than the satin sarongs purchased in the market from Vietnamese. They do not generally wear blouses unless they are cold or are going to town.

A woman never leaves her village without a carrying basket. The most widely used basket is the large back basket (sah) for carrying anything from firewood to gourds of drinking water, unhusked rice, or items bought in the market.

Adornments. Men wear brass hand-tooled bracelets. If their hair is long, they tie it in a little bun around a wide aluminum blade used as ornamentation. A man sometimes wears a single strand of beads. At puberty, Stieng boys and girls have their four upper front teeth chopped out at the gum line, and the bottom four filed to a point and lacquered black. By 1960, however, that custom was seldom practiced

in the village and surrounding area where we lived. Some older
men have become self-conscious of their filed teeth when around
outsiders and have had them gold-capped by Vietnamese practitioners.

Women wear aluminum bracelets and anklets, sometimes only
a couple, but often many on both arms; these are never removed. Most women wear solid aluminum necklaces. One of the
most interesting adornments that Stieng women wear is their
ivory ear plugs (pi blửc) made from the tusk of an elephant
or wild boar. Ear lobes are pierced when girls are infants,
and a string is inserted into the hole. Then as a girl grows,
the hole is gradually stretched with a small bamboo plug or
even a hand-rolled cigarette. At puberty, girls usually receive small ivory plugs to insert in their already stretched
lobes. Later, in adulthood, they may purchase a larger pair,
which are considered very valuable.

In recent years, new plugs have been impossible to obtain
because wild animals have moved deeper into jungle areas to
escape bombardment, where it is unsafe to hunt. Neither
Stieng men nor women scarify themselves or use paint or makeup
of any kind.

Young girls wear their hair hanging loosely, but teenagers
and women wear their hair in a loose bun at the nape of their
necks. Women in the Sông Bé area do not cut their hair unless their spouse dies. Women from Đức Phồng can be recog-
nized by their distinctive hairstyle--they cut a fringe of
bangs all the way around their head, but then allow the rest
to grow long and tie it into a bun at the back of their head.

Housing. Since the Stieng people live in a forested area
with an especially heavy growth of bamboo, it is natural that
they build their houses using this versatile material. A
house often measures as much as sixty feet in length, but
only about twenty feet in width. Trees six to eight inches
in diameter are sufficiently sturdy to be used as main house
posts, planted in holes three feet deep. Bamboo poles are
lashed to the main posts to make side frames and rafters.
Rattan, split into one-eighth inch cords, is the material of
choice for tying frames together. When rattan is not obtain-
able, the outer layer of green bamboo is the second choice,
and makes an excellent tie. The outer one-eighth inch layer
is peeled from the bamboo pole into strips. The strip breaks

at the knot, so in effect, comes premeasured long enough for
ties. It is pliable when green, stiff and tight when dried
in place, and does not need to be braided into cords.

For the outer walls and partitions, many large bamboo
poles are carried long distances from the forest. The men
split them while still green, dry the strips to protect
against weevils, and then weave them neatly into large sheets
for walls and partitions. Usually two men work together on
the weaving. The outside walls are tied to the bamboo framework with rattan or bamboo cord.

The thatch roof is completed as soon as possible so that
the house may be occupied immediately while the interior is
being finished. Thatch ('ja) is a waist-high wild grass with
a serrated edge. When it is tied in clumps, each piece clings
to the next and makes a waterproof covering. Thatch is
gathered in bundles and carried to the village where it is
dried. If it is not dried well, it will rot during the rainy
season or develop leaks as it dries and contracts. Dried
thatch is laid out in neat rows on the ground and clamped together in three-to-four-foot sheets by means of interlaced
splits of bamboo. When many of these roofing sheets are
finished, then two or three men work together fastening the
grass to the rafters with bamboo ties. A roof in a Stieng
house has a very steep pitch in order to allow the heavy
rains to run off quickly. The roof of the house is thus more
prominent than are the walls. Doorways are usually cut
opposite each other at the narrow ends of the house.

The house does not include furniture as Euroamericans
think of it. The main item of furniture is a sleeping platform from eight to ten feet wide, made of split bamboo laid
across a frame of bamboo poles along the entire length of
one side of the house. The sleeping platform also serves as
a storage area for valuables such as wine jars, blankets,
gongs, and clothing.

After the sleeping platform is built, partitions of woven
bamboo may be put up for privacy. Each compartment is large
enough for one of the nuclear families of the extended family
which occupies the house. If a man has two or more wives,
each wife and her children have a separate compartment.

A girl sleeps in her parents' compartment, whereas a boy
sleeps separately. Married children living in the same house
with their parents have separate compartments of their own.
When someone dies, his section of sleeping platform is chopped
away, leaving a vacant space.

The unpartitioned side of the house is simply a dirt floor
with a cooking fire for each wife.

Tools. A man seldom goes anywhere without his shoulder
axe (wiêh) and small knife (pêh). The shoulder axe is his
most useful tool. With it, he clears his field, chops his
firewood, and builds his house. An axe blade is bought in
the market and fitted to the end of a curved portion of a
bamboo shoot. The shape of the handle is a modified letter
J which allows it to rest neatly on the shoulder. The blade,
which is closer in size to a wide knife blade than an axe
blade, is held tightly in the knot of the bamboo shoot with a
small peg of wood. A shoulder axe blade that is broken, or
can no longer be sharpened, is fitted to a two-foot long
bamboo handle to make a small, efficient hoe used for weeding corn, tobacco or other plants. A commercial hoe blade,
available at Vietnamese markets, is used for digging holes
and gardening. This large blade is eight inches wide and
twelve inches long.

Another axe (sung) is about half the size of a medium-
sized American axe and has a heavier head than the shoulder
axe blade. The back of the head is hollow, allowing a
three-foot curved piece of wood to be inserted. This in-
creases the weight of the head with a minimum use of iron
and results in a heavy axe capable of felling trees or
splitting large pieces of firewood.

A man makes his own knife handle from a small curved portion of bamboo shoot. The blade is five inches long and has
a sheath made of two flat pieces of wood tied together with
braided rattan cord. He tucks this knife into the waist-
band of his loincloth, always on the right side.

Weapons. Besides shoulder axes, knives, and clubs, Stiengs
have spears and crossbows in their arsenal. Spears are used
ceremonially to kill water buffalo. Crossbows (sơna) made of

hard wood are used to hunt small game such as squirrels,
porcupines, and groundhogs. The bow of the crossbow measures
from four to six feet in length, and the stock is similar in
length. It has a trigger of bone and a slot on top for
placing a poison tipped bamboo arrow. The tip of the stock
is often decorated with carvings, as well as blood and fur
from the first kill. A poison which apparently attacks the
nerve center of the animal is made from the bark of the 'jar
tree, and is very effective. The crossbow is more powerful
than accurate since arrows made of bamboo splits are irregular
in shape. The advantage, when hunting, is in having the
cover of thick jungle. The hunter never has to shoot across
an open field, but can get within a few yards of his target.

Basketry. In a land where bamboo is plentiful, it is no
surprise that quite a variety of baskets are made. Boys
learn the skills of basketry, beginning by making the sim-
plest types first.

The back basket (sah) is tightly woven of fine strips of
bamboo, with two shoulder straps of strong, flexible braided
rattan. It is used by the women for carrying heavy loads of
wood, rice, or water. A loosely woven basket (waas) is used
only to carry gourds of water. Baskets of various shapes
and sizes are woven for specific purposes. A quart-sized
basket (cupiêng) with fitted lid and one shoulder strap is
used to carry cooked rice to the field. A long and narrow
basket (sôôr) with two straps and pointed bottom is used as
a quiver and for carrying small game. A gallon-sized harvesting basket (khiêu) of tightly woven bamboo is carried
over one shoulder and tied to the waist while harvesting. A
flat basket (dôông) with one slightly pointed side measuring
four to five feet in diameter is used for winnowing.

We were especially impressed with the speed with which
hundreds of small baskets were made at a wedding feast, to be
used for dividing up the meat that was butchered. Young men
are also adept at weaving fish traps, complete with a bamboo
spring which pulls the opening shut after the fish enters.

Figure 14.   Sah.

Weaving. Women are skilled in weaving loincloths, skirts, blankets, and a cloth for carrying an infant on one's hip. A woman, sitting on a blanket on the ground, holds a simple wooden loom with her feet, resting it on her lap and tying it to her waist. Material is woven with rather intricate designs of red, black, white, and yellow thread. In former days, women grew their own cotton in the village, spun the yarn, dyed it, and then wove it. Today they buy yarn from the Vietnamese. This art is fast dying out as it is cheaper for them to buy cloth than to make their own.

Pottery. A few older women still are skilled in making clay pots. A white clay sediment from a stream is shaped into pots by hand without the use of a wheel. After drying the pot for a time, it is fired by placing it directly into a fire. The pots are used for cooking rice and are made with lids. This craft is no longer common as it is more customary to buy aluminum pots in the market.

Musical Instruments. Most minority peoples of South Viet Nam have gongs as part of their inventory of musical instruments. The Stieng people have two sets of gongs, one set called gong consisting of five separate gongs with convex centers, and another set called chênh consisting of six separate flat-centered gongs. These are purchased from Chinese merchants in large towns or in Saigon. Each individual gong has its own pitch and is played separately by one man. It is taboo to play these outside the house except under certain circumstances, such as when a water buffalo is sacrificed. Wine flows freely when gongs are played, since gongs summon the spirits, and the spirits must be offered wine at the very least. On such occasions, which last through the night, the same tune is played continuously, with no variation.

The khôôm buôt (literally, 'blow-joined') is a wind instrument made of a gourd into which six varied lengths of bamboo are inserted and held in place with pitch. The musician blows through the top of the narrow neck of the gourd varying the pitch by fingering notches in the sides of the bamboo.

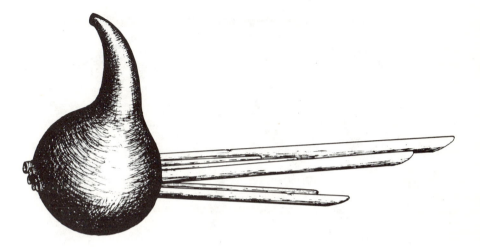

Figure 15.   Khôôm Buôt.

The chênh kêy (literally, 'gong horn') is made of hollowed-out buffalo horns.   There are six to a set, and they have pitch levels which correspond to the six gongs called chênh. Each horn is played individually, and they can only be blown outside the village at night during harvest season.   We enjoyed listening to their flutelike sound as the men returned from the field.

Every young boy learns to make and play a six-stringed banjo (đênhdut).   It is made from an eighteen-inch piece of bamboo.   Strands of the outer layer of the bamboo are lifted from the circumference of the tube, extending to its entire length.   Variously sized frets of bamboo are inserted under each strand to determine its pitch.

Toys. Men make very large kites (clêêng) using a bamboo frame and covering of paper bought in the market.   They add several long tails with tassels.   A bull-roarer which vibrates in the wind, making a musical sound, is attached to the frame.   Kites are flown during the windy season, in February and March, and may be kept airborne through the night when the wind is strong.

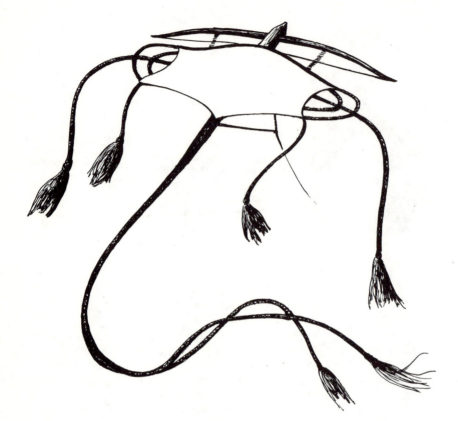

Figure 16. Clêêng.

Stieng boys carve small tops (pi blir) of wood, and make special string for them of vine. Two or more boys play together with their tops as a competitive sport.

As the war machinery came closer and closer to the Stieng area and children saw machine guns, artillery, planes, and parachutes, they began copying these. The center rib of a banana leaf was used to make toy repeating rifles. They cut a series of slits, lifted them up, and then in pretending to shoot, ran their forefinger quickly down the barrel. This made a sharp 'rat a tat tat' sound. Once, after they had observed paratroops practice jumping at a nearby airstrip for the first time, all the children cleverly made their own parachutes out of bits of cloth and string.

ECONOMIC ORGANIZATION

A few Stiengs have recently (1974) been moving away from
their traditional nonmarket economy. In each village one
finds someone selling wine, tobacco, rice, or dried fish.
Before this, only Vietnamese would buy and sell to the Stieng.
Stiengs live at a subsistence level, made more difficult because of the long period of war. Vietnamese money has come
into wide use, both for market purchases as well as for
borrowing and paying of debts.

Work and Labor. As in many agricultural societies, the
Stiengs have periods when they work very hard, and other
times when they are free. During planting and harvesting
season, they work from dawn until dusk, walking long distances
to and from their fields as well. At those times everyone
in the family--men, women and children--works together in the
household fields.

Division of Labor. Some types of work--pounding rice,
winnowing, cooking meals, chopping firewood, hauling water,
and weaving cloth--are specifically done by the women of the
society. Young girls receive training in these practices,
and take responsibility in accordance with their age.

Men hunt, trap, fish, build houses and fences, make tools,
and clear the fields. They also make most of the artifacts
of the society, such as baskets, traps, kites, shoulder axes
knives, pipes and musical instruments.

Young people, both boys and girls, herd cattle and water
buffalo, if the household has such.

Wealth. Prosperity is measured by the number of wives a
man has and by material possessions such as wine jars, slaves,
gongs, cattle, water buffalo, and pigs.

The most valuable of the wine jars (srung) may be worth as
much as five slaves. The diameter of a wine jar measured in
cubits (that is, the length of the forearm from the elbow to
the tip of the middle finger) determines its value. A wine
jar which measures one cubit in diameter is normally equal to
one slave; a jar of two cubits would be worth two slaves.

Stieng men of the bulđ division feel that the bride price
in their area is extremely high compared with that of other
parts of Indochina. Even so, having two wives is not uncommon, and a man in Sơn Trung village had seven wives.

Consumption. War and the resettlement of Stiengs into
overcrowded hamlets have caused the people to consume much
less food than they really need. In recent years, they have
not grown enough food to feed themselves because their fields
have always been in contested areas.

FOOD

The main food is rice, grown by swidden agriculture. Corn
and a favorite type of elongated squash (plai đien) is also
grown. The Stieng raise animals such as pigs, ducks, and
chickens, and grow bananas, papaya, and chili peppers in
small quantities. Hunting for wild boar and other small game
gives them another source of food, along with fishing.
Stiengs also gather edible plants such as bamboo shoots, in-
sects from the forest, and algae from the rocks in the river.

Fishing. Although the Stieng are adept at many types of
fishing, it provides only a minor portion of their food
supply. One form of fishing is by means of a trap made from
woven strips of bamboo complete with a small gate. Bread or
rice is placed inside the trap in order to attract fish, which
then enter through the small opening. The trap is placed at
the bottom of a stream. It is often left there all day with
no catch at all.

A second common way of fishing is by scooping small fish
out of a shallow stream using a woven bamboo scoop the size
of a large straw hat. Usually, only a few small fish are
caught in this way.

A third method is with line and hook, and a fourth method
is by poison. This latter method is done by an entire village and is an enjoyable community affair. First, the river
is dammed up, causing it to become shallow on the downstream
side. Then a pungent reddish root from the forest is pounded
and tossed into the river. This poison stuns the fish, bringing them to the surface, where they can be grabbed. Sometimes
they have a good catch, but they are often disappointed.

Agriculture. Once a field is prepared, it is customarily
used to plant crops for three years before being abandoned
and allowed to lie fallow. Each family usually works three
fields at the same time. These include the present year's
newly prepared field, last year's field, and a field from
the year before.

In late February, Stieng men go to the field and clear
the underbrush. Then they chop down any trees in a new field.
The wood is stacked for housebuilding or firewood, and brush
is piled up to dry and burn.

Just before the rains begin in May, rice is planted. Corn
is planted between the rows of rice as well. It grows quickly and can be harvested long before there is danger of it
shading the rice plants. Families work together in planting.
A man walks back and forth across the field making holes with
a dibble stick in each hand, while a woman follows him, dropping three or four grains of rice into each hole, then covering the hole with her foot.

Since it rains every day, five or six months a year, there
is always sufficient water for growth. Harvesting a large
crop, however, does not only depend on rain, but on a Stieng's
ingenuity in keeping away pests and wild animals. Therefore,
as soon as planting begins, someone must stay in the field
day and night in order to keep the animals and birds away. A
noisemaker (pôôh) of bamboo clackers is connected with systems
of twine around the field that one person can operate from a
little field house. It is used to scare off little black
birds considered to be a major pest. Young people and women
take turns watching the fields, freeing the men to seek cash
income while waiting for harvest.[2]

Men, women, and young people all help with the harvesting,
and each person carries a khiêu basket. The rice plant is
not cut, but each ripened head is picked by hand. This takes
longer than cutting, but the Stieng have a taboo against
cutting the rice stalk. An exceptional harvest would be a
hundred back baskets of grain per family.

Gardening. Each Stieng family has a small garden behind
the house where it grows its favorite squash year round.

All parts of this plant are eaten--the fruit, vine and leaves.
Besides squash, the garden produces gourds used to store
drinking water, betel leaves, mint, chili peppers, leeks,
bananas, jackfruit, and papaya.

Domestic Animals. Water buffalo, pigs, ducks, and chickens are raised in and around the village. Buffalo are raised
only for sacrifice and wealth, but are not used for plowing.
Dogs are raised as pets, as well as for meat.

Problems. I would like to emphasize that what has been
described is typical of good times. But during much of the
time we lived among the Stieng people, they were not able to
farm in their usual manner. Many Vietnamese had moved into
the area, precipitating land disputes and forcing the Stieng
to go further from their villages to plant. Available land
was often too far from the village to permit travel back and
forth each day, or the land was in an area contested by war-
ring parties where they were not permitted to travel. Another difficulty was that the government would not allow them
to stay in the fields at night, which meant that they lost
much of their crop to predators.

Cash Income. During the years when it was safe for Stieng
men to go into the forest, they cut down great quantities of
bamboo and sold it to Vietnamese traders. The traders paid
the men by the piece and then hauled heavily loaded trucks
to the coast, or to Saigon to sell to other Vietnamese who
specialized in furniture making or house building. After
1963, it was no longer possible to earn much money in this
way because of the constant danger of war activity.

A second means of obtaining cash is through the sale of
sesame seed which the Stieng plant in their rice fields.
They sell this seed to Chinese merchants.

A third important way to earn money is to collect the sap
of the huge, tŏŏm raach tree in five gallon cans, and sell it
to Vietnamese traders, who then sell it to boatmakers. The
Vietnamese call this type of tree cay bau. To get the sap,
the tree is notched and a fire is built in the notch. When
the fire cools, the sap runs into the notch and is collected.

A fourth means of earning money is to lead loggers to very
large trees deep in the forest. Since Vietnamese are not
familiar with the forest, they pay Stieng men to scout out
the best sources. A great deal of commercial lumbering has
been done in the area by the Vietnamese. Of course, war
hampered this activity too, as no one dared go deep into the
jungle.

MARRIAGE AND THE FAMILY

Courting. Courting as we know it is not part of Stieng
culture. Young people do chores and other activities together, but it is never proper for an unmarried couple to be
alone. Group activities which bring young people together
include herding water buffalo or cattle, fishing, hunting,
and gathering edible roots, nuts, and berries in the forest.
If an unmarried couple is found alone together, they are
assumed to be having illicit sexual relations, and will be
so accused.

Selection of a Spouse. Marriage with the daughter of a
mother's brother is preferred, but is not obligatory. Marriages are often arranged by parents while boys and girls
are still infants. The purpose of such a marriage is pri-
marily economic. The bride price and gift exchange are taken
care of then, and the children grow up together in the boy's
home as brother and sister. When the girl reaches marriageable age, right after puberty, she may be given in marriage
to some other man and her bride price used to pay for a girl
to be wife to the boy with whom she grew up. This is probably due to the fact that they feel more like brother and
sister, and an actual marriage relationship would seem
strange to them. In some cases, however, when the young
couple reaches adulthood, they do marry.

Some opportunity to choose a marriage partner is open to
a young man since it is possible for him to see a girl that
he finds attractive in a village that he is visiting, in-
quire about her--whether she's married, if she's skilled,
and if she can work hard in the field--and, if she meets his
standards, begin arranging for a marriage.

Once a girl has been chosen, it is necessary for the parents to give permission and begin making arrangements for the
marriage. It is possible that parents may refuse to arrange
a marriage, either because they cannot afford the bride price
at that time, or because the girl is the child of a witch
(chaac).

Bride Price. In arranging the details of the marriage,
two intermediaries each are chosen by the parents of both
bride and groom. These men must not be members of their
families and must be acceptable to both sides. The groom's
parents and their intermediaries go to the bride's village
to discuss the proposed marriage with the bride's parents.
After this initial contact, which may or may not settle the
bride price, the parents return to their own village and entrust everything into the hands of their intermediaries.

Intermediaries have a great deal of responsibility. They
not only are witnesses to the marriage agreement, but they
must see that the bride price is paid. In a situation where
the price cannot be paid, and the groom is not able to serve
in his father-in-law's household, then the intermediary is
liable.

In spite of much bargaining, the bride price is quite
rigid, and follows the price paid for the bride's mother. A
normal price would be one bond slave, one expensive jar
(srung), a water buffalo, three or four pigs, 20 small wine
jars, five bush axes, and five spears. Bargaining takes a
lot of time, because, if there is no bond slave or wine jar,
they must figure the equivalent in money. The devaluation
of money has caused much difficulty in figuring current
equivalents.

As an alternative to the bride price, the couple takes up
residence with the bride's family, and the groom contributes
his labor to his father-in-law's household.

Most men complain about the high bride price, and some
men therefore choose to take a Cambodian wife to avoid having
to pay it.

When the bargaining is completed, a wedding date is set.
It can take place within a few days or after as long as a

month. The marriage, however, cannot take place three or
thirteen days after the agreement is made. These days are
taboo.

    An interesting economic feature connected with the bride
price is called trading (toh laas). This means that a
brother of the bride can borrow from the groom at an advantage. If a man is in debt, if he needs a wine jug or water
buffalo, or plans to get married and is in need of his own
bride price, he can ask his married sister for any of these
and she and her husband are obligated to help with the debt.
The brother, however, must check the financial situation of
his sister before asking. Otherwise, because the obliga-
tion is so strong, the brother-in-law might be forced to
make his own wife a bond slave. If the request for help is
agreeable, a month is allowed for the sister and brother-in-
law to procure what is needed. The brother will return to
his sister's house bringing baskets of glutinous rice. The
rice is divided by the sister among all the children who are
related to her husband. Then the sister butchers a pig so
that they can feast and drink together. Killing a pig is
compulsory in this situation.

    Long before borrowing takes place, brothers have recipro-
cal obligations to their newly married sister. They must
help the new couple get financially established by bringing
gifts--pigs, chickens, or other basic household necessities.

    Elopement. A young couple from wealthy families may fall
in love and decide to marry on their own. Early some morning,
while the girl is pounding rice, he will sneak to her village and carry her off. Later, when the girl's parents miss
her, they send out search parties. Eventually they will find
that the couple has eloped. Then all the relatives go to the
groom's village where the full bride price is paid, plus a
little extra. There they join in a time of feasting and
drinking.

    Marriage Ceremonies. The first feast known as 'bringing
gifts to them' (Jên drap a bu), is the main marriage ceremony, after which the couple may engage in sexual intercourse.
The ceremony takes place at the village of the bride. Three

pigs, which are part of the bride price, are brought to the
bride's parents by the groom or groom's parents. These pigs
are known as the 'sacrificial pig', the 'looking for a wife
pig', and the 'spear and axe pig'; the last of these relates
to an engagement present which includes a spear and a sacrificial shoulder axe with a curved handle (wiêh ửͬr).

All the animals brought are butchered that day and are
shared equally by both families. Most of the meat is con-
sumed by wedding guests.

Before any of the meat is eaten, there is an elaborate
ceremony. When evening begins, the intermediary has the
responsibility of calling on the spirits. The bride and groom
stand facing each other with their right feet on a buffalo
horn. The intermediary mixes together pig's blood, a mashed
tuber, a little wine, and a piece of the pig's liver, using
the same knife which he used to kill the pigs. Taking the
knife, he smears some of this mixture on the bride's foot,
and then on the groom's foot. While anointing their feet,
the intermediary calls to the spirits of the sky, the grave,
the house, and all the deceased relatives, and asks them for
their blessings on the marriage, requesting that the spirits
prevent sickness and guard the new home. He also asks that
the spirits make the union prosperous. This special knife
becomes the property of the groom. He must not lose it,
sell it, or trade it.

The second part of the ceremony involves the drinking of
rice wine. A wine jar is filled with wine, using a hollowed-
out buffalo horn as a measure. The groom uses a reed to
drink from the jar. As he drinks, someone pours water into
the jar of wine, using a buffalo horn to measure exactly how
much is added. In this way they can tell how much the groom
has drunk. He can drink either two or four hornfuls of wine;
three is taboo. While he's drinking, the bride places a
string of red beads around his neck. When the groom finishes,
the bride drinks wine in the same manner. The groom removes
the beads from his neck and places them around the bride's
neck. She wears those beads all that night and the next day.
She can wear them longer if she chooses, but usually removes
them after the first day or two.

After this ceremony is completed, all the guests are served
rice and roast pork. The bride ceremonially gives her husband
a handful of rice; and he reciprocates, signifying their
pledge to live and work together.

At the end of the first ceremony, the couple takes up
temporary residence in the bride's parent's house. The parents prepare a separate compartment for the newlyweds, and
they are permitted to have sexual intercourse.

The second ceremony takes place immediately after rice
harvest at the groom's village, and is a regular part of the
harvest ceremony. It is called 'our son brings his wife
home' (jên coon seq a sai). It refers to the fact that the
bride price has been paid, and the couple takes up residence
in the groom's village. From that point, they begin to contribute to the economic welfare of the groom's family. It
is important that the second ceremony occur after rice harvest because of the significance of making fresh wine from
that year's rice. It insures the success of the marriage.
Commercial wine sold by the Vietnamese is not considered
legitimate for the purpose, since the Stieng believe that the
spirits are not accustomed to Vietnamese wine.

Three pigs are brought and butchered for the feast. Also,
a type of glutinous rice considered especially delicious is
carried by the guests to the groom's village, where it is
cooked in bamboo tubes. There is a special term for each
pig. One is called the 'sticky rice pig', referring to the
fact that all the bride's relatives can go to the groom's
village. The second pig is known as 'stepping on the sleeping
mat pig', indicating that a new household is to be established
in the groom's village. The third pig is named 'entering
the bedroom pig' which symbolizes that the couple may engage
in sexual intercourse in the groom's village.

As the years pass, the intermediaries keep a record of the
payment of the bride price. In most cases, it is years before a groom is able to procure the valuable jar or bond-
slave. In this situation, the groom lives in his father-in-
law's house and contributes to that family's economy. This
may continue indefinitely, or the full bride price may in
fact be paid. In the latter case, another feast takes place

at the village of the bride, for which the bride's parents
are responsible to provide the meat.

In recent war years, the extremely costly bride price has
added greatly to the burden of debt that Stieng households
carry. We have observed that they are never free of debt,
and some of their debts are beyond their ability to ever repay.

Number of Spouses. Stieng marriages are often polygamous.[3] The suggestion that a man take a second wife may come
from the first wife, who wants help with the work. In a
polygamous household, each wife and her children have a separate compartment within the same house. They also each keep
separate their own rice, cooking utensils, pigs, chickens,
and gardens. The husband owns all these things in common
with each wife, but ownership is not shared between wives.
A man eats and sleeps with each wife in turn.

Men also acquire additional wives through the levirate,
that is, by taking the widows of their deceased brothers.
When a man dies, the preference is for his brother or other
male relative to take the widow as wife. The brothers may
divide the possessions of the deceased among themselves, and
they are obligated to also take the widow. If a widow does
not agree to live with one of her husband's male relatives,
she can return the bride price and marry someone else or return to her parents' village. A son may take his father's
widow as his own wife, providing she is not his biological
mother.

Whoever takes a widow as wife also assumes the debts of
the dead husband.

Avoidance. The Stieng have strict sex avoidance rules.
This especially applies to affinal relatives. A man must
never have physical contact with the wife of his brother or
his son. A Stieng family unit living together in a long house
includes all members of the patrilineally extended family,
as well as couples whose bride price has not been completely
paid. Still it is important that certain relatives never
touch each other. If they do, even inadvertently, the
younger is always considered at fault.

Divorce and Adultery. Divorce is very uncommon.[4] About
the only real cause for divorce is adultery. If a wife is

unfaithful, she is believed to cause her husband to become
sick or otherwise have trouble. So if a husband is on a
fishing or hunting trip, or arranging a loan, and is unsuccessful, he will suspect his wife of infidelity.

The female partner in a case of adultery is severely punished. If a husband believes his wife is guilty, he may beat
her until she confesses. Then he may demand that she go with
her parents and sue for settlement from the guilty male
partner. The interloper may be required to pay a jar (srung)
or pig as indemnity. The wronged husband may choose to go
along and watch the proceedings, but he has no right to make
any charges. In the case of repeated adultery with the same
man, the payment may be a bond slave, which may be the man
himself. If that happens, the bond slave must live and work
in the house of the woman with whom he has had the affair.

A wife can do no more than scold her husband if he is suspected of adultery; but she can threaten to tell the husband
of the woman involved, in which case suit could be brought
against him. This is one way wives keep their husbands in
line.

Men and women are very careful not to be seen alone with
someone of the opposite sex. They would never go to their
fields together, walk back from a river together, or perform
any other ordinary daily task in the company of someone who
was not their spouse. If they did, they would be accused of
adultery. There must always be a third person present in any
such situation.

If divorce does occur, the bride price must be returned.
If the wife's parents cannot make payment, then the intermediaries chosen by the wife's parents are responsible for
the debt.

Mistresses. Although dating, as Americans think of it, is
not part of Stieng culture, a young unmarried man may have a
mistress. He must make arrangements for the rendevous
through an intermediary--another girl. He pays something to
both girls, and the couple meet at a prearranged spot in
the forest. A relationship like this can last from between
one meeting to a couple of years, or even marriage. If the

girl becomes pregnant, they must marry, and the bride price
must be paid. The alternative is to pay a penalty.

   The Stieng have a legend about a girl sent out to the
field each morning to keep doves from eating the newly
planted rice seed. While there she had opportunity to meet
her boyfriend. But as the rice sprouted, she cut it down
and told the family that it had not yet sprouted. When the
rice sprouts, the doves are no longer a problem. In this
way she continued her rendevous for a long time.

   Single People. A person does not remain single unless
crippled, disfigured, or unusually ugly. All other women
marry; and all other men marry, even if the bride price is
exorbitant and they are very poor. Foreign single women--
whether Vietnamese, French, or American--are assumed by the
Stieng to be someone's mistress.

   Orphans. An orphan is usually cared for by the brother
of the child's deceased father. If the child has no such
kinsman, the mother's brother takes responsibility. There
are situations, however, where an orphan will not be cared
for because its family has caused others trouble, and the
relatives do not feel pity for the child. An orphan, when
becoming a part of a new household, helps by working in the
field.

RELIGIOUS BELIEFS IN RICE PLANTING

   There are three major ceremonies connected with the planting and harvesting of rice. They are: the ceremony for finding a field, the sprinkling ceremony, and the harvest ceremony.

   Ceremony for Finding a Field (Pê Lnoong). In January, when
the rains have stopped, the head of the household begins to
look for a field. He looks close to his own village first,
but more often must search a one or two hour walk from his village. Ideally, he chooses a field adjacent to his present
one, since he tries to work three fields at the same time.
It is necessary to choose one that has been fallow for fifteen or twenty years. He can judge this by the size of the
trees. He is also alert for a certain grasslike weed (la siêt),

the presence of which indicates favorable soil conditions.
He also prefers terrain free of rocks or difficult slopes.

When he has chosen a field, he marks it as such by cutting
a small four-foot square clearing in which he plants a bamboo pole. The bamboo is split at the top into four strips,
one pointing down with la siêt grass placed in the splits.
He offers a prayer at the site which goes something like this:
"I am trusting here. I haven't dreamed, I haven't had a
nightmare, I haven't had anything to show me not to plant.
I want to plant. Even if I should plant the hardwood tree,
have it bear fruit. If I should plant a pestle used for
pounding rice, let it sprout."

When the man returns to the village, it is taboo for him
to speak to visitors, and visitors are forbidden to enter his
house. If either of these happen, it is believed that wild
pigs or deer will ruin his field after it is planted.

After staking out his field, a man waits a night or two
for omens in his dreams. Bad dreams would reverse his deci-
sion. If he dreams of clear running water, that would be a
good sign; but if he dreams of falling or some other accident, then he would take that as a warning not to plant there.
He would then choose another field. After two or three days
of uneventful dreams, however, he returns to his new field
and performs the second part of this first ritual called
'the testing' (Pê Lnoong). An area of ten to fifteen feet
square is cleared. While clearing, the man continually
watches for bad omens warning him not to plant the field. A
bad omen, for example, might be the sound of a falling tree,
which the Stieng believe to be the sound of one's own coffin
being made. He also watches for certain birds which are bad
omens. No prayer is offered at this particular time. If he
clears this small area and nothing happens to warn him, he
then returns and begins to clear the entire field.

The small area which was originally staked out is the spot
where he erects his field house. It becomes his shelter and
home for much of the year while he is planting and harvesting.
He even spends some of his nights there protecting his fields
against predators.

Ceremony of the Sprinkling of Rice (Broh Ba). When the
rice is about two feet tall, but before the seed appears, a
sacrifice is made in the village. Both a pig and a chicken
are killed and a spirit pole (cdnhjoh) is made within the
village. Spirit poles are made of bamboo and are used in all
Stieng sacrifices. The bottom is split into several parts
into which other strips of bamboo are woven, producing the
shape of a lamp base. The top of the pole is also split into
many thin shavings, so thin that they curl.

One split, used to pierce the liver of the chicken, is not
curled. It stands in the center of what appears to be tassels
of curled bamboo. These curlicued tassels are smeared with
blood from the sacrifice, and this pole then becomes the focal
point of the worship ceremony. Though the pig and chicken are
killed in the village, they are carried to the field for the
remainder of the ceremony.

In the original four foot square clearing, a small replica
of the rice house, called the 'rice spirit's house', is
erected. The sacrificed meat is placed alongside this small
spirit house, and a handful of freshly cooked rice from the
top of the pot is offered to the spirits. Basic ingredients
used in making betel chew--including the betel nut, betel
leaf, lime, and tobacco--are placed in a little dish and set
inside the spirit house. The meat from the sacrifice is also
placed within the spirit house at this time.

The farmer has previously planted a tuber (gun) believed
to have magical properties alongside his field house. Such
a tuber is now pulled up, mashed together with water, and
placed in a bamboo tube. In the actual 'sprinkling ceremony', the owner of the field sprinkles some of this sub-
stance on all four sides of his field and on the path that
he uses to go to the field. While sprinkling, he calls upon
the rice spirit to give him a good rice harvest.

When he finishes, he places the empty bamboo tube inside
the spirit's house and removes the meat, leaving the rice
and betel chew ingredients for the rice spirit. In the evening, back in the village while his wife cooks the evening
meal, the man takes a little part of the sacrificed meat,
makes another small spirit pole, and goes to the spring where

he normally bathes each day. He calls on the spirit of the
water and offers it a sacrifice too. He leaves a little
rice and betel chew ingredients, which are part of all
sacrifice ceremonies.

The Harvest Ceremony (Pư Ba Khiêu). This third ceremony
also begins in the same little square that was first cleared.
The harvest ceremony takes place anytime after all the rice
is harvested, either immediately or some months later. Evi-
dently the ceremony is postponed as long as possible to show
abundant harvest and to avoid the immediate cost of a sacrifice. The ceremony is named after the particular basket
(khiêu) used to harvest rice.

Each household builds a storehouse high off the ground,
either within the village or in the field. As the rice is
harvested, the storehouse is filled first, except for what
is eaten that day. None of the storehouse rice can be eaten
until the harvest ceremony is completed. Once the storehouse
is filled, then the remainder of the rice is stored in large
baskets in the house. This extra rice can be eaten before
the harvest ceremony.

If there is a good harvest of one hundred or more large
back baskets, the harvest ceremony must take place or else
the owner cannot leave his village. His family may leave,
but it is taboo for him to leave until the sacrifice is
offered.

During the harvesting, the rice around the spirit's house
is harvested last. It is put into an old basket, and that
particular rice is considered to be the spirit's rice and
is kept in the storehouse.

For this sacrifice, the owner of the field makes a new
spirit pole, which is anointed with the blood of a chicken
and pig. The basket of rice for the spirit is brought from
the storehouse, and the head of the roasted pig and a whole
chicken are put on top of the basket. Then the spirit pole
is placed on top of the rice. Every type of food found in
a Stieng household is also placed in the basket. One special
preparation is the cooking of sticky rice (pênjêng) in a
finger-thin bamboo tube. After cooking, the tubing is cut

every inch or so to make it flexible, and then it is wound
around the top and sides of the spirit pole. Three other
items of importance in the sacrifice are a dish of betel nut
chew, a dish of wine, and some drinking water for the spirit.
After these are all in place, the man calls upon the spirit
of the rice. He especially asks for protection and health
for the new family if his son and daughter-in-law have returned to his home. He also asks for good luck, freedom from
sickness for his family during the coming year, and then calls
attention to all the parts of the sacrifice he has just made--
the pig, the chicken, the wine, and the betel he has given
to the spirit to use. After that, he retrieves the chicken
and the pig's head for the guests to eat along with rice that
has been prepared.

SICKNESS AND DEATH

Sickness and death are believed to be caused by a witch
or sorcerer (chaac). In Stieng eyes, all people are divided
into two classes, sorcerers and good people (joh). Any illness or misfortune is attributed to the curse of a real person, often an individual of one's own village. Furthermore,
death is divided into two categories, violent death (chhêt
briêng) and death from sickness, both caused by sorcery,
with the possible exception of death in battle. If a person
is killed by a tiger, it is believed that the tiger was
raised and fed rice by a sorcerer. It is believed that if
the tiger's stomach were cut open, cooked rice would be
found, proving that a sorcerer had been feeding it. If there
is an auto accident, sorcery is believed to have influenced
the vehicle by causing the driver to temporarily lose his
vision. Or if a person becomes ill, it is believed that a
sorcerer is eating his liver or brain. The sorcerer is believed to subsist on liver or brain of other people.

Healing Techniques. There are several ceremonies used in
healing. The mhom ceremony is performed by a 'spirit woman'
(mê brah), a woman who, by visitation of the spirits, is
claimed as their wife, and to whom they entrust a special
white stone (tmau tlaar). The stone has magical powers used
in healing and authenticates her status as a shaman. She
carries it in a small shaman's bag. A spirit woman is called
upon to hold the mhom ceremony and to divine the type of

sacrifice required to appease the sorcerer and stop him or
her from further harming the sick person.

The spirit woman orders a chicken and possibly a dog to
be killed for sacrifice prior to her arrival. These are
roasted on a spit. A spirit pole is made, and the chicken
is hung on a wall to the left of the pole, above the sleeping
platform of the patient. The entrails of the chicken are
attached to the wall to the right of the pole. The dog is
hung to the left of the chicken. A miniature bamboo ladder
is made and leaned against the spirit pole. On the right of
the pole is a bamboo tube of water and an empty bowl. Around
the spirit pole is a large dish of uncooked rice, two bowls
of cooked rice, a plate of food and a gourd of water.

When all of these items are assembled, the spirit woman
begins a chant, with heavy breathing and calling of the
spirits. During this chant, she falls into a trance and is
believed to make contact with the sorcerer, who tells her the
cause of the illness. When the trance ends, she begins to
heal by sucking the stone, stick or string which has caused
the illness out of the person's body. This ceremony may last
all night since, as soon as the prime patient has been attended,
everyone in the village with any and all ailments comes for
a brief treatment.

In the prồng ceremony, a sick person's body is rubbed with
homegrown cotton wet with saliva, by a male shaman (chồndrồng)
who has contact with the spirit world. This shaman discerns
what animal must be sacrificed in order for the person to be
healed by holding the wet cotton behind a candle. He then
receives insight as to the sacrifice the spirits require.

After an animal is killed and roasted, a sliver of each
part of the animal--leg, tail, eye, skin, etc.--is placed on
a tray along with rice and wine, and taken to the village
gate and left. Then each family in the village is given a
piece of meat from the sacrificed animal. It is essential
that this be done; otherwise the sacrifice will not be
effective. It often happens that several animals, such as
water buffalo, cattle, pigs or chicken, are required.

Because animals are very costly, this system of animal
sacrifice is a tremendous financial burden; but intense cultural pressure induces the people to be willing to suffer
debt or poverty in order to perform them.

In a more simple ceremony than the previous two mentioned,
the individual householder functions as priest by praying to
the spirits (bon brah) himself. The head of the family kills
a chicken for sacrifice, spreading the blood on the spirit
pole and putting the spirit pole outside the village gate.
He then calls the spirits of the forest, mountains, rivers,
rocks, trees, and dead relatives to request pity on him because a member of his family is sick. He promises the spirits
a sacrifice if the person is healed. This is financially
more advantageous than the previous two ceremonies, as a man
is not obligated to sacrifice unless the sick person becomes
well.

Trial by Ordeal. Occasionally, someone who is extremely
ill may dream that a particular person in the village is a
sorcerer. In the dream, he sees the sorcerer coming to eat
him. Each fireplace in the village is then given a notched
piece of bamboo (khaac) as a warning that someone is suspected of sorcery. The village is told that the sick person
had better improve or there will be an open accusation. If
the person does not improve, a close relative goes to the
person and accuses him or her of being a sorcerer, demanding
a trial by ordeal.

In one form of trial by ordeal, seven layers of leaves are
put on the accused person's hand. A razor sharp bushaxe is
held to the person's wrist to keep him from moving while
molten lead is poured onto the hand. If the lead, burning
through the layers of leaves and then the hand, drops to the
ground in the shape of a water buffalo horn, then the person
is guilty of causing the illness. If the person suffers only
a minor burn, however, the charges are dropped.

If the accuser wishes to be doubly sure, he goes to the
forest and drops molten lead on a round section of bamboo.
It too must form the shape of a water buffalo horn while he
is calling out the name of the accused. If that happens,
the accuser announces the fact to the entire village.

A person usually confesses to being a sorcerer when presented with this evidence since, if he does not, he is beaten
or tortured until he does. If the sorcerer can heal the sick
person, he is released; but if not, he may be sold into
slavery, killed, have his fingers chopped off, or be tortured
to death by making cuts on his body and rubbing red pepper
into them.

Another variation of the ordeal is to see if a person can
hold his breath under water. A sorcerer will not be able to
hold his breath at all. In 1968 there were young men in
their twenties who had witnessed the trial by ordeal, although the government no longer permitted sorcerers to be
killed. We are told that the French government did allow
these killings as a part of the Stieng system of justice.

Medicine. Although the Stieng perform all the foregoing
ceremonies, they also accept Vietnamese or Western medicine.
There seems to be no incongruity with this practice. We have
attended healing ceremonies, and have given an injection to
the sick person immediately afterwards. The person is believed to recover if the spirit allows him to do so; but if
the spirit wants him to die, he will, no matter what medicine
is given.

Magical Charms (gun). One means of avoiding sickness and
death is the wearing of charms. A charm is made from the
tuber, mentioned earlier, (gun) which is considered to have
magical powers. The tuber is sliced into small pieces one
quarter inch in circumference and one eighth inch thick.
After being dried, these pieces are worn on a string around
the neck to ward off evil powers.

The tuber can also be made into a special potion to perform other desired functions--anything from a love potion
furtively given to a girl whom one wants as a mistress, to a
potion to cause a dog to bite someone unwanted in the village.

Infant Mortality. The rate of infant mortality is extremely high among the Stieng. There is a lack of knowledge
of basic sanitation, and babies often die of pneumonia because they are exposed to rainy or cold weather when newborn.

Of the babies born during the three years (1960 to 1963) we
were living in a Stieng village, perhaps fifty percent died.

The people have responded to this problem in a number of
ways. First, babies are not named until about three years
old, when their chances of survival are better. They also
believe in reincarnation, that is, that dead infants return
to life in the form of another baby. They mark a dead infant with charcoal or ink and look for a birthmark in that
spot when a new child is born to see if it is the reincarnated child.

This marking of a child is not obligatory; but it is believed that if a reincarnated child is born and the parents
do not give it the right name, the baby will cry a lot until
it is given the name of the dead child. The dead child may
appear to them in a dream and tell them which name to give.

Death. If none of the healing remedies previously discussed are effective, the quietness of a Stieng village is
broken by the death wail. All of the relatives of the deceased run to the deceased person's sleeping platform.
They gather around the body, and as they wail, each person
simply calls out the term of relationship he had with the
deceased. If he was the father, then "father, father,
father" is called out. Wailing continues day and night
until burial. The people purposefully remain awake to keep
the dead one company. The men drink and kid each other a
bit in order to keep themselves awake, but often fall asleep
by morning. If a Stieng person dies in the province hospi-
tal and is laid in the morgue, the relatives do not always
stay with the body.

Able-bodied male relatives of the deceased prepare the
coffin. It is sometimes made of purchased lumber, but
typically the men choose a large tree and chop it down. A
log is squared off at the sides, split in half, and hollowed
out to fit the corpse. The work party divides itself, and
one group hollows out the top half while the other group
hollows out the bottom. If the family is too poor to afford
a sacrifice feast, the body may be wrapped in only a few
strips of bamboo or put into a broken wine jar which is
sealed for burial.

Each man who works on the coffin cooks his own food separately in the forest. He fears he will contract the disease of the dead person if food is prepared in the village and carried out to him. The family of the deceased person provides a little meat for each man in the working party if they have it.

The coffin is carried back to the village when ready. Stiengs do not wash the body, change the clothing, or make any other special preparations for burial. The body is not embalmed, but is simply put into the coffin and the coffin sealed. If the person's death is caused by an accident, then only the closest relatives are willing to handle the body.

A water buffalo or pig is sacrificed and roasted. Then when the coffin is sealed, a ceremony is performed (seen cdmôôch). Each person attending the funeral takes a bit of meat, a little rice, and a small piece of tobacco and places it on top of the coffin just before it is carried to the graveyard. Some of the men have dug a grave about three or four feet deep, and then the coffin is placed into the hole. The dead person's personal belongings--such as clothing, crossbow, shoulder axe, and water jug--are buried with him. His back basket is burned, and his wine jar broken. The grave is heaped with dirt as high as two or three feet above the ground.

A bamboo shelter is erected over the grave with a waterproof roof over it. Then other possessions of the deceased are placed at the grave. The items placed there are always very battered and worn. It is believed that things are opposite in the next life, so if the deceased has broken items at the grave, then in the next life, he will have good things. This also has a practical purpose in that people will not steal broken things from a grave.

As the burial party returns from the graveyard, all the members stop at a stream and bathe and wash their clothes (ôm bôôc) before entering the village. As soon as they arrive at the village, the closest relative of the deceased must light a fire. The sleeping platform of the deceased is burned, and the fire is closely watched to keep it burning --six days if a woman has died, and seven if a man.

Immediately after the burial, as an outward sign of
mourning, a widow cuts her hair off and smears ashes on her
face. A husband or child cuts a lock of hair from his forehead.

The name, or any word rhyming with the name, of a deceased person must not be mentioned in the hearing of the deceased person's relatives. If the name is Mê, for example,
rhymes of the name such as bê or tê would become bay or tay.
The dead person is always referred to as 'the deceased'
(cmôôch).

Two days after burial, the closest adult relative takes a
finger-sized tube of cooked rice and shrimp to the grave site
and places it on top of the grave. This is the final symbolic
act performed at the grave.

On the sixth or seventh day, a closed bamboo tube is put
on the fire. The relatives stand around the fire, and when
the tube explodes, a gourd of water is thrown into the fire.
The gourd breaks and the fire is extinguished. This signifies the end of burial rites.

NOTES

[1]The material for this paper is based on observations and interviews collected over a fourteen year period from 1960 to 1974. My husband Ralph and I, along with our three children, lived with Stieng people nine of those fourteen years. We lived five of the nine years in the village of Bukrêoai and then in the capital city of Sông Bé, both in Phước Long Province. Our purpose in living in close contact with the Stieng was to learn the Stieng language in order to develop a written language, prepare literacy materials, and translate the New Testament portion of the Bible. In order to accomplish these goals, we also spent time studying the culture of the Stieng people. Neither of us had any professional anthropological training, so there are gaps in our notes.

[2]Describing Stieng life in the 1860s among the Bu Dêh Stieng (Azemar 1886), reported little care taken to ward off pests, and little opportunity for cash income.

[3]Azemar (1886) found little polygamy, except among chiefs. Le Bar et al. (1964:157), quoting Gerber, report little polygamy because of the high bride price. We found wide differences in the marriage customs of the Bu Dêh and Bu Lơ.

[4]Azemar (1886) says divorce was not permitted except for sterility. In cases of adultery, the woman was presumed innocent.

REFERENCES

Azemar, (Pere) H. 1886. "Les Stiengs de Brolam." *Excursions et Reconnaissances,* pp. 147-60, 215-50.

De Barthelemy, P. 1904. *Au Pays Moi.* Paris, Plon.
---1899. "Au Pays des Mois." *Bulletin de la Société de Géographie de Paris,* 7th ser., 20:330-93.
---1901a. "Reconnaissance chez les Mois-Stiengs et aux Environs du Mont Djambre." *La Géographie* 3:489-98.
---1901b. "Un Voyage chez les Moi-Stiengs Vivant au Pied de la Chaine Djambra." *Revue Indochinois* 129:300-302 and 130:327-28.

Embree, John F. and Lillian Ota Dotson. 1950. *Bibliography of the Peoples and Cultures of Mainland Southeast Asia. (Southeast Asia Studies.)* New Haven: Yale University Press.

Gerber, T. 1951. "Coutumier Stieng." *Bulletin de l'Ecole Française d'Extrême Orient* 45:228-69.

Le Bar, Frank M., Gerald C. Hickey, and John K. Musgrave. 1964. *Ethnic Groups of Mainland Southeast Asia.* New Haven: HRAF Press. Esp. pp. 157-58.

Raulin, Henri P. 1946. "L'Evolution des Stieng de la Delegation de Hon-quan." *Bulletin de la Société des Etudes Indochinoises* 21:2.67-71.
---1947. "Les Technique de la Percussion et de la Production du Feu chez les Stieng." *Bulletin de la Société Etudes Indochinoises* 22:2.111-21.

SEDANG ASTRONOMY

Wanda Jennings

The enduring effects of war, recent contacts with American soldiers, former associations with French soldiers, the continuing influence of Catholic priests, the unsettling impact of resettlement, and the encroaching Vietnamese society, although strong catalysts in most aspects of Sedang[1] life, haven't changed comments on Sedang past as told from the stars. However, knowledge of man's space explorations and moon expeditions has begun to penetrate the context of their astronomy. Nevertheless, general content remains intact, and facts of former culture are free to mutate as fiction in the new.

In this paper I identify some of the heavenly bodies—mostly stars—that the Sedang have named, and I comment on how these names relate to culture, folklore, and language.[2]

STARS AND PLANETS

Sedang friends did not readily volunteer information regarding what they could see but once someone had mentioned a constellation, other comments were forthcoming. Older people were the more valuable informants.

General

Stars that are either circumpolar, short-lived, or in some other way not closely related to the planting and harvesting cycle by which the Sedang would otherwise identify them will be considered first.

Upstream Star (Hơlóng Kơnhóng). Plei Mnang, the village where this research was done, is approximately 13.5° latitude in old Phu Bon Province, Viet Nam. Circumpolar stars (those of greater than 76.5° latitude) are understandably not prominent in Sedang skies (Nicolson 1972:119). Consequently, the Sedang name only one such star, Polaris, the North Star. Their way of expressing the northerly direction is 'upstream' (konhóng), and this star is so designated. As a result of

177

its low position on the horizon, this star is often blocked
from view by trees.

Mirror Stars (Hơlóng Nhéng). While no one ever volunteered
a name for the Milky Way, when I asked what a possible name
might be, they said 'Mirror (glass) stars'.

A Star Defecates (Hơlóng Eak). Falling stars or meteors
are said to be ordinary stars defecating.[3] The feces are then
seen on the earth in the form of snails, called 'Star Feces'
(Eak Hơlóng). Such land snails are considered contaminated
by the Sedang.

Although tektites, thought to be extraterrestrial in origin,
can be found in parts of Viet Nam (including Kontum Province,
the home territory of the Sedang), no specific incidents have
been recorded from the Sedang telling of rocks or other large
matter having fallen from the heavens.

Spirit Ghost (Kia Xeáng). Comets which seem to be horizontal to the earth's surface are distinguished from 'star
feces' by several terms, 'Spirit Ghost' being but one. Another explanation is that of a ghost propelling himself
through the air like a spear (Kia Xông). But more interesting is the imagery of the ghost of a lizard (Kia Kơxôm)
wobbling and blinking its way toward the waterfalls. The
sight of this ghost is said to result in sickness.

Very Bright Star (Hơlóng Nheang). One of my colleagues
asked me to check with the Sedang to see if they knew that
Venus was both the morning and the evening star. For a long
time, no one spoke of an 'evening star' as such. I only got
names for Venus such as 'Dawn Star' (Hơlóng Ga) or 'Day-
break Star' (Hơlóng Lo). Then all of a sudden on hearing
these names, one Sedang friend recited this poem, revealing
that they do indeed know that Venus does double duty:

> Glowing Star,
> One leaving, one arriving,
> One arriving it comes out in the direction of
> the morning;
> One leaving it comes out in the direction of
> the evening.[4]

Stars Of The Rice Harvest Season
(Họ́lóng Rớnó́ Sua Báu)

Viet Nam has two seasons, wet and dry. The rainy season
comes at different times in different parts of the country.
The Sedang 'almanac' follows the planting cycle. Harvest
corresponds roughly to late fall and early winter in North
America.

Pig Basket, Chicken Coop (Tớdrong Chu, Tớdrong Í). The
people of Viet Nam make little domed baskets for transporting small animals such as baby pigs, chickens, and birds to
the market or to corral them at home. These are woven with
spaces to give lots of air. Varying in size from slightly
smaller to slightly larger than the circle one makes with
his arms (the Sedang always measure circumference in preference to length or height), they are easily transported and
nearly every home has at least one. The animal may be removed through a hole at the top or by a door at the side.

Figure 17.   Chicken and Pig Basket.

It is an understandable metaphor, therefore, that the open
cluster of stars we call Pleiades should be called 'pig
basket' by some villagers and 'chicken basket' by others.
Some, however, do not accept the ambiguity and want to call
Hyades the 'pig basket', arguing that it has five stars as
opposed to the six in Pleiades,which is obviously the
'chicken basket'. Actually, Pleiades is seven stars, but
only a few Sedang I questioned saw seven; most counted only
six.

Blacksmith's Forge (Tǒniam). Blacksmithing appears to have
been a part of Sedang technology for a long time. In the
past, local craftsmen produced a variety of items, such as
brass rings for arm and ankle, smoking pipes, jewelry and
mouth harps; but due to the availability of Vietnamese goods
today, their efforts are mainly concentrated on hammering
out garden tools for themselves and ornamental knives for
foreigners.

With smithery as a familiar Sedang occupation, it is not
too surprising that the forge should be the imagery used to
describe the stars forming the group known to Westerners as
Hyades. The forge is described as being between the Chicken
Basket and the Spear Strap (see below). The picture they
draw of the constellation, however, is as unlike the arrangement of stars as a picture of a bull is to Taurus, the corresponding Graeco-Roman constellation of which Hyades is a
part (Rey 1956:43).

This constellation was explained by one Sedang in the
following terms:

```
                b                      f
                                         f
        a            ccc        d    e    f
                                         f
                b                      f
```

a	person	e	rock on which metal is beaten
b	bellows		
c	pipe	f	people, one of whom is the blacksmith
d	fire		

Figure 18. Blacksmith Shop.

If the Sedang drawing does not seem to correspond with
what the reader sees in the sky, perhaps a description from
a western cultural orientation will help one locate the constellation Hyades and consequently the Sedang constellation
(Moore 1965:75):

> Aldebaran is of the first magnitude and is
> strongly orange-red... Several members of the
> cluster are visible, extending from Aldebaran
> in a sort of V shape; most of them are of
> between the third and fourth magnitude, while
> one, theta, is a double wide enough to be split
> by anyone with average eyesight.

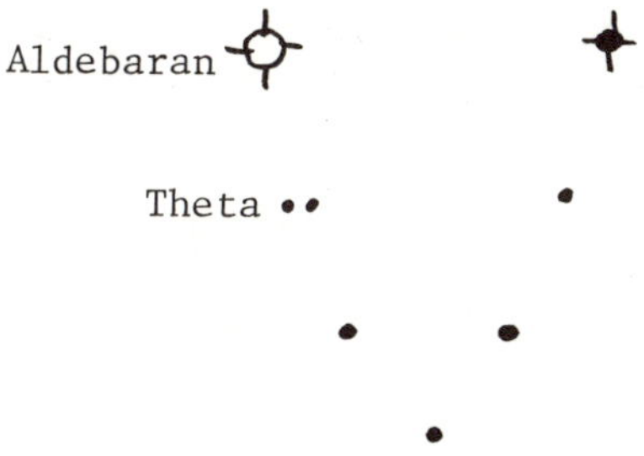

Figure 19.   The Forge.

By comparing Figures 19 and 20, we can visualize the two
tubes of the bellows, formerly made of bamboo but more recently of metal shell casings, being represented by the two
blinking stars (theta) in the 'V'. Aldebaran, the brightest
star, portrays the fire. The other top star in the 'V'
would be the smith. His helper and observers are the neighboring stars.

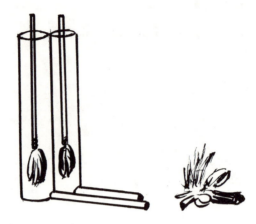

Figure 20.   Forge Bellows.

Spear Trap (Ta). This seems to be the constellation most
widely known to the whole range of Sedang villages and dialects.   It consists of the three stars which constitute
Orion's belt in Western mythology. This stellar arrangement is to the Sedang reminiscent of the foundation poles of
the bamboo trap used to spear wild pigs, deer, etc. By
comparison, the three stars of Orion's belt become the poles
supporting the spear in Sedang imagery.

Figure 21.   Sedang Spear Trap.

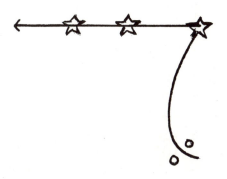

Figure 22.   Spear Trap Constellation.

In recent years because of the war, hunting grounds have
been dangerous territory. As villagers were resettled in
strange areas, game locations were unfamiliar; forested areas
were at great distance and unsafe. Consequently, to set a
trap and return to check it came to involve twice as much
work as formerly. The rifle, therefore, at least during the
war, was replacing the spear trap and crossbow for Sedang
hunters.

Almost all men and older boys still know how to make spear
traps. Nonetheless, the rifle is used more and more, and if
game becomes more scarce in overpopulated resettlement areas,
this trap may well be forgotten except for its position in
the night sky.

Barking Deer (Chiu).   Orion had dogs, but for the Sedang
it is the Spear Trap that gets a deer. There it is, the
star Betelgeuse or Rigel (Nicolson 1972:129), walking toward
its ill fate.

Children, especially girls, are usually vague about what
a Barking Deer is. They are found in the area, but the
Jorai, who traditionally inhabited the area, still control
the hunting grounds. In any case, at least a few people
still see a chiu up in the heavens.

Shield (Khia).   Information on the Shield is rather ob-
scure.   Perhaps it is only proper that it should be so, since
real shields are also lost from the modern culture.   In times
past the Montagnards had intertribal battles using crossbows and spears.   Wooden shields covered with goat hair were
their standard protection.   But today, a search for one in an
area with 7,000 Sedang only yielded the comment, "I hear
there is a man who used to have one, but I don't know his
village."

Definite indications of the constellation place it in the
very low southernmost sky at the same time of the year that
Ta is visible.   It may possibly be identified with the
Southern Cross.

The drawings in Figure 7 were made by Sedang friends to
describe the shield and the constellation with the comment
that there might be more stars in the lower curve.

Figure 23.   Shield.

Planting Season Stars
(Hơlóng Rơnó Chói)

The five Sedang star pictures appearing in the dry season
can be matched with only two Western terms. These five stars
tend to be connected with myths which we might call ghost
stories (tối kia; literally, 'tell about deceased spirits').

Granny Pia's Sacrifice Pole (Loáng Kang Ja Pía). Pia or
Apia is the heroine or princess of Sedang folk tales. Sometimes she is an animal or part of an animal (as Apia Elephant
Tusk) which becomes human. On the other hand, she sometimes
changes an animal into her Prince Charming, usually by roast-
ing it in a bamboo tube (as in a story called Apia Squirrel).
Apia is also simply a designation for all the young girls,
most likely sisters, in a given story, where some descriptive
term will be added as a means of distinction, such as Apia
Messy Hair, Apia Bright Flower, etc.

The Decorative Post (Loáng Kang) is the post to which the
water buffalo about to be sacrificed is tied during the
ritual killing of the animal.

A Hơdang-Rengao[5] neighbor of mine once said that they call
the same constellation 'The Sacrifice Pole of Der' (Lông Gang
Dêr).[6] The story goes further that when Der built his pole,
he was transformed into a handsome fellow with golden hair.
As he began to beat the bass drum, water started to rise and
flood the earth. When the water receded, Der and his pole
were ghosts in sky. Instead of a hook (see below) to stand
up the pole, Dak Ri villagers see a rope to tie the buffalo.

A young Sedang boy illustrated the Sacrifice Pole as in
Figure 24.

Figure 24.   Sacrifice Pole.

Apia's Pole is made up of stars corresponding to Scorpius, an easily distinguished constellation (Ebbighaussen 1966: 177).   Compare Figure 25 with Figure 24.

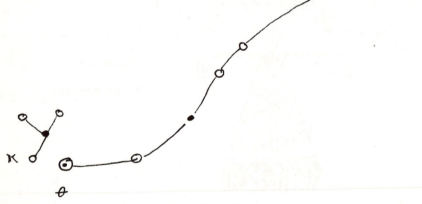

Figure 25.   Scorpius.

During the period that this research was being conducted,
the village of Tea Hodro held a preharvest celebration at
which they tried to recreate some of the former customs,
omitting elements of their traditional animistic religion.
They sang during the night, telling the young people they
wanted to teach them some of their culture that had been lost
as a result of recurrent flight during the war. The decorative post which they made was a simplification of former ones.
Made only of bamboo, it still sported color, relief carving,
weaving, and beautifully done fringes. In this case, since
this was a Christian village, instead of calling to the
spirits as in olden times, they sang in thanks to Father
Spirit (the Christian God).

Among Catholics, who constitute the majority of those in
more populated areas, sacrifices to placate spirits are no
longer openly practiced. Also non-Catholics have been left
without animals to sacrifice due to the war. As a result,
the sacrifice pole has lost its original purpose. Simplified
versions are used to decorate the roadway and village mall to
welcome visiting dignitaries or for festive occasions.

Bird (Chem). The bird on the sacrifice pole is not left
out (see Figure 24). The star Antares is so identified.
Swinging free from the pole is the Snake Buzzard (Kơkléang
Pah). On the real pole it is made of woven bamboo with
lovely designs. A Sedang drew it as in Figure 26.

Figure 26.

Snake Buzzard.

The Hook (Kolei). Continuing with Sedang concepts of
Scorpius, four stars of his tail are known to those from
Dak To as The Hook. Hooks were made from forked bamboo sap-
lings (pɗlái) and were used to get fruit from the tops of
trees or to lift sacrifice poles into place. That is why
the hook appears at the base of the pole.

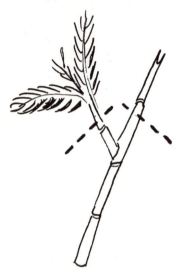

Figure 27.   Bamboo Hook.

A *Shoulder Pole for Two to Carry Grandmother's Corpse*
(Tɗnong Tong Ja, Tɗnong Tong Kia). Tɗnong is a word meaning
a 'shoulder pole used between two people for carrying', derived from tong 'two people carry on shoulders' and the
nominalizing infix -ɗn-. To westerners this is the big dipper of Ursa Major. To the Sedang, folklore Princess Apia's
corpse is being borne to its burial. There it appears in
the northern sky at her spirit pole.

Shoulder poles are still in common usage to carry water
or heavy bags of rice. Every day, in season, men may be
seen carrying tree sap (chá) to the market for pitching boats.

The Fly (Rɔ́i). The second star down the dipper's handle,
Mizar, has a faint star, Alcor, that appears to be touching

it. Because it is in the Grandmother's Corpse group, a few
Sedang say it is flies swarming on grandmother's corpse (rối
chum kia ja). Others say it is flies swarming on a deer
speared by the trap (rối chum chiu tro ta). This fly motif
may be related to a custom of previous decades. During
sacrifices the Sedang would take the liver of the water
buffalo, place it on a leaf, then spear it with a long bamboo
pole. This was placed upright in the air. If a fly lit on
it, it was believed that 'Thunder Spirit' (Xeáng Tơro), the
greatest of the spirits, was landing there and accepting
their sacrifice.

THE MOON

The moon (khế) plays an integral part in Sedang culture
because its cycles define the times for planting.

Full Moon, Brightest Moon (Khế Vó, Khế Mơnia). Sedang
say that if on the night of a full moon one puts water in a
basin and catches the moon's reflection, one can see a banyan
tree (loáng trai) and Apia husking rice by pounding it in a
hollow log mortar in Sedang fashion with a long pole pestle.
The moon is believed to have been hotter than the sun in
former times and no one could sleep while it was in the night
sky. But now the banyan tree gives shade from the worst of
the heat.

Two young Catholic ladies discussing this commented that
once the old people thought it was Apia, but now they know
it was really Maria (Mary). Such syncretism of traditional
beliefs with Christian ones constitutes an important but un-
studied area of Sedang culture.

The new moon was a time for celebrating death anniver-
saries and playing gongs. Often our Jorai neighbors would
play gongs throughout the phase of the new moon. Sedang
comments indicated that if they had still had their gongs,
they would have used them on this occasion.

Other moon phases of significance are:

suspended moon (khế topeáng)   new moon
big moon (khế kan)   quarter moon waxing

middle moon (khế dế)   half moon
frog belly moon (khế pơtok ket)   quarter moon waning

Use of the phrase 'frog belly moon' may relate to the
metaphorical designation of the ball of the finger as a 'tad-
pole stomach' (klea plon).

Kau *Fish Eats the Moon* (Kau Ka Khế). When the darkness
of the eclipse comes, the Sedang say they fear 'Grandfather's
Ghost' (Kia Ki Poa) who is very powerful and greatly feared.
His medicine or sorcery is administered in the black of
night. If such a ghost enters a person, that person's head
is likely to be separated from his body. He eats the livers
of his victims, causing eventual death. One hamlet of
Kayong people resettled in Plei Mnang are accused of having
a sorcerer who is possessed by Grandfather's Ghost. She is
quite normal in the daytime; but at night, they say her head
has been seen floating about. The Christian Sedang do not
admit to sorcerers in their own villages.

The kau fish, abundant in traditional Sedang territory
but not available at the resettlement site of Plei Mnang, is
said to be a small catfish-like species and has been identified as the 'serpent head fish' (ophiocephale) by Smith (n.d.).

SUN (hài)

As the term for moon is used with numbers to designate
months, so the word for sun is numbered to designate days,
as in 'day one' (hài môi), i.e., Monday. The time of day is
described in terms of the position of the sun:

coming out sun	(hài lo)	sunrise
hot sun	(hài tô)	midmorning/afternoon
middle sun	(hài dế)	high noon
falling sun	(hài klêh)	late afternoon
flooded sun	(hài luô)	sunset

Hours and minutes are being used more frequently as the
younger generation obtains watches.

Centipede Eats the Sun (Kơpế Ka Hài). This denotes a
solar eclipse and is heard as the second part of a medial

rhyme phrase (Smith, to appear) referring to the lunar
eclipse as well (see above).

Fish eats the moon;	(Kau ka khế);
Centipede eats the sun.	(Kờpế ka hài).

The Sedang feared an eclipse of the sun, believing it
brought some major disaster or final doom (tap mang ling).
They feared they would no longer be able to make a fire and
they would all die in the dark and the cold, not being able
to make rice fields.

During an eclipse the sun was thought to be being eaten
by a centipede from whom it had borrowed a water buffalo.
When the centipede asked the sun to return the buffalo, an
argument ensued. So when a solar eclipse occurred, the villagers all joined in to help the sun in its battle. They
pounded their mortars, beat their gongs and drums, shot guns,
and yelled. Note the similarity of this practice with ancient
Chinese culture:

> When an eclipse occurred the Chinese thought that
> the sun was being swallowed by a huge dragon.
> The whole population joined in making as much
> noise as possible to scare it away. They always
> succeeded! (Nicolson 1972:7)

Women's Days, Men's Days (Hài Kờdrai, Hài Kờnõu). When
the days are long and it stays light later, the men stay out
setting and checking their traps, busy caring for the needs
of their families. For this reason, the Sedang say that the
sun 'is not able to become evening quickly'. It must wait
for the men to finish their work. These days are known as
'men's days'. By the same token, the shortest days in the
year are called 'women's days'. This is based on the tend-
ency of the women to return home early from their tasks of
scooping fish or hunting bamboo sprouts in order to nurse
the baby, who otherwise would cry, and to cook the evening
rice for the husband, who otherwise might complain.

NOTES

[1]The Sedang, as the Vietnamese call them (and as they have
been called in the literature with the exception of Devereax,
who called them 'Ha(rh)ndea(ng)' or 'Ha(rhn)de:A(ng)', call
themselves Rơteáng. The Sedang traditional homeland is the
Central Highlands of South Viet Nam, north of Kontum. They
have an estimated population of 40,000. Their language is
North Bahnaric within the Mon-Khmer language family. For
additional information consult materials listed in SIL, Viet
Nam bibliography.

[2]The ethnographic present is 1974.

[3]A similar belief has been noted among the Dusun (Williams
1965:10).

[4]Hơlóng Nheang,
Môi Pra, môi Preáng,
Môi Preáng gá lo peáng ga;
Môi Pra gá lo peáng kơsei.

[5]Hơdang-Rengao is closely related to Sedang.

[6]Der in Chrau, a South Bahnaric language, means 'dragon'.
He drinks up rivers and lakes and is probably related to
this man who caused a flood.

REFERENCES

Ebbighausen, E.G. 1966. *Astronomy*. Columbus, Ohio: Charles
  E. Merrill Books, Inc.

Izikowitz. 1951. *Lamet: Hill Peasants in Indochina*.
  Goteberg: Ethnografiska.

Moore, Patrick. 1965. *Naked Eye Astronomy*. New York:
  Norton and Company.

Nicolson, Ian. 1972. *Astronomy*. Toronto: Bantam Books.

Rey, H.A. 1956. *The Stars: A New Way to See Them*. 1956.
  Boston: Houghton and Mifflin.

Smith, Kenneth D. n.d. *Sedang Dictionary*. Dallas, Texas:
  Summer Institute of Linguistics. Microfiche.

---To appear. *Sedang Poetics*.

Williams, Thomas Rhys. 1965. *The Dusun: A North Borneo
  Society*. New York: Holt, Rinehart, and Winston.

NUNG WEDDINGS

Janice E. Saul

The Nung are a Tai speaking minority group whose original homeland was in South China, (Schrock, et al. 1972:367).[1] Many now live in the Lang Son and Bac Giang areas of North Vietnam. In 1954, several thousand of them went south as refugees and were resettled in Tuyen Duc, Long Khanh, and Bien Hoa provinces. Over 2,000 of the Nung Fan Slihng group were resettled near Tung Nghia in the Quan Duc district, Tuyen Duc province.

The Nung are patrilineal and practice patrilocal residence. A bride leaves her home to live with her husband's family. It is very rare for a newly married couple to have their own separate home. Nung men sometimes marry Vietnamese or Chinese wives, but Nung women rarely, if ever, marry outside Nung circles. Nung men, especially wealthy ones, may have more than one wife. These co-wives live in the same house. Divorce consists simply of the separation of a husband and wife, and is usually initiated by the husband.

Preliminaries to a Wedding. A Nung suitor, having decided whom he wants for his wife, has an intermediary go to her parents and ask for her consent. The girl or her parents may, of course, reject the proposal; but if they are willing, the two families agree on the bride price. The groom pays the bride price and provides food (e.g., ducks and pigs) for the wedding feasts.

Next, a Taoist priest examines the birth dates of the boy and girl and comparing them with the signs of the Zodiac to see if they are compatible for marriage. If they are, the priest then determines, by the stars, a propitious day for the wedding. After the date is fixed, if the groom cannot be present (e.g., because of army duty), the bride may be married by proxy.

The girl's parents accept the bride price and give some to the girl to buy clothing. The bride sews her own bridal clothes, usually about ten outfits. Her parents also give

195

her a ring, a cooking pot, two basins, a trunk, mosquito net, blanket, lamp, a tray with four glass cups, ten rice bowls, a teapot and cozy, a teakettle, several pairs of sandals, and kerosene for the lamp.

When the wedding date is set, the prospective bride and groom ask friends and neighbors to assist. They also make invitations for friends and relatives to attend the feast (kĭhn làu).

The First Day. The wedding takes three days. On the evening of the first day, the groom (khởi) goes to the home of the bride (mê lu) to present the parents with meat, betelnut, and glutinous rice. Close friends of the bride join her at a supper provided by an uncle or older brother.

The Second Day. Next morning, the groom goes to the bride's house accompanied by his best man, the intermediary, a person to welcome the bride, and a girl to carry a sacrificed chicken. At ten o'clock, another feast is held at the bride's house with relatives and friends. The bride and her friends sit on her bed to eat and drink wine, after which the groom distributes betelnut and cigarettes to the family and relatives of the bride. Then he and the best man go home, leaving the intermediary and the greeter to accompany the bride.

It is then time for the bride to prepare to leave her home. This is a sad occasion, and the bride often cries for over an hour, for her leaving involves not only leaving her own family but also being removed from the guardian care of her ancestors' spirits. For the procession to the groom's house, she dresses in black satin trousers, a black blouse open at the side with mandarin collar and long wide sleeves, a long wide black sash tied in the back, socks, sandals, and a black scarf tied under the chin. (In recent years the Nung in the Nam Son hamlet have changed to having brides and bridesmaids wear Vietnamese-style long dresses with trousers for the wedding.) The bride wears earrings presented by the groom. She sticks a needle with red thread into her sash, symbolizing her willingness to provide for her husband. It is customary that she wear her hair long, twisting it and wrapping it inside a black velvet cloth, then placing it in a circlet on top of the head in typical northern Vietnamese style. The bridesmaids also wear black blouses and trousers,

but their scarves are tied behind their heads in the fashion of
the typical Nung woman's headdress.

At three o'clock in the afternoon, the bride is led to
the groom's house by one of the men of the village. She is
accompanied by two bridesmaids, a girl or two to carry a
sleeping mat, suitcase, mosquito net, and blanket. The intermediary and greeter from the groom's side also go with
her. A priest follows the bride to bind all the spirits
during the wedding procession to prevent an attack on anyone
either in the procession or a bystander. Preceding the
bride is a girl carrying a chicken which was sent by the
groom and blessed by the priest. The bride and bridesmaids
carry large black umbrellas, the bride's umbrella having a
red bow if she is wearing the needle with red thread. The
bride lowers her umbrella so that her face is not seen. The
procession is very slow because there are frequent stops
along the way while a bridesmaid distributes betelnut chew
to women bystanders and cigarettes to men. Two girls walk
with the bride, supporting her arms.

Upon arrival at the groom's house, they must wait outside
until someone invites them in. As the bride enters the doorway, firecrackers explode and there is much merrymaking.

The house is gaily decorated with streamers, evergreens,
and small flags. On the door posts are red papers with
blessings written in Chinese characters by a priest. In the
main room there are two or three large new mirrors decorated
with painted flowers.

A bridal chamber has been prepared with colorful curtains
providing privacy. That evening the bride eats supper on
her newly built bed with her maids, and the curtains remain
closed. She sleeps with her maids that night. The groom
eats supper with close friends.

That evening the male helpers kill pigs for a sacrifice
and roast them for a feast. They also kill ducks and steam
them in large vats. At one feast ten pigs and thirty ducks
were prepared. Rice rolls with meat, vegetable dishes,
steamed white rice and red glutinous rice are also prepared.

The Third Day. On the third morning, guests arrive about
ten o'clock for another feast (slàn làu). The groom eats in

the main room at a table with his friends. A priest and
several selected men sit on a bed by the ancestral altar. A
pig has been sacrificed and its head placed on the altar, for
the bride must be accepted by the groom's ancestor spirits.
The bride again eats with her friends on her bed in the bridal chamber, secluded by curtains.

The male helpers prepare the food and set the tables.
Usually 200 to 300 guests are invited, and these eat in the
house or outside where temporary shelter has been constructed
to cover the courtyard. There may be thirty tables of guests,
and some may eat in neighbors' houses. When guests are
seated, one or two members of the groom's family (usually the
father or an uncle) go to each table to invite the guests to
eat. After one group of people has eaten, the tables are
cleared and reset with food for the next group.

When everyone has eaten, the bride is led by her mother-
in-law and accompanied by one of the bridesmaids to each
table. She carries a tray with bowls filled with gifts of
betelnut and cigarettes, covered with folded hand towels.
The men are served first. Each guest accepts a bowl and
wraps a gift in a towel, then places in the bowl a conventional sum of money for the newlyweds. The guests all register (khau pu) and pay a customary price for the meal.

Afterwards, the men usually amuse themselves with some
gambling. In the North, the bride would also sing to the
groom's parents, and they in turn would sing to her. In the
South, however, the young people no longer know these songs.

When the guests have left, the helpers eat, clear tables,
and then return everything that was borrowed. Women helpers
wash the dishes and return them. In the evening, the helpers come back again to eat supper with the family. Later,
the temporary shelter over the courtyard is also dismantled.

On the following day, the bride and groom customarily pay
a visit to the bride's parents' home (thọi hoi).[2]

Nung weddings involve no further formalities other than
having the event registered at the government office.

NOTES

1. Janice Saul worked in South Vietnam with the Summer Institute of Linguistics from 1962 to 1975. This information was obtained from 1963 to 1966 by personal observation and interviews while living in the Nung village of Nam Son near Tung Nghia, Tuyen Duc province, South Vietnam.

2. In the North the bride lives at her own house until she becomes pregnant (LeBar, et al., 1964:237).

REFERENCES

Schrock, Joann, et al. 1972. *Ethnographic Study Series: Minority Groups of North Vietnam*. DA PAM 550-110. Washington: U.S. Government Printing Office.

LeBar, Frank, Gerald C. Hickey, and John K. Musgrave. *Ethnic Groups of Mainland Southeast Asia*. 1964. New Haven: Human Relations Area Files Press.

NUNG PRIESTS AND SPIRITS

Janice Saul
Kenneth Gregerson

Nung[1] religion revolves around ancestor worship and animism with influences from Buddhism, Confucianism and Taoism (Schrock, et al. 1972:388-90). The reader acquainted with Chinese or Vietnamese religious life will note familiar features, though we will make no attempt to identify them individually in this paper.

Ceremonies for the family worship of ancestral spirits are presided over by the head of the household, usually the father. The altar to the ancestors typically stands in the main room opposite the doorway and consists of two shelves for the ancestors and one for the spirit of the hearth. At the altar, the family presents sacrifices, other offerings and invocations to the spirits of deceased ancestors of within three or four generations, to induce them to protect the house and its inhabitants. Each lunar new year the ancestral spirits are invited back and feasted. New red papers with blessings in Chinese characters are then tacked to the doorway of each home. There are also special feasts for the ancestors at the first and fifteenth days of the lunar months. Should such rituals be neglected, the Nung believe that the ancestors will bring sickness or tragedy upon them.

The Nung are animists. They believe spirits (phi) live in mountains, rocks, trees, water and fields. Priests must have power to control all of these spirits and to protect people from them. There is a single, small building with an altar to the spirit which protects the village. This stands immediately outside the village and is the only religious edifice found in the Nung village.

THE SUPERNATURAL IN EVERYDAY LIFE

Unlike people of Western cultures, the Nung consider it completely normal to recognize their spiritual world and their material world as interlocking realities. The daily round of life routinely takes spirits into account. As

examples of the functional impact of this view on other areas
of culture, consider the following brief accounts of some
aspects of health care and house building in the village of
Nam Son.

The Nung consider sickness to be the result of retaliation
by an offended spirit. Priests or mediums may be summoned to
conduct seances to determine just which spirit was offended
and precisely what sacrifices will suffice as an appeasement.

Pregnancy is viewed from spiritual perspective also. Ex-
pectant mothers must observe specific taboos on certain foods
and habits. At the birth of the baby, there is a heightened
sense of apprehension over the possibility that malevolent
spirits may be present. Consequently, it is unusual for anyone to help the mother during the actual delivery, though her
mother is permitted to do so, if available. Although the
delivery normally occurs at home, the child cannot be born
within, nor even carried into, a newly built house for a
month according to restrictions set out by the spirits.

Like the people of many other non-Western cultures, the
Nung have learned to accomodate Western medicine to their own
advantage. Before I (JS) arrived in Nam Son, a Nung man had
been trained by the government to be a village medical officer. When I, as a nurse, entered the village, I worked with
him in the clinic. I also enabled him to get three months'
training in medical work with an American doctor. There
were about thirty Nung priests in the village who routinely
conducted seances to determine cause of illness, although I
never heard of them using magic or supernatural power to heal
the sick. Some were said to be able to pronounce a curse or
cause a girl to love a fellow. I never experienced any open
opposition from the priests. In fact, I would often enter a
home where a priest would be calling on the spirits in a
ceremony for the sick. He would interrupt his chanting to
welcome me, tell me to give the injection, and then resume
chanting. One priest said that he and I made a good team
with his appeasing the spirits and my dispensing the medicine.
Gradually, the priests also began to come for medicine. They
told me that they observed that we got better when we took
medicine even though we did not fear the spirits. As people
got relief and many recovered through medicine, the medical
work greatly increased. Women even began to trust me to help
deliver their babies.

Another everyday instance in which the Nung are obliged to
offer sacrifices to the spirits occurs when they disturb the
ground to build a new house. The process begins as the walls
of the house are nailed together lying on the ground. The
priest then enters the picture to decide what hour of the
night the house should be raised. Usually it is 1 or 2 a.m.
when one hears the shouts of the people as the walls are
raised. A pig is then sacrificed outside. As the beams are
erected and the roof is being laid, a Nung priest takes
smoking incense around to each beam and offers a prayer to
the spirit. A large red banner is hung on the long middle
horizontal beam of the house. This is inscribed with Chinese characters invoking blessings for the new house. The
front door posts and mantel are also decked with red papers
bearing appropriate Chinese words. (Similar inscriptions are
used at their New Year's celebrations.)

In the center of the main room of the new house, an altar
with three shelves is erected, each shelf for a different
spirit. Alternatively, only a table is set up as an altar.
All altars have a large red paper as a backdrop and many have
other fancy articles arranged on them.

Each house has a platform altar in front or in back.
There the father or head of the house (mother, if the father
is deceased) sits priest-like to offer prayers and sacrifices
and burn incense placed in bowls of rice to the family spirits.
The official Nung priest is called, however, when someone is
sick or dies. The recompense for such services is usually
quite costly, involving the slaughter of pigs, chickens,
ducks, or whatever the priest advises.

RELIGIOUS PRACTICIONERS

Nung religious practicioners include priests, mediums
(priestesses) and, to a lesser extent, sorcerers.

Priests are referred to as 'bright eyes' (sláy thả hụhng)
because of their knowledge of things spiritual; they are thus
distinguished from the 'dark eyes' (thả dáhm), the common
people. Priests are chosen for their office by the chief
priest and other priests under the guidance of the spirits.
In order to be a priest, a man is trained by a chief priest
for approximately five years. He learns the prayers and

chants and is taught to read the books of incantations and ceremonies written in Chinese script. At the end of this training period, the student priest observes a four-month period of abstinence. During this time, he can only perform sacrifices to the spirits; no other work is permitted. Other restrictions are as follows: 1) He cannot enter a house where a woman is confined after giving birth. 2) He cannot use the same area of the village to relieve himself as other villagers. 3) He must have someone else prepare his food, for he is not allowed to enter the kitchen. 4) He may not walk under a clothes pole. 5) No one can sit on his bed other than himself. 6) He may not speak to a woman, nor may he have sexual relations with his wife. At the completion of this period, the priests and relatives are invited to the feast and ceremony of ordination (cải tạo). After the feast, the chief priest cuts a cord attached to a replica of a woman's womb, symbolizing thereby the new priest's 'second birth' into the spirit world.

When conducting ceremonies, priests wear a unique garment, which may either be an embroidered robe or a solid blue robe. He also wears an embroidered, mitre-shaped hat. When communicating with the spirits, the priest sits on a mat spread before the ancestral spirit altar in the house, making incantations and finally falling into a trance. On one occasion I (JS) saw a priest, seated on a wooden bench, twirl around several times after lighting several papers, and fall onto the bench, moving his legs rapidly as though astride a galloping horse. He was, they explained, riding a spirit mount to the sky to contact another spirit there.

Women mediums or priestesses are known as dạ thển. A woman who feels called to be a priestess makes frequent trips to a body of water where she bathes to be cleansed. There the spirits enable her to find some token which will give her power as a medium. This she brings home to be placed on her altar. She then goes through a period of fasting. On the first and fifteenth day of the lunar month she may eat no fat. She also invites three priests and two priestesses for a ceremony of rebirth like that of a priest. After that ceremony, she too observes a period of abstinence for four months like that of a priest. She is forbidden to go anywhere and may not have relations with her husband. If she does, the spirits may punish her with death. She may say nothing bad.

If she disobeys, she must sacrifice a rooster to ask forgiveness of the spirits. If she continues to do wrong, the spirits may cause her to beat herself, even to the point of death. The priestess has power to appease evil spirits to bring healing for the sick. On a typical visit to a patient she is accompanied by someone with a guitar and a chain of bells wrapped in a cloth. She plays the guitar and sings and chants while shaking the bells. Then she falls into a trance in order to communicate with the spirits in an effort to effect a cure.

While magic and sorcery are less prominent, some priests also have power to make love potions and evil potions. They can also pronounce curses on people. In fact, if a sorcerer fails to exercise his skills for as long as a month, the spirits, it is reported, will punish him.

SPIRITS

The Nung live in a world of spirits, and these spirit beings have unique identities as sketched briefly for some of them below.

The Three Spirits of the Sky (Slam Ke Nheu Vang). Nung informants say these spirits have the most power. They can forgive sin and help people. Every one is obliged to worship these spirits, offering chickens or ducks. When an individual enters the priesthood, these three spirits are invited to testify that this person is able to be a spiritual ruler or priest.

Ancestor Spirits (Cohng Cho). The Nung worship their departed ancestors for from three to four generations. As soon as an old person dies, he is ceremonially venerated at the altar. At the lunar new year, the spirits of the ancestors are invited back to a feast. Ducks and chickens are sacrificed for them. If this is not done, it is feared that the ancestral spirits will attack the children of the household, causing illness. Then the head of the household can offer this sacrifice. But if a sin has been committed, the priest is called to sacrifice and offer ducks, chickens or pigs to beg the pardon of the spirit. In addition, the person who is guilty of the infraction must confess it before the priest.

Only then can the sick person be healed. Sometimes the offended spirit may take the sick person's spirit to punish him. In
this case, the priest offers a sacrifice and calls the spirit
of the sick one to return. If the spirit permits the sick
one's spirit to return, that person is assured of recovery.
Sometimes the priest also calls on the three spirits of the
sky to help.

The Spirit of the Old Man (Cohng Ke). The spirit that is
worshipped on the table in the courtyard is called the spirit
of the old man. It is especially in times of danger that the
Nung call on this spirit for help. Those who call on this
being, whether he helps or not, must perform a sacrifice.
Some households offer a chicken, or sometimes a duck and
chicken. If one fails to sacrifice, the spirit is sure to
wreak vengeance on the children of the house. If this spirit
becomes very angry, the sacrifice of a pig is required; non-
compliance in this case may result in death. Many times when
a sacrifice is offered, the spirit rejects it. Another animal
is then sacrificed; each time it must be a pig. The following
notes are true only for the particular spirit mentioned, but in
general it is believed that if a person gets sick and dies, the
family must learn which spirit was responsible and make an appropriate sacrifice. Otherwise, the spirit of the departed must
follow the malevolent spirit and be punished forever. The only
remedy is to call a priest to redeem the dead person's spirit,
and thus deliver him.

The Spirit of the Kitchen (Phi Hehn Fay). This is a rather
potent spirit which, if offended, may only be placated by the
sacrifice of an abundance of chickens.

The Spirit at Birth (Me Va/Me Slihng). Every Nung recog-
nizes a spirit at the birth of a child that has given the
child life and will guard him and rule his life. The parents
are careful to perform acts of worship toward this spirit at
birth. Later, however, when a person marries, this spirit no
longer rules him.

The Spirit of the House or Hearth (Phi Hon). The spirit
of the hearth is worshipped by placing tokens on the top
shelf of the altar. Every lunar new year this spirit is
venerated. Some spirits of the hearth will accept no meat
with fat and if offered, the spirit will cause the person to

vomit. Other spirits will accept any meat. Some households
must buy a goat to sacrifice. But if the spirit comes and
demands a sacrifice, the family must offer it according to
the idiosyncracies of that spirit. The Nung forbid eating
beef and buffalo. If anyone eats such, the spirit of the
house says it has been defiled and causes the partaker to experience chills or vomiting. If the violater is sick a long
time and becomes weaker with more frequent chills, the Nung
say his spirit has fled. The sick one's spirit has followed
the offended spirit, thus rendering the person weak.

Parenthetically, regarding the departure of one's spirit,
the Nung say that if a child sees something startling and upon returning home becomes sick for a long time, the reason is
that his spirit has fled. The parents must then take some
rice with fish and meat and go call the child's spirit. If
that doesn't work, a priest must take a duck and chicken and
call the spirit. Similarly, when an elderly person gets sick,
they say his spirit has gone down below and again a priest
must call him back. If the spirit flees in this way, the
spirit is said to have gone four places (all over). If it
has gone into the water, the priest calls into the water to
bring him back up. If a spirit enters a grave, the priest
must call into the grave. If that grave is far from the village, the priest takes unhusked rice and pours it into a basket, making a mound to represent the grave. The priest can
then insert a knife into the mound to release the spirit of
the sick person from the distant grave.

Returning now to the roster of spirits, the spirit known
as phi phahn is described as one that can attack and possess
an individual. In case of such possession many trays of food
must be offered; some spirits demand three trays and some
five. Many ducks and chickens must be killed, and the whole
animal is offered, including feathers and intestines.

Finally, another spirit, phi an fu is said to be resident
in every Nung house. Failure to do homage to this spirit
may also result in an attack on one of the members of the
family.

It is apparent from what has been said above that staying
on good terms with the spirit world involves knowing the proper spirit 'prescriptions'. Those who know among the Nung

give the following summary of sacrifices for the various
spirits:

The spirit of the old man: a chicken

A spirit offended by a wrong sacrifice: a pig

The spirit of the kitchen: a chicken or duck

The ancestral spirits: a chicken or duck

The departed spirit of a sick person: a duck

A sick person's spirit in a grave: a chicken

A guardian spirit: a chicken

For spirit possession: a chicken or duck

The spirit of the house: a goose or a cow

A spirit causing injury: meat, eggs or fish

A spirit who attacks a woman confined after childbirth: a chicken

A spirit who curses a place of sleep: rice, snails
or fish

THE AFTERLIFE

When a priest or priestess ('bright eyes') dies, he or she
is believed to go to the sky to work with the three spirits
of the sky. That is, one of the priest's spirits will go to
the sky, while another will dwell in the houses that the family made, and the third spirit will enter the corpse.

When a common person ('dark eyes') dies, his spirit goes
to work the fields in the place of the dead. When a child
dies, his family requests a priest or priestess to make a pen
and paper for the child's spirit. The child's spirit is thus
led by the priest to a place to study. If unmarried teen-agers
die, the priest leads them to an uninhabited place. Every day
they are free to play, but when they return in the evening

they have no place to sleep, for there are no houses. If an
orphan dies, the priest or priestess must redeem his spirit,
or he will suffer forever. The child or unmarried person who
dies is not venerated. If a married adult dies and has daughters but no sons, then nobody will venerate him, unless there
are grandsons, for a daughter cannot venerate her parents.
If a person dies without anyone to venerate his spirit, bowls
of incense are placed in the grave to signify a desire to be
rid of a spirit which could potentially bring trouble.

Normally, when a family member dies, the family lights incense so the spirit can find his way and other spirits will
come to greet the new spirit. Followers of the 'King of the
Sky' (Christians) do not burn incense, so the Nung say that
they will be unable to see their way clearly; neither will
they have a house or any provision for their spirits.

A PRIEST'S FUNERAL

I (JS) have reported elsewhere (Saul, 1972) on some aspects
of Nung funeral customs in general. Here I restrict myself
to an account of the more specialized rites surrounding the
death of priests.

When a priest dies, his children place cooked rice in his
mouth to provide food for his journey. They bring water with
citronella and wash his body and cut his hair. Then they
dress him in his priestly robe and place him in a chair. The
other priests are invited to come and bid him farewell. They
write Chinese characters on papers and banners. Then they
kill a chicken and smear its blood over the paper, which is
placed around the coffin. The body is placed on a mat on the
bed, where the priest in charge of the ceremony takes water
and washes the dead man's face. White cloth is used to wrap
the body, though in addition the wives and daughters-in-law
usually supply some red cloth for part of the wrapping.

Then the priest, using a sword, scoops up ashes and throws
them into the coffin. Each priest also drops a joss stick
into the coffin. Then the officiating priest takes ashes and
charcoal and places them in the coffin. While he does so, he
recites a sentence, and the eldest son repeats after him.
Following that the corpse is placed into the coffin and a
chicken is killed and offered at the head of the coffin to

signify the feeding of the spirit of the deceased. The children of the priest also pour out wine onto a tray to offer to
his spirit. Each mealtime thereafter the children pour out
wine, first the sons, then the wives and grandchildren. The
sons and grandsons then prostrate themselves before the coffin
while the priest finishes reading, beats a drum and clangs
cymbals, and the people wait. This is called weeping at
lunch and supper (phohn ngai, phohn pau).

Sticks with strings attached are given to the priest to
ignite and place inside rice bowls with paper money. These
bowls are placed at the ends of the coffin. This ceremony is
called lighting lamps (tem tuhng-chi). The sons' lamps are
lit first, then those of other relatives, and finally the
lamps of the daughters and granddaughters. When a lamp is
lit, the priest reads the names of the mourners, thus inform-
ing the dead spirit that these are the people who have
brought chickens and made lamps to light the way for him.
Friends of the sons and daughters contribute money to buy the
chickens, and other relatives together contribute to light
their lamps.

Two evenings before burial, one of the priests performs
the caht pu ma ceremony, in which he goes into a trance,
leaving his body in order to go tell spirit soldiers that the
deceased priest's spirit is about to arrive at the place of
the dead--like announcing the arrival of a ruler--so the
soldiers will guard him. This must be performed three times.
The first evening it is done nearby, the second evening far-
ther away, and the third time the priest must go all the way
to the grave site.

The day before the burial is called tan seu or lam slang.
On the afternoon of that day, a goat is sacrificed and its
intestines cleaned and placed on the back of the goat. The
priest then lights lamps in front of the coffin. This ceremony is called khau cong. The goat provides transportation
for the dead priest's spirit to ride, to meet the three
spirits of the sky. That evening a pig is killed and offered
beside the coffin. Then the priest reads a list of names on
a large sheet of white paper. These, the names of all the
relatives attending the funeral, are read to the spirit.
After the priest finishes reading, the people begin wailing.
Then each relative pours out wine in a gesture called thu lau

tan seu, signifying that each one is bidding farewell to the
deceased. The wife also pours out wine as her final farewell.

The evening before burial, the daughters of the priest present a money tree, a tall pole decked with colored streamers
and paper money. The priest fastens to the top of this pole
a list of the names of those who made it. Then the priest
marches around the tree followed by the sons-in-law. Again
the relatives--men, women and children--pour out wine. The
priest reads the names listed on the money tree, then clangs
cymbals, and the people wail (phohn sen), signifying that the
daughters are repaying the departed parent for his trouble in
raising them.

The wife's relatives customarily make a paper horse for
the spirit of the dead person to ride. If the priest has
several wives, he normally receives that many horses. Paper
houses (hon si) as well as the paper horse must be presented
by a priest to the spirit of the deceased the evening before
burial. The priest calls the spirit and presents the houses
and horse for his use in the land of the dead. Then the relatives parade around (called phohn si). Silver and gold paper
is also offered this way. After burial, the money tree, silver and gold-colored paper money, houses, and paper horse will
all be burned to enter the land of the dead for the spirit's
use.

The morning of burial a chicken is killed, and the blood
is used to paint eyes on a piece of cloth. When a person is
ordained into priesthood, this cloth is painted for him with
pictures of humans and tigers drawn on it. The eyes of the
humans, however, are not painted on the cloth until the time
of the priest's death. If the priest dies first, only part
of the picture will be painted, and the remainder completed
when his wife dies. If the priest and his wife are both dead,
then the whole picture is painted. The painting of the eyes
is to enable the spirit soldiers to see the way and follow
the dead priest, taking him to the land of the dead. If the
wife remains, a portion of the cloth is left to protect her.
If they are both dead, the completed picture enables them to
travel together.

When the procession to the grave is about to begin, the
relatives on the wife's side bring the paper horse and place
the clothing of the dead priest on the horse, after which
they all wail. Then they take the horse out to the road, and
again they cry. This signifies giving the spirit of the deceased a horse to ride to the land of the dead, the final
separation. They say, "You go to the land of the dead; I will
stay in the land of the living."

A chicken is carried on someone's shoulder to the grave,
and upon return, the chicken is given to the priest who performed the caht pu ma ceremony of announcing the priest's
arrival among the spirits.

Children of priests and priestesses carry toy guns in the
funeral procession, a pantomime of soldiers guarding an
officer on the way to the king. During the funeral procession
(oc phi), men also frequently shoot guns to signal that the
spirit is leaving his house, or that they are feeding the
spirit enroute, or simply that it is the time of burial.

Halfway to the grave, the procession stops so the children
can pour out wine to the spirit. Upon arrival at the grave,
they again offer wine (thu lau to hong), as the final farewell.

The priests and sons of the deceased march around the
grave. The eldest son and officiating priest next step down
into the grave to pray to the spirit of the ground. After
they step out, the coffin is lowered and a tall pole is
placed at the grave to indicate to the spirits that those
present will serve this spirit. A priestess or priest's
wife who dies usually has a banana plant with a human figure
on it planted by the grave. This is called lau-li and has
the same significance as the tall pole. There are also three
round objects in the shape of conical hats placed by the
grave. For a priest, a lamp is lit at the grave for three
evenings.

All the people who made the paper houses, paper money,
paper horse, and money tree are given a slice of meat by the
children of the deceased. They are also given two bowls con-
taining money in exchange for the things they gave for the
deceased.

When the chief priest in Nam Son died, he had many 'spiritual children'-priests and priestesses that he had trained.
All of them came to his house to light lamps and bid farewell.
Each one held a stick with ribbons (fan) and marched around
the coffin. They contributed money to make the house for the
spirit. They constructed a large gateway, and on the morning
of the burial, all, including the son of the chief priest,
passed through this gateway in a ceremony known as tu lau.
They explained that the gateway portrays the place where the
spirits greet this new spiritual ruler.

The day of the funeral, the priests wore blue robes and
mitered hats while the officiating priest wore a red embroidered robe. The priestesses wore tan robes and hats with long,
colored streamers hanging to the ground in back. Each carried
a ribboned stick and they walked side by side in an even row,
with the officiating priest out ahead.

Upon arrival at the grave, the priestesses danced around
the grave and then raced to their respective homes, for the
one who arrives home before the coffin is lowered receives
much power from the chief priest's spirit to appease spirits
and do good. This is called bihng ma.

There was no wailing at the funeral procession of the chief
priest, for the Nung said he would go to the sky and become a
ruler of the spirits, like a king or president.

NOTE

[1]Janice Saul and Kenneth Gregerson worked in South Vietnam
under the auspices of the Summer Institute of Linguistics.
Janice Saul lived among the Nung and has studied their language and culture extensively (see "Nung Weddings," also in
this volume). Kenneth Gregerson, who has done extensive research among the Rengao, a Mon-Khmer group in Kontum Province, assisted Miss Saul in writing up these field notes.

The Nung are a minority Tai group whose original homeland
was in South China. Many live in the Lang Son and Bac Giang
areas of North Vietnam. In 1954, about 10,000 went south and
were resettled in Tuyen Duc, Long Khanh and Bien Hoa provinces. The 2,000 Nung who resettled in Nam Son speak the
Fan Slihng dialect.

REFERENCES

Saul, Janice E. 1972. *Nung Funerals* in *Southeast Asia* 2:1.
    Southern Illinois University.

Schrock, Joann, et al. 1972. *Minority Groups of North Viet-
    nam: Ethnographic Study Series*. DA PAM 550-110.
    Washington: U.S. Government Printing Office.

NOTES ON CHRAU ETHNOGEOGRAPHY

David Thomas

The Chrau (Jro) people live east of Saigon in an area comprising parts of former Long Khánh, Bình Tuy, Phước Tuy, and Biên Hòa provinces.[1] Their language belongs to the South Bahnaric group of Mon-Khmer languages. The Chrau have, by their own accounts, lived in their present location since time immemorial, nor have I uncovered any traditions of migration from anywhere else.

Recently Vietnamese have been settling in this area in larger and larger numbers, so that the Chrau are now only a small minority of the present population, resulting in the Chrau language and the original Chrau place names being almost completely submerged.

With the increasingly strong Vietnamese cultural influence, and with dislocation of old patterns due to wartime resettlement, Chrau clans and settlement patterns are little more than memories, as very few Chrau are still able to live in their old clan homes, and postwar settlement patterns are bound to be drastically different from the prewar patterns.

On maps of the area, particularly the eastern half, it is not uncommon to see several locations given the same name. These generally reflect the clan name and clan area, as members of a clan often did not live in a close cluster, but their houses may have been separated from each other by a mile or two of jungle.

CLAN AREAS

The Chrau region, before the Second World War, was divided into areas (palây) within which a family that had proper kin ties could farm freely. Some of these areas had clear boundaries, while others appear to have had clear centers but less clear boundaries. Some of these areas, seemingly the older Chrau areas, appear to have been restricted to a single matrilineal clan, while others seem to have several clans represented. The fighting from 1945 to 1975 has completely broken up the Chrau cultural and settlement patterns, but

215

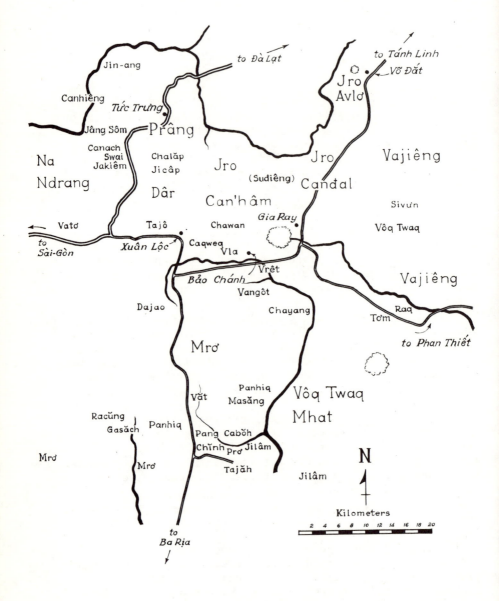

Map 3.   Chrau Clan Areas.

many Chrau still long to go back to their ancestral areas
where they used to farm. It has not always been clear to me
which names are simply area names and which are also clan
names, as the clan picture has been muddied by the resettlements and by the shifting towards a (Vietnamese-like) patrilineal system. Some names are clearly clans, with an area
and a lineage having the same name. Other names seem to be
solely areas, and others solely lineages. Tơm 'trunk' and
chồng 'tip' are often used to distinguish, respectively,
primary clan areas from secondary areas of the same clan, or
people living in their main clan area from people who have
moved to a different area.

     Palây Jro is by far the largest of the areas and is
divided into three sub-areas. It is said that 50 years ago
a chief, or influential person, ruled in each of these three
areas. Palây Jro Maq Avlơ (Upper Jro, Jro Tơm Ca, Jro Ramvuh)[2]
is centered around Võ Đất, extending S to the upper branch of
Daq Cawêng. This is considered by many Chrau to be the
original Chrau homeland, and is rivaled in prestige only by
Palây Prâng as a fount of Chrau culture.

     Palây Jro Canđal (Central Jro, Jro Nchar) is centered
around Trần Tao, including Trà Tân and the areas of Daq
Cawêng and Daq Gasĕt to about 5 km. S of Võ Đất. Nchar is
possibly derived from Gũng Char, the most prominent geographical feature in the Jro area and bordering on the Central Jro
area.

     Palây Jro Maq Can'hâm (Lower Jro, Jro Ca-i) is centered
around Tho Vực, extending N to Daq Nlê and E to Gia Ray.
Palây Ngao is a subsection of Lower Jro around Tho Vực and
Daq Vrêt. The Chaluh subclan has a taboo against eating
crocodile meat because of an ancestor's having been helped
by a crocodile; this is the only such taboo that I have
found among the Chrau. Chaluh people are scattered from
Bao Chánh to Túc Trưng. There are also Jro Camĕc and N'he
subclans reported.

     Palây Vajiêng, Võq Yiêng (Bà Giêng) covers a large area E
of Palây Jro in western Bình Tuy province, including Tánh
Linh, Gia Huynh, Suối Kiết, and down to Highway 1. There
are many subclans of Vajiêng, including the Cŭh, Siêng, Dâr,
Daq, and they have scattered far and wide throughout the
Chrau area, so that Vajiêngs are found from W of Túc Trưng to

Xuân Lộc and down to southern Bình Tuy. Vajiêng Siêng are
found in Palây Vajiêng and southern Bình Tuy.

   In the Túc Trưng area, Vajiêng Cŭh are found in Vôq Juôc
(Daq Juôc), Vôq Khlong (Daq Khlang), Vôq Prâng (Cây Xăng,
Đức Thặng), Vi Gadayh (upper Daq Gadayh), Vumdăn (Daq Vumdăn),
Unghiên (Daq Unghiên), and Daq Hợp. Vajiêng Cŭh are also
found in Palây Vajiêng. Vajiêngs are also found in Phú Mỹ,
Bảo Mỹ, and Giềng Học near Xuân Lộc, as well as in other
places.

   Palây Sivưn is the area around Suối Kiết and Gia Hùynh,
S of Palây Jro and N of Palây Vôq Twaq in Bình Tuy.

   Palây Tơm Raq (Simjơ, Vn. Rừng Lá) is the area N of Gŭng
Jrwŏng, extending to N of Highway 1. Raq (Vn. lá buông)
'latenier palm leaves': This area abounds in palms. I know
of no clan lineage with this name.

   Palây Vôq Twaq (Vn. Thanh Tóa) is an area between Daq
Calêu, Daq Lŭq Si-ăt, and Phong Gle in northern Phước Tuy.
(toa [twá].) The Vôq Twaq clan is also found in Gia Ray,
Palây Vajiêng, Palây Jilâm, and as far as Tánh Linh. A sec-
tion S of Suối Kiết and Gia Huynh is also known as Palây Vôq
Twaq (twaq 'latenier palm tree').

   Palây Mhat (Vn. Thưa Tích) is the area S of Palây Vôq Twaq
and E of Daq Calêu, including Bảo Bổ and Đất Đỏ. The area
(or its inhabitants?) is also known as Mrơ Thưa Tích, which
may indicate a relationship with (part of) the Mrơ clan.

   Palây Masăng (Vn. Lâm Xuân) is the area W of Daq Calêu
opposite Palây Mhat, and S of Palây Panhiq. Masăng subclans
include Masăng Mơ (mơ 'paddy field') and Masăng Prâng (prâng
'red clay'). There may have originally been a phonological
connection between masăng and lâm xuân, though their present
forms are rather different.

   Palây Panhiq apparently comprises two area, one lying near
the Phước Tuy-Long Khánh border, W of Daq Calêu and N of Palây
Masăng and Ngai Giao. The other area includes Cụ Bị and Cụ
Khánh N of Daq Simônh and E of Daq Njrang.

   Palây Jilâm (Lâm, Vn. Bảo Lâm) apparently comprises two
areas, one around Xuân Mộc and Như Lâm and the other W of

Daq Calêu and S of Daq Cabŏh. Như lâm seems to be derived
from jilâm, with j → nh and the neutral presyllable i → ư.
Palây Jilâm was mainly occupied by people of the Vôq Twaq
clan.

    Palây Tajăh (Vn. Bình Giả) is in the area of Bình Giả and
SE to Gŭng Glao. There may also be a Tajăh area in south
central Long Khánh. With j → gi, -h → (hỏi tone), and
(presyllable) → (huyền tone), a connection between the two
names is quite possible, though the t → b is anomalous. The
epenthetic nh is not unusual.

    Palây Prơ (Prưa, Vn. Bàu Trơ) is the area between Daq
Cabŏh and Bình Giả. It is N of Palây Tajăh, S of Palây Cabŏh,
and E of Palây Chỉnh. Lacking a pr-, the shift to Vn. tr-
is not surprising. ưa is a local Chrau phonemic variant of ơ.

    Palây Chỉnh (Vn. Bảo Chinh) lies NW of Bình Giả, W of Palây
Prơ and S of Palây Pang.

    Palây Cabŏh (Vn. Tầm Bó) is between Daq Cabŏh and Daq
Yarwec, N of Palây Prơ and E of Palây Pang. (See Daq Cabŏh
for the phonological derivation of Cabŏh.)

    Palây Pang lies W of Daq Cabŏh and Palây Cabŏh and N of
Palây Chỉnh.

    Palây Văt (Văch) is in the upper reaches of Daq Cabŏh, SE
of Núi Lé.

    Palây Gasăch (Kisăch, Vn. Hát Dịch) lies between Daq Njrang
Swai and Daq Châu Pha, W of Palây Panhiq, N of Palây Mrơ, and
E of Palây Racŭng, E of the Biên Hòa-Phước Tuy border. There
may possibly be a phonological relationship between săch and
dịch.

    Palây Racŭng (Vn. Hát Dịch) lies on the Biên Hòa-Phước
Tuy border W of Palây Gasăch.

    Palây Mrơ consists of at least three large widely-separated
areas. Mrơ Can'hâm (Lower Mrơ) is E of Long Thành, covering
a large area, and also has a small section N of the confluence of the Daq Swai and Daq Vluq (S of Palây Gasăch). Mrơ
Avlơ (Upper Mrơ) is in southern Long Khánh around Câm Mỹ and

Câm Tiêm. Palây Mhat is also known as Mrơ Thừa Tích, probably
implying that people of the Mrơ clan have settled there in
large numbers. Mrơ people are now also found in Ôn Cung.
Subclans Mrơ Kê Thi and Mrơ Ngăn have been reported, probably
from the Upper Mrơ area.

Palây Tamŭm (Dimŭm, Camŭm; Vn. Cà Mum) is N of Palây Dijao
and Palây Tijah. The t~d~c variation in the presyllable is
not uncommon in Chrau; t and d tend to neutralize in that
position. The Vn name is a close approximation of the Chrau
name.

Palây Chayang (Vn. Thoại Hương) is beside Daq Calêu SE of
Palây Vangôt. It is tempting to see a dim resemblance between
chay and Vn. thoai, and yang and Vn. hương, though this is
not certain.

Palây Vangôt (Vn. La Minh) lies S of Palây Vrêt, S of Daq
Swai and W of Daq Calêu. It was apparently populated by a
mixture of clans, including Jro.

Palây Vrêt (Vn. Bảo Liệt) lies S of Palây Chawan and Gũng
Char, and N of Palây Vangôt. It is bounded on the NW and SE
by Daq Calêu, and on the SW by Daq Swai. Vn lacks vr-, so
vr- → bao l- and e → ie, plus adding tones. It is not
clear whether there is any connection between Palây Vrêt
and Daq Vrêt in Palây Jro Can'hâm.

Palây Tajô (Dijô, Vn. Lưng Tài), lies W and NW of Xuân Lộc,
in the An Lộc, Suối Tre, Núi Đỏ, Ấp Bình Lộc area. The Tajô
clan is said to use peculiar intonation.

Palây Dajao (Tijao, Vn. Thời Giao) is a clan area in south
central Long Khánh, around Thời Giao and Ong Quê, and perhaps
also an area near Bình Giả and Gũng Giao in N Phước Tuy.
j → gi is the normal equivalence, as is low tone for a presyllable; and t → th in a presyllable is close.

Palây Vla (Vôq Vla) is around Ôn Cung in central Long
Khánh. Subclans include Vla Daq.

Palây Suđiêng, between Gia Ray and Daq Nlê, was the home
of a semilegendary clan said to have lived there 150-200

years ago, who fled to Bà Rịa and Bình Dương. A potsherd
site 7 km. NW of Gia Ray is said to be their remains. They
are said to have fled from a dragon that they disturbed while
digging a well (Ntu Dangvěh). This story is probably a remi-
niscence of the Jro who fled (were forcibly resettled by?)
the French 100 years ago and settled in the Bình Dương--Bình
Long area, the Stiêng (Sođiêng) area (Bourotte 1955:31-41).
The Chrau in the Bình Long-Tây Ninh area still refer to
themselves as Jro and are sometimes listed in official records under the name Tamun (Chr. tamun 'person'). The Bình
Long Chrau tell of their two ancient chiefs who fought against
the French but were defeated. Such tales of the 'Sưđiêng'
probably have some historical basis.

Palây Caqwěq (Paqwěq) is the area around Xuân Lộc, Tân Phú,
and the upper end of Daq Calêu, including Mơ Dâr Sinh, Mơ
Tamrach, and Mơ Lamsai.

Palây Chawan is bounded on the W by Daq N'hap, on the N by
Palây Jro Ca-i, on the E by Bảo Chanh, and on the S by Palây
Vrêt. It includes the sources of Daq Simrong, Daq Ca-it and
Daq Vrêt, and the paddy areas Mơ Jri, Mơ Jâng Khla, and Mơ
Câu. It is tempting to see a resemblance between chawan and
the chanh of Bảo Chanh.

Palây Prâng (Vôq Prâng) is the area around Túc Trưng and
Daq Lawa. This is an area of prestige and of fairly heavy
population, so that the whole northwestern section of the
Chrau area is sometimes referred to loosely as Prâng. This
area has a distinctive dialect (Thomas 1971:220-1). If
there were a Prâng river, I might have been tempted to see a
connection between Daq Prâng and Túc Trưng; but this does not
seem to be so. prâng 'red clay'. There does not seem to be
a Prâng clan; Palây Prâng seems to be most heavily populated
by Vajiêng Cǔh, with a Chalưh settlement on Daq Ndu and a
Bà Thâu settlement on Daq Mongcăq.

Palây Dâr (Vôq Dâr) is basically the Bình Lộc area, extending loosely to Đồng Xoài. (dâr 'fertile, luxuriant forest'). The population is apparently Vajiêng Dâr, and other
Vajiêng Dâr are reported down near Long Thành.

Palây Swai (Đồng Xoài) is the area N and NW of Gia Tân
and E of Dộc Mơ hill (Gǔng Vam Vlôr). The Vn Đồng may have

been added on analogy with the better known Đồng Xoài in
Phước Long.

Palây Jakiêm (Vn. Gia Kiệm) is between Gia Tân and Gia
Kiệm, W of Highway 20. j ➝ gi is normal.

Palây Canach (Ganach) lies between Palây Swai and Palây
Jângsôm, NW of Gia Tân. It is between Gŭng Vam Vlôr and Daq
Ranơm.

Palây Jâng Sôm (Nsôm, Sŭm, Tơm Sŭc; Vn. Bến Nôm) is the
area E of Bến Nôm and Cây Gạo and S of Daq Ranơm. Palây
Jâng Sôm, though small, has a reputation for being the home
of wise men and a center of Chrau traditional culture and
knowledge. (tơm sŭc 'source village'.) It is the home of
the Sŭm clan.

Palây Yayong (Vn. Võ Dông) is apparently a general term
including Palâys Canach, Jâng Sôm, Swai, Ấp Jro, and Jakiêm.
The relationship between these is not clear.

Palây Canhiêng (Canhêng) is the area W of Palây Prâng and
N of Palây Jâng Sôm and Palây Na Ndrang on both sides of Daq
Nlê. This is apparently the only exception to the rule that
Daq Nlê is the boundary of the Chrau area. Palây Canhiêng
is both vague and extensive, but with a very small population
(30 people?).

Palây Jin-ang (Vn. Vĩnh An) lies beside Daq Nlê NW of Túc
Trưng. j ➝ SVN v[y], -ang ➝ SVN an[aŋ]. It is possible
that the Chrau name is derived from the Vn. name.

Palây Na Ndrang (Vn. Bầu Hàm) is the westernmost part of
the Chrau area. It is said to have originally extended from
Bến Nôm to Hố Nai (and perhaps Biên Hòa), including Dầu Giây,
Hưng Lộc, Bầu Hàm, Bầu Cá and Trắng Bôm. (Factual information about Palây Ndrang was not easy to elicit.)

Palây Vatơ (Patơ, Bò-tơ; Vn. Bầu Cá) is a settlement area
N of Highway 1 at the Long Khánh-Biên Hòa border.

Palây Vaglao is unidentified but perhaps N of Bình Lộc.
The Vu Glao people have all moved to Túc Trưng.

Palây Jicâp (Vn. Gia Cấp) is just N of Bình Lộc. Its inhabitants, Vajiêng Cŭh and Vu Glao, have moved to Túc Trưng.

Palây Chalăp (Vn. Võ Định) is along Daq Tambŭng. Its inhabitants have also moved to Túc Trưng.

Clan lineage names have been mentioned under several of
the clan areas, including Jro (Tơm, Ngao, Camêc, Ramvuh,
Chalưh), Vajiêng (Cŭh, Dâr, Siêng, Daq), Twaq (Ngăn), Masăng
(Mơ, Prâng), Mrơ (Kê Thi, Ngăn), Tajô, Dajao, Vla (Daq),
Suđiêng, Vatơ.

Other lineage names are reported for which no clan area of
that name has been found. The Chalăh live in Palây Chawan.
The Valang live near Túc Trưng. The Vavrăch and the Vayai
live in the direction of Long Thành. The Bà Thâu (the same
as Vatơ?) live on Daq Mongcăq near Túc Trưng. The Suh Ratiêng
(Suđiêng?) live in northwestern Phước Tuy. No location was
specified for the Vacŭh.

CITIES AND TOWNS

The Chrau have no cities, but they do have names for some
of the nearby towns and cities.

Masưt (Vn. Phan Thiết). Phan Thiết has probably always
been the major source of salt for the Chrau, so it is tempting to postulate an ancient Cham word *masin 'salty' (cf.
Tagalog maasin 'salty'), which filtered through the Roglai
n → t shift and the Chrau i → ư shift yielding masưt.

Dâng Kho or Vi Chăm (Vn. Tánh Linh). Tánh Linh has a
fairly large Cham population, so Vi Chăm 'Cham place' is not
an unexpected name. The source of Dâng Kho is not clear.

Mơ Vŏh or Bầu Ria (Vn. Bà Rịa). Mơ Vŏh may be translated
'salt paddy field', probably indicating that the site of Bà
Rịa was once a rice field that was too salty to be usable.
Bầu Rịa is probably just an alteration of the Vietnamese
name to fit the local Vietnamese pattern of using bầu (for
mơ or tamăn) in place names.

Vahwa (Vn. Biên Hòa). These two names are clearly related, but it is difficult to say whether Vahwa is a shortening of Biên Hòa to fit Chrau patterns, or whether Biên Hòa is an expansion of Vahwa to fit Vietnamese patterns. Both are normal patterns. The h of Hòa is not pronounced in modern southern Vietnamese, but the borrowing may have taken place before the loss of h.

Sigor (Sài Gòn). The Chrau form clearly underlies the Vietnamese form, as the unidirectional r → n shift shows. The modern Khmer form (Nokor) also attests the final r. It is unlikely, though not impossible, that the Chrau area once extended to Saigon, so the Chrau form is probably derived from a Khmer form that had s rather than n in the presyllable.

NORTHEAST SECTION

For convenience of description we will call the 'northeast section' that part of the Chrau area bounded roughly by Võ Dắt, Tánh Linh, Đá Mài, Highway 1 to Xuân Lộc, northeast again to the Langa River. This comprises essentially the area of the Jro Tơm Ca, Jro Nchar, Jro Ca-i, and Chawan clans. The Jro area is considered by many people to be the true home of the Chrau and the place where the purest Chrau language is spoken. It is also by far the largest of the clan areas, so that many Chrau use Jro as the name for the whole ethnic group.

MOUNTAINS AND HILLS (gŭng)

Gŭng Char (Vn. Núi Chứa Chan). The highest mountain (837 m.) in the Chrau area. char is also used of a huge lone elephant, and of the huge rice paddies near Bảo Chánh. Note the r → n sound shift. The source of the Chứa is not clear.

Gŭng Tambong (Vn. Núi Con). A small hill 1 km. NW of Gia Ray.

Gŭng Cang (Vn. Núi Hàm). A hill 1 km. N of Gia Ray.

Gŭng Raq (Vn. Núi Lá?). A twin-peaked hill 1 km. NE of Gia Ray, the source of the Daq Sivừr River. raq (Vn. lá buông) 'latenier palm'.

Gŭng Gle (Vn. Núi Le). gle 'small bamboo'. Vn. lacks a
gl- cluster, so gl →1. A hill just N of Highway 1, 3 km. E
of the Gia Ray junction.

Gŭng Glăq (Vn. Núi Le). The smaller peak of Gung Gle.

Gŭng Gate (Vn. Núi Gỗ). Unidentified.

Gŭng Long (Vn. Núi Chồn). Unidentified.

Gŭng Krai (Vn. Núi Chồn). Unidentified.

Gŭng Krênh (Vn. Núi Chồn). Unidentified.

Gŭng Hôc (Vn. Núi Hôk). A hill halfway between Trần Tao
and Highway 1. No change in name.

Gŭng Con Sŏh (Vn. Núi Võ Đất). No apparent connection
between the Chrau and Vn. names. Võ Đất is apparently derived
from the town Võ Đất at its foot.

Gŭng Grao (Vn. Núi Grao, Núi Rao). Two hills halfway between Gia Huynh and Đá Mài on the Long Khánh-Bình Tuy border.
The Chrau distinguish them as Grao Mê and Grao Con (mê
'mother', con 'child'). Grao has no meaning. Vn. lacks a
gr- cluster, so gr → r.

Gŭng Săq Iĕr (Vn. Núi Sương Gà). Unidentified, N of Highway 1, E of the Long Khánh-Bình Tuy border. iĕr (gà) 'chicken';
the shift from săq 'body, name' to sương (xương 'bone'?) is
unexplained.

RIVERS AND STREAMS (daq)

The Upper Daq Nlê System.

Daq Nlê (Vn. Sông Đồng-Nài, Sông La Nga). Flows from E of
Tánh Linh to Biên Hòa and Vũng Tàu. It forms the northern
and eastern boundary of the Chrau area.

Daq Vrêt, Vrêch (Vn. Suối Rết). Flows from Xuân Lộc, E
then N into the Daq Nlê. Vn. lacks a vr- cluster, so vr → r.

Phong Mơ Jikwar. A small stream flowing from Mơ Jikwar
(S of Bảo Chánh) NW into D. Vrêt.

Daq Mơ Măq.   Presumably a stream flowing through Mơ Măq
into D. Vrêt.

Daq Ca-ĭt (Vn. Suối Gia Ích).   Flows from Xuân Lộc NE,
joining D. Vrêt near Tho Vực.   Chr. ĭt → Vn. ich [ĭt].

Daq Glao (Vn. Suối Gia Lao).   Flows from Gŭng Char NW
under Cầu Gia Lao bridge, and into D. Vrêt near Tho Vực.   A
branch, Glao Con, flows from Gŭng Char, past Sơ Ga-âm, then
E into Glao Mê.   The Vn. Gia apparently reflects Daq, and
gl → l. glao 'large bamboo'.

Daq Simrong (Vn. Suối Yon, Suối Tăm Rong).   Flows from
5 km. NE of Xuân Lộc, NE into D. Vrêt N of Tho Vực.   Chrau
presyllables are unstable, so that the second Vn. name
might well represent a local Chrau variant Tamrong.

Daq Tong Sung (Vn. Suối Đầu Rìu).   A tributary of D.
Simrong, flowing SE into it from Mơ Tong Sung, 5 km. E of
Tho Vực.

Daq Machic, Machit (Vn. Suối Con).   Northernmost tributary of D. Simrong, flowing E into it.

Daq Ramvăch (Vn. Suối Con).   Three linked streams (Ramvăch
Mê, Ramvăch Ntu, Ramvăch Con) flowing E into D. Vrêt from S
of Gŭng Sipiq.

Daq Rây (Vn. Suối Gia Ray).   Flows from Gŭng Char at
Gia Ray, N into D. Nlê.   Vn. Gia reflects Daq, and Rây was
changed to Ray.

Talŭng Klăp Canđaq.   A deep hole in the Daq Rây river 5
km. NW of Gia Ray.   canđaq 'crow'.   There is said to be a
tunnel leading from it to D. Nlê.

Daq Por (Vn. Suối Cơm).   Flows N from Gŭng Char,
approaching the highway in Gia Ray, then N into D. Rây.
por is 'soup' in most Chrau dialects, including the Gia
Ray area dialect, but is 'rice' (Vn. cơm) in some southern dialects.   In central Chrau compounds, however, por
is sometimes equivalent to Vn. cơm, as in vran por (Vn.
trùng cơm) 'angleworm'.

Daq Plŏh Vŭr (Vn. Suối Dái Bò). Flows NE from Gŭng Char,
joining D. Rây just N of Gia Ray. (Vn. dái bò 'bull testicles', Chrau plŏh vŭr 'gaur testicles').

Daq Ca Rắch (Vn. Suối Con). Flows N from Gŭng Tambong
(1 km. NW of Gia Ray) into D. Rây.

Daq Talo (Vn. Suối Cát). Talo Mê flows N from Gŭng Char
into D. Rây. A smaller tributary, Talo Con, flows into Talo
Mê on the east side.

Daq Jrang (Vn. Suối Chà Rang). Flows into D. Rây on the
W (E?) side, due E of Tho Vực. Vn. lacks j, so j ⟶ ch.

Daq Pai Vŏq (Vn. Suối Ba Gió). Flows N into the Nlê between D. Rây and D. Ranga. Vn. lacks p-, so p ⟶ b; -i merged
with gi-; v, like Vn. v, ⟶ [y]; and Vn. lacks final glottal
stop, so q ⟶ (high tone).

Daq Ranga (Vn. Suối Me). Flows N into the Nlê between D.
Pai Vŏq and D. Hợp. ranga (Vn. me)'sesame'.

Daq Simrông (Vn. Suối Bào Sình). Unidentified but apparently
different from Daq Simrong above. Connected with Tanlô Simrông?
(Same as D. Ramvắch, flowing into D. Ranga?)

Daq Caweng (Vn. Suối Gia Hùynh, Dar K'Huṇh). Two branches,
one rising halfway between Gia Hùynh and Suối Kiết, the other
rising 10 km. N of Gia Hùynh, flowing W and joining not far
from the Nlê, then emptying into the Nlê. The second name is
apparently a French adaptation of the Chrau.

Daq Nduq (Vn. Suối Cha). Flows from halfway between Gia Ray
and Bảo Sen N into D. Cawêng. No evident connection between
the names. With D. Cawêng, it forms the boundary between
Palây Jro Ca-i and Palây Jro Nchar.

Daq Uq (Vn. Suối Đất). Flows from 3 km. SW of Trần Tao
into D. Nduq. Vn. đất 'earth' for uq 'clay'.

Daq Vryĕng (Vn. Suối Ktoul). E. of Gia Ray, flowing N into
D. Nduq.

Daq Gatửl (Vn. Suối Gáo, Suối Ktoul). Flows N intermit-
tently from the highway, 7 km. NE of Gia Ray, into the
southern branch of D. Cawêng. gatửl (Vn. gáo) 'a species of
tree'.

Daq Gasĕt (Vn. Suối Chết, Dar Sat). Flows W from 5 km. SE
of Võ Đất, then SW into D. Cawêng. Its lower section is con-
fluent with the northern branch of D. Cawêng. Chết shows the
shifts s →ch and ĕ →ê.

Daq Nji (Vn. Suối Cây Da, S. Di). Flows W from Bình Tuy
into D. Gasĕt. cây da 'banyan tree' is translated from the
somewhat similar sounding jri 'banyan', possibly an avoidance
of ji 'sick'. di is a phonological adaptation j →d.

Daq Pajal (Vn. Suối Cây Da). Unidentified. Possibly jal
→da (j → [y], l → ∅), or possibly some confusion with Daq
Nji. Or possibly the Suối Da that joins D. Cawêng 3 km. NE
of Gia Hùynh.

Daq Sivửr (Vn. Suối Cao). Flows N from Gŭng Raq (2 km. NE
of Gia Ray) to a junction with D. Cawêng near D. Hớp. The
connection (if any) between the names is not clear.

Daq Camen (Vn. Suối Ca Mên). Flows N from 3 km. N of Gia
Ray into D. Sivửr. Chrau e is often close to Vn. ê.

Daq Rŏh Poq (Vn. Suối Mo, Suối Con). Flows N from 4 km.
NW of Gia Ray into D. Sivửr, joining it just N of the D.
Camen junction. Vn. mơ is possibly from Mơ GaMŭc, a nearby
swamp area.

Daq Hớp (Vn. Dar Hôp). Flows N from E of Mơ GaMŭc (4 km.
NW of Gia Ray) to a junction with D. Cawêng near the Langa.
The Vn. name is apparently a French adaptation of the Chrau.

Daq Canach (Vn. Suối Con). Unidentified. D. Swai/Calêu?

Daq Gatăng (Vn. Suối Con). Unidentified.

Daq Pôngngŏh (Vn. Suối Con). Unidentified.

Daq Panoch (Vn. Suối Con). Unidentified.

Daq Pagar (Vn. Suối Háp). Unidentified.

Daq Pan'ho (Vn. Suối Con). Unidentified.

Daq Pagap (Vn. Suối Gáp). Unidentified. gap →gáp.

Daq Ndôq (Vn. Suối Khỉ). Unidentified. dôq, khỉ 'monkey'.

Daq Talŭng Ma (Vn. Suối Nhím). Unidentified. sima, nhím 'porcupine'. talŭng ma 'porcupine waterhole'.

Daq Gaphe (Vn. Suối Gạo). Unidentified. Vn. name from the main syllable of the Chr. name, phe, gạo 'rice'.

The Daq Uây *System.*

Daq Uây (Vn. Suối Gia Ui̇̀, Song Oi). Flows E from Gŭng Char, then SE into the Sông Dinh near Đá Mài. Daq → Gia, Uâ →u,o.

Daq Sikwêch (Vn. Suối Quết, Gia Quếch). Flows E from Gŭng Char, joining D. Uây at the foot of Gŭng Char. Southern Vn. lacks a sequence êch, so êch →êt.

Daq Mvrông (Vn. Suối Con). A rivulet flowing E from Gŭng Char, joining D. Uây just E of D. Sikwêch.

Daq Chaloq (Vn. Suối Gia Lố). Flows S from Tanlô Chaloq (2 km. SE of Gia Ray) into D. Uây. Vn. lacks final glottal, so oq →ố.

Daq Nđăch (Vn. Suối Sen). Flows S from Tanlô Nđăch (Bảo Sen) into D. Uây.

Daq Vrech, Vrăch. Unidentified, an upstream tributary of Daq Uây.

Daq Yân (Vn. Suối Giêng). Flows S from NW of Suối Kiết into D. Uây. ý →gi is normal Vn. spelling. yâ →giê is not an exact equivalence, but is probably as close as southern Vn. can come. n →ng is probably a southern Vn. confusion of n and ng.

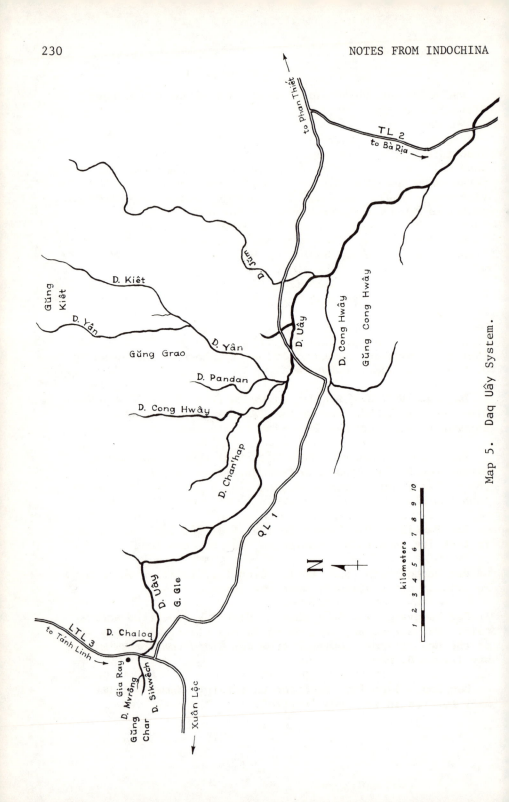

Map 5. Daq Uây System.

Ɖaq Kiêt (Vn. Suối Kiết). Flows S from Núi Kiết, near Suối Kiết, into D. Yân. kiêt 'itchy'.

Daq Pandan (Vn. Da Prin Danh, Suối Cát). Flows S from Gũng Grao into D. Yân, joining it just N of the junction with D. Cong Hoi. ri is probably a misreading of written ư, the normal Chrau vowel quality in pan- [pɨn]. d →d is unusual for a Vietnamese shift, but would be a normal French transcription. nh is normal southern Vn. spelling for n.

Daq Chan'hap (Vn. Da Chanh Hấp). Flows SE from 8 km. S of Trần Tao into D. Cong Hwây.

Daq Cong Hwây (Vn. Suối Công Hôi). Flows S from 4 km. S of Gia Hùynh into D. Yân near its confluence with D. Uây. wây → ôi.

Daq Cong Hwây (Vn. Suối Gia-Ôi). Rises in Gũng Cong-Hwây (Núi Bé) just S of Highway 1, flows E into the confluence of D. Uây and D. Jŭm. hwây →ôi.

Daq Jŭm (Vn. Sông Dinh). Flows SW from 10 km. N of Sông Dinh, then SE to the sea at Hàm Tân. j →d is a normal correspondence, but the ŭm →inh is strange.

Daq Cacat, Tacat (Vn. Suối Cát, Suối Lạnh). Unclear: either the S. Cát flowing S from Núi Xã Dủ into D. Jŭm, or the S. Cát flowing from S of Sông Dinh S into D. Jŭm. cacat, lạnh 'cold'.

Daq Damvlang, Daq Camvôq Bo (Vn. Suối Ɖầu Bò). Location in Bình Tuy uncertain. camvôq bo, đầu bò 'cow head'.

Daq Danggừr (Vn. Suối Ɖôi). Bình Tuy, location uncertain. No evident correlation between the names.

Daq Dangyang (Vn. Suối Nhan). Bình Tuy, location uncertain. Vn. has no ngy, but nh is fairly close. Probably one of the two streams flowing S from Núi Giang Lớn across Highway 1 into D. Uây.

Daq Cop. Bình Tuy, location uncertain. Names for the many turtles in it. cop 'turtle'.

PONDS AND PADDY AREAS

Mơ Tamăn Char, Mơ Trăm Đông (Vn. Đồng Bảo Chánh). Large
marshy paddy area immediately S of Bảo Chánh. mơ 'rice paddy'
tamăn 'open area'. Char may be derived from Gŭng Char right
beside it, or both may mean 'huge' (see under Gŭng Char).
Vn. lacks -r, so r ⟶nh.

Mơ Jikwar. Paddy area S of Mơ Tamăn Char. The source of
Daq Mơ Jikwar.

Mơ Siđe. Paddy area S of Mơ Jikwar and N of Daq Calêu.
The source of Daq Mơ Siđe.

Mơ Mphu (Vn. Ruộng Âm-phủ). Paddy area between Daq Vrêt
and the railroad track, just W of Bảo Chánh. m ⟶am.

Mơ Câu. Paddy area in Palây Chawan just S of the railroad, NW of Ôn Cung.

Mơ Sa Jưl. Paddy area S of D. Ca-it. sa jưl 'eat barking
deer'.

Sơ Ga-âm. Plantation 3 km. NE of Bảo Chánh. so probably
from Vn. sở 'place of work'. Ga- is a name prefix, so Âm is
very likely the name of someone originally connected with the
plantation.

Mơ Pănh Cop (Vn. Ruộng Lớn Tho Vực). Paddy area 2 km. NNE
of Tho Vực. pănh cop 'shoot turtle'.

Tanlô Rao Răm (Vn. Bàu Con). A pond 1 km. N of Gia Ray.
tanlo 'pond', rao răm 'wash field'.

Tanlô Simrông (Vn. Bàu Sình). A pond near D. Ranga and D.
Sivưr.

Mơ GaMŭc (Vn. Ruộng Mức). Paddy area between D. Rŏh Poq
and Ntu Ramvăch, 4 km. N of Gia Ray. Ga- is probably the
name prefix, so Mŭc was probably a person originally connected
with the area.

Mơ (Tanlô) Chaloq (Vn. Bàu Gia-lô). A marshy area 2 km. SE of Gia Ray, and the source of D. Chaloq. cha →gia, loq →lô.

Mơ (Tanlô) Nđăch (Vn. Bàu Sen). A marshy area E of Gia Ray, and the source of D. Nđăch.

Ntu Dangvěh. A semilegendary well, said to have been dug long ago by the Suđiêng, near D. Nlê between D. Hơp and D. Ranga.

Ntu Ramvăch. A well near the confluence of D. Ramvăch Mê and D. Ramvăch Ntu.

Tanlô Chăp Maih. Unidentified. chăp maih 'golden egg'.

Tanlô Rěh (Vn. Bảo Mây). Unidentified. rěh, mây 'rattan'.

Tanlô Ca-ai (Vn. Bảo Ca-ai). Unidentified.

Mơ Măq (Vn. Ruộng Lớn). Paddy area across the river from Mơ Mphu, E of Bảo Vinh. măq, lớn 'large'.

Mơ Cala (Vn. Ruộng Tre). Paddy area on both sides of Daq Ca-ĩt, 4 km. WNW of Bảo Chánh. cala, tre 'bamboo'.

Mơ Sa Jưl (Vn. Ruộng Trạng Đồng). Paddy area E of D. Vrêt near Tho Vực. sa jưl 'eat barking deer'.

Mơ Jâng Khla (Vn. Ruộng Lắc Chiếu). Paddy area in Palây Chawan on both sides of Daq Ca-ĩt, 2 km. NNW of Bảo Vinh B. jâng 'foot'.

Mơ Tong Sung (Vn. Ruộng Đầu Rìu). Paddy area 6 km. NW of Bảo Chánh. tong sung 'axe handle', đầu rìu 'axe head'. Daq Tong Sung flows through it.

Mơ Tung Moq, Dung Moq (Vn. Ruộng Gia Mó). A paddy area near Bảo Chánh, N of D. Simrong, just E of Mơ Tong Sung. Apparently the original name tung moq 'carry bark' became weakened to dungmoq; the Vn. then substituted gia for the presyllable as in other names, and a sắc tone was substituted for -q.

Mơ̆ Cănh, Canh (Vn. Ruộng Tràm). Paddy area S across Ḍ.
Simrong from Mơ̆ Tong Sung and Mơ̆ Dung Moq, 5 km. NW of Bảo
Chánh.

Mơ̆ Trao. Paddy area 5 km. NW of Tho Vực. trao 'a tuber'.

Mơ̆ Tamăn Jrŭng (Vn. Ruộng Bảo Vinh A). Paddy area near
Bảo Vinh A.

SOUTHEAST SECTION

In the Southeast Section we include everything south of
Highway 1 in Biên Hòa, Phước Tuy, Long Khánh, and Bình Tuy
provinces. This area is divided among many small groups and
clans, whose dialects are fairly close to Jro speech.

MOUNTAINS AND HILLS

Gŭng Jrwŏng (Vn. Núi Mây Tào). A large mountain (704 m.)
near the Long Khánh-Phước Tuy-Bình Tuy border, second in
importance only to G. Char. jrwŏng is the name of a strong
rattan found in the area, and Vn. mây tào is a translation
of this. The mountain is also occasionally referred to as
Gŭng Rĕh 'rattan'.

Gŭng Cong-hwây, Gŭng Vacăh (Vn. Núi Bê). A large mountain
(874 m.) just E of G. Jrwŏng, named for the Cong-hwây River
(Suối Gia Ổi) that rises in it and circles around the north
side of it. It is higher than G. Jrwŏng, but doesn't seem
as important to the Chrau; perhaps it is on the fringe of the
Chrau area. There is no apparent connection between the
Chrau and Vn. names for it.

Gŭng Camhâr. An unidentified hill or mountain in central
Bình Tuy.

Gŭng Pachăh Nggan (Vn. Núi Bễ, Núi Bê Bắc, Núi La Minh).
A mountain (324 m.) S of Suối Cát. Bễ 'broken' is a partial
translation of pachăh nggan 'broken dish'. Bắc is probably a
SVn. pronunciation of Vn. bát 'dish', or perhaps a Chrau pro-
nunciation of the Vietnamese, also dropping the tone ˜ on bễ.
The history behind the Chrau name is unknown.

Gŭng Grong. A hill (189 m.) in Palây Vrêt (S of Suối Cát)
near the junction of D. Calêu and D. Vangmang (Glao Mang?).

Gŭng Glang (Vn. Núi Đất). A hill (161 m.) between Mơ Vrêt and Daq Calêu, opposite D. Vongchong and D. Swai.

Gŭng Gavô (Vn. Núi Mẩu, Núi Trà Vô). A hill (209 m.) S of Suối Cát. Trà Vô is clearly derived from Gavô; the pre-syllable in Chrau words is often unstable, so Vietnamese explorers may have been given a form with something other than ga-, though tra is not a permitted Chrau presyllable. The huyền tone on trà is the normal reflex of a Chrau pre-syllable with its de-emphasized lowered pitch (Thomas 1971: 59). And the Vn. v (y) for Chr. v (lenis b) is interesting.

Gŭng Vađang. A hill in Palây Dijô, unidentified.

Gŭng Glao (Vn. Núi Nửa). A hill (152 m.) S of Quang Giao in Xã Bình Giả, Phước Tuy. glao, nửa 'large bamboo'.

Gŭng Yang (Vn. Núi Nhân). A hill (184 m.) W of Quận Đức Thạnh. The Vn. form could be derived from the meaning of yang 'spirit', if the Vn. form may be assumed to have been originally nhang 'joss stick'. But perhaps it is easier just to take it as a deformation of the Chrau form, with y →ñ and ng →n [ŋ].

Gŭng Prho (Vn. Núi Đỏ). Phước Tuy. The Vn. is a straight translation of prho 'red'.

Gŭng Uq (Vn. Núi Nghê). A mountain (203 m.) N of Bà Rịa called uq because the Ji-uq River rises near it and flows by it.

RIVERS AND STREAMS

The Daq Calêu *System.*

Daq Calêu (Vn. Suối Gia Lêu, Sông Ray). Rising S of Xuân Lộc, flows E through Ôn Cung, near Suối Cát, then S through Phước Tuy to the ocean. The Gia could reflect either the Daq of the Ca-. This is the southern boundary of Palây Chawan, and the main river in the southeastern area. Streams in the eastern end of the area flow into the D. Uây-Sông Dinh, while in the western end, several flow into the lower Đồng Nai River.

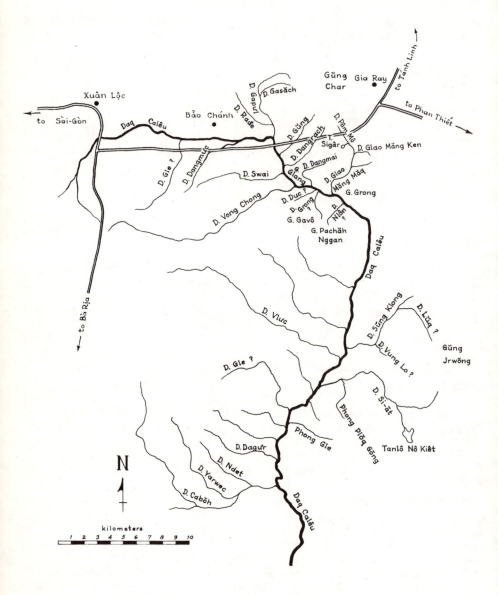

Map 6.   Daq Calêu System.

Daq Gle (Vn. Suối Lé). Flows N across Highway 1 into D. Calêu between Bảo Đinh and Ôn Cung.

Daq Dangmực (Vn. Suối Đửng Một). Flows N across Highway 1 into D. Calêu E of Ôn Cung. The main stream, Dangmực Mê, is fed by a smaller stream Dangmực Con. It is difficult to decide which language was the source of the name, as -ực is extremely rare in native Chrau words, but neither is Vn. đửng một obviously meaningful.

Daq Gapử1 (Vn. Suối Mon Coum). Flows S into D. Calêu from E of Bảo Chánh, fed by D. Rađe and D. Gasêch. The source of the Vn. (French?) name is uncertain.

Daq Gasêch, Gasăch (Vn. Suối Sách, Suối Muồng). This is the northernmost tributary of D. Gapử1, flowing W from Gửng Char. Chr. săch [săč] is phonetically equivalent to NVn. sach [săč].

Daq Rađe, Daq Mở Siđe. This is a southern tributary of D. Gapử1, flowing E from Mở Siđe (S of Bảo Chánh).

Daq Gửng (Vn. Suối Giɑ Gung). Flows from G. Char SW across Highway 1 into D. Calêu. Vn. lacks ử, so ử →u.

Daq Năh Tửng (Vn. Suối Na Tung). This is a small stream in Palây Vrêt, flowing from G. Char across Highway 1 into D. Calêu. Vn. lacks final -h.

Daq Simwŏt (Vn. Suối Đa). Unidentified. Below D. Dangrach, flows W into D. Calêu. No apparent connection between Chrau and Vn. names.

Daq Dangrach, Singrach (Vn. Suối Cát). Flows S from G. Char across Highway 1 at Suối Cát and then westerly into D. Calêu.

Daq Swai (Vn. Suối Sai, Suối Cát). Flows E into D. Calêu, S of Highway 1, and forms Vangôt-Vrêt boundary. Some southern Vn. dialects lack sw-, so sw →s.

Daq Canach? (Vn. Suối Gia Nach). The westernmost tributary of D. Swai?

Daq Dangmai, D. Damai (Vn. Suối Đồng Mai). Flows W below and through Mơ Vrêt into D. Calêu.

Daq Vongchong (Vn. Sông Vong). Flows E through Mơ Vangôt into D. Calêu S of D. Swai.

Daq Duc. A small stream in Vangôt, flowing E into D. Calêu S of D. Vongchong.

Daq Grong (Vn. Suối Rôn). Flows E into D. Calêu S of D. Duc in Vangôt. Vn. has no gr-, so gr →r, and Vn. -n is [ŋ], so ng →n.

Daq Nlôn. Small stream in Vangôt flowing E into D. Calêu.

Daq Pâm Mô (Vn. Suối Đá). Flows from G. Char SE across Highway 1, then into D. Glao Măng. Mô is possibly from tamô (Vn. đá) stone. May be from pâm tamô 'hit stone'.

Daq Glao Măng Măq (Vn. Suối Gia Măng). Flows S from G. Char, across Highway 1, then somewhat southwesterly into D. Calêu. Gia is apparently a substitute for glao.

Daq Ửng Yơ (Vn. Suối Ổng Dư). A stream S of D. Glao Măng Ken, flowing W into D. Pâm Mô. The Chrau name is unusual in that it is two words and has no meaning, but the Vn. name is quite ordinary, so I assume the Chrau name was borrowed from the Vietnamese (the shifts would be regular).

Daq Glao Măng Ken. A small stream, rising S of the Gia Ray intersection on Highway 1, flows a short distance W into D. Pâm Mô.

(Vn. Suối Sáp). Flows from G. Gavô S then E into D. Calêu.

. (Vn. Suối Sách). Flows from E of Cẩm Tiêm E into D. Calêu.

Daq Sửng Klong (Vn. Sông Trong). Flows from G. Jrwŏng W into D. Calêu. Vn. lacks ŭ and kl, so ŭ →ô and kl →tr. sông 'river' is obviously semantically fitting. Phonologically, it could have been borrowed either direction, but since this stream is small, sông is probably not original.

Daq Vung Lo. Small stream flowing into D. Sửng Klong.

Daq Lŭq. Small stream flowing from W of Gŭng Jrwŏng into D. Sŭng Klong.

Daq Vlưc (Vn. Suối Lúc). Flows E from Cẩm Tiêm into D. Calêu. Vn. lacks vl-, so vl ➝ l. The reason for the ư ➝ u shift is not clear, as Vn. has -ức.

Daq Si-ăt (Vn. Suối Bà Lú, Suối Sa Ác). Flows NW from Tanlô Nô Kiêt in NE Phước Tuy into D. Calêu. The first Vn. name seems unconnected. The second is clearly derived from the Chrau, with the neutralized presyllable vowel i [i~ə~a] becoming a fully syllabic a, since Vn. is monosyllabic. The reason for the ăt ➝ ác shift is not clear.

Phong Plŏq Gong. Small stream in Vôqtwaq, flowing N into D. Si-ăt.

(Vn. Suối La Hoa). Flows E into D. Calêu, junction just S of D. Si-ăt. I was unable to get the Chrau name for it.

(Vn. Suối Chàm). Flows NW into D. Calêu in Vôqtwaq. I was unable to get the Chrau name for it.

Daq Gle? (Vn. Suối Lé). Flows from NE of Cẩm Mỹ E into D. Calêu.

Phong Gle (Vn. Suối Lé). Flows W from N of Thừa Tích into D. Calêu. It is not clear whether this is basically a lexical or a phonological equivalence. le 'small bamboo' would be a translation of Chrau gle, but gl ➝ l and e ➝ é would also be natural phonological shifts.

Daq Mpra. Small stream below D. Le. Flows into D. Calêu?

Daq Tanho. A stream N of D. Dagưr. Flows into D. Calêu?

Daq Dagưr (Vn. Suối Sao). Flows E from Núi Sao into D. Calêu. dagưr, sao 'a hardwood tree'.

Daq Cabŏh (Vn. Suối Tầm Bố). Flows S from near Cẩm Mỹ to near Bình Giả, then E into D. Calêu. The low tone and short vowel of Tầm match the low tone and short vowel of the presyllable Ca, t~k shifting in Chrau presyllables is not uncommon; Vn. must separate into two words and must add a

final consonant after the short vowel, of which m would be
most natural before b. High tone for h is expected. In
short, there is close phonological equivalence between the
names.

Daq Yarwec (Vn. Suối Youert). Flows S from Núi Lé into
D. Caboh. The Vn. name is apparently a French transcription
of the Chrau name.

Daq Khlim. Small stream; flows into D. Yarwec (?).

Daq Ndêt (Vn. Suối Gia Hoét). Flows from Núi Sao SE into
D. Caboh. The et in the two names matches, but the rest
doesn't match.

Daq Mvưl (Vn. Suối Re). In N Phước Tuy. Flows into D.
Calêu (?).

Daq Đar. S of D. Mvưl. Flows into D. Calêu (?).

Daq Vit (Vn. Suối Langa). Flows into D. Calêu (?).

Daq Jri (Vn. Suối Sao). Unidentified. May be the same as
D. Dagưr.

The Daq Swai *System.*

Daq Swai (Vn. Suối Xoài, Sông Ca, Sông Sai, Sông Dinh).
The major river in western Phước Tuy, flowing through Bà Rịa.
Xoài and Sai are both variants of Swai. Chrau s varies between [s] (Vn. x) and [š] (Vn. s); some dialects of Vn. lack
sw.

Daq Njrăng (Vn. Suối Chá Răng). Flows SW from W of Đồn
Điền Courtenay into D. Swai. I expect Chá should properly be
Chà, reflecting the low pitch on Chrau presyllables. Vn.
lacks j, so j →ch.

Daq Simônh (Vn. Suối Xà Môn). Flows SW from N of Ấp Cụ Bị
into D. Swai. Chr. s [s] is equivalent to Vn. x. The presyllable vowel shows the same shift as in D. Si-ăt, discussed
above. Vn. lacks ônh, so nh →n.

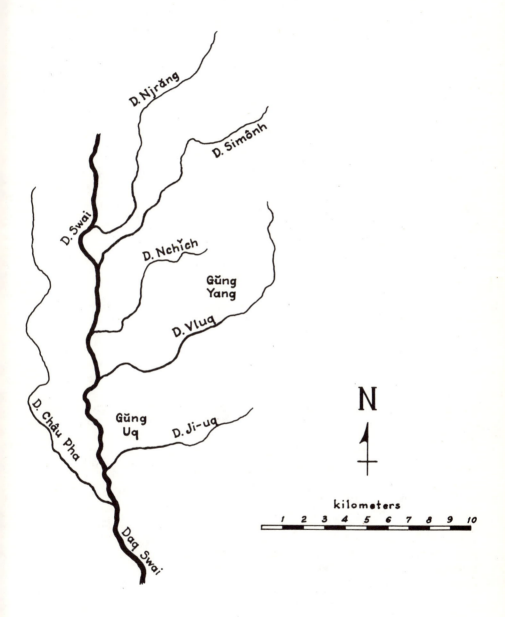

Map 7. Daq Swai System.

Daq Nchїch, Daq Nchit (Vn. Suối Tít). Flows from S of Ấp Cụ Bị into D. Swai. Vn. lacks prenasals, and ch →t is fairly close, though both languages have both phonemes.

Daq Vluq, Vluc, Vruc? (Vn. Suối Lup, Suối Đá Đen). Flows SW from just E of Quận Đức Thạnh into Daq Swai. Vn. lacks vl so vl → l. One would normally expect Vn. c for Chrau q, but the apparent confusion in the names Lúp and Lút (a small tributary) indicates that the transcriber heard a stop phoneme that he couldn't identify.

Daq Châu Pha (Vn. Suối Chau Pha). Rises on the Phước Tuy-Biên Hòa border and flows SE into D. Swai. The name is identical in both languages, but the form seems more typically Vietnamese than Chrau.

Daq Ji-uq (Vn. Suối Soui). Flows W into D. Swai S of G. Uq. No apparent connection between the names.

Others.

Daq Sôc (Vn. Suối Sốc). Flows SE from E of Cẩm Mỹ into Sông Cá. Exact phonological equivalents (plus the necessary high tone before a final stop).

PONDS AND PADDY AREAS

Tamăn Gavô. Just S of Highway 1 in Palây Tơmraq, about 7 km. W of the Bình Tuy border.

Dâr Cavlưng (Vn. Trang ?) A fertile forested area between Daq Glao Măng Măq and Tanlô Sigâr (SE of Gǔng Char).

Tanlô Tagưr (Vn. Bàu Sao). A pond E of D. Ũng Yơ and S of Highway 1. tagưr,(dagur), sao 'a hardwood tree'.

Tanlô Sigâr (Vn. Bào Trống). A pond S of the intersection on Highway 1 near Gia Ray. Its outlet flows NE just a short distance into D. Pâm Mô just above the D. Glao Măng Ken confluence. sigâr, trống 'drum'.

Tanlô Meo (Vn. Bàu Mèo). Unidentified. meo, mèo 'cat'.

Tanlô Ntui (Vn. Hồ Mướp). Unidentified.

Tanlô Jun (Vn. Bau Nai). Unidentified. jun, nai 'deer'.

Mơ Vangôt (Vn. Ruộng La-Minh). Paddy area S of Suối Cát, near D. Calêu. The center of the Vangôt clan area. No apparent connection between the names.

Mơ Vrêt, Mơ Dangmai (Vn. Bảo Liệt). Paddy area just S across D. Calêu from Mơ Vangôt. The center of the Vrêt clan area. Vn. lacks vr- and br-, so the single syllable becomes disyllabic, and r → l.

Tanlô Nô Kiêt (Vn. Bàu Ngứa). Pond in Phước Tuy 5 km. NE of Thưa Tích, the source of D. Si-ăt. kiêt, ngứa 'itchy'. The form nô kiêt would lead one to expect that both words have meaning, but I know no meaning for nô, and Vn. has dropped it.

Tamăn Nô Kiêt (Vn. Bàu Hàm). Marshy area W and S of Tanlô Nô Kiêt.

Mơ Vŏh (Vn. Bà Rịa). (vŏh 'salt') There is no apparent connection between the names.

NORTHWEST SECTION

The northwest section is that part of the Chrau area generally west of Daq Vrêt (Vn. Suối Rết), south and east of Daq Nlê (Vn. Sông Là Nga, Sông Đồng Nai), and north of Highway 1. Túc Trưng and Bình Lộc are the main Chrau centers of this area, and it is sometimes referred to generally as Palây Prâng, though the term Prâng refers properly only to the area just east of Túc Trưng. Dialectally this area is somewhat different from the rest of the Chrau area (Thomas 1971:219-222).

MOUNTAINS AND HILLS

Gŭng Sipiq (Vn. Núi Sa Bi). A hill between D. Vrêt, D. Canduôr, and D. Ramvăch. (sipiq 'weasel') Vn. has no initial p or final glottal, so p → b and q is lost.

Gŭng Padôc, Cađôc (Vn. Núi Đốt). A mountain (248 m. W of
Highway 20 just N of Tuc Trung. The phonological equivalence
is close, dropping the presyllable, d → đ, and southern Vn.
transcription of [k] as t.

Gŭng Jun, Gŭng Vam Vlôr (Vn. Núi Cui). A hill (97 m.) between Highway 20, D. Glao, and the road to Bến Nom. The first
Chrau name (jun 'deer') is unrelated to the second (vlôr, cui
'small bear'). The first word (presyllable?) is dropped in the
Vn. name.

Gŭng Yayông (Vn. Võ Đông). A mountain (236 m.) midway between Gia Tân and Cây Gạo. If the đ is a printing error for
d, then there is close correspondence between southern Vn.
and the Chrau.

Gŭng Paglơ, Payglơ. Apparently the hilly area 3 km. W of
G. Klăn, the source of D. Nwa.

Gŭng Nwa. Small hill (75 m.) 4 km. NW of G. Klăn.

Gŭng Klăn (Vn. Núi Tràn). A mountain (225 m.) beside Highway 20, halfway between Túc Trưng and D. Nlê. Probably Tràn
is a printing error for trăn. klăn, trăn 'python'.

Gŭng Canach (Vn. Núi Tăm Rong). Unidentified. canach
'puddle'.

Gŭng Goq (Vn. Núi Điếu). Unidentified. goq, điếu 'pipe'.

Gŭng Catrơ (Vn. Núi Trơ Trơ). Unidentified.

Gŭng Jong (Vn. Núi Con). Unidentified.

Gŭng Sindôc. A mountain (396 m.) between Bình Lộc and
Highway 1. The source of D. Sindôc.

Gŭng Wiq, Wit (Vn. Núi Dơi). An unidentified hill W of
Xuân Lộc. wiq, dơi 'bat'.

RIVERS AND STREAMS

All rivers and streams in this section form part of the
lower Daq Nlê system.

Daq Canduôr (Vn. Dar Kontour, Suối Con). The main river (Canduôr Mê) flows NE from Mơ Canduôr Mê (SW of Gŭng Sipiq) then NW into D. Nlê. A small tributary (Canduôr Con) flows W into Canduôr Mê near the confluence with D. Nlê. Dar Kontour is apparently a French adaptation of the Chrau form.

Daq Lawa (Vn. Dar Klap, Suối Con). Flows N into D. Nlê just W of D. Canduôr. The Dar Klap (French) name apparently reflects an older or alternate name for the river. It is the western boundary of Palây Jro Ca-ĭt and eastern boundary of Palây Prâng.

Daq N'hap, Daq Cahap (Vn. Suối Háp). Flows N from Xuân Lộc into D. Nlê. It is the western boundary of Palây Chawan. Vn. lacks a n'h cluster, so n'h → h.

Daq Sipiq (Vn. Suối Chồn). Unidentified. Perhaps a tributary of D. N'hap. sipiq, chồn 'weasel'.

Daq Pai Vŏq. Flows NE from just N of Ấp Núi Tung (NW of Xuân Lộc) into D. N'hap.

Daq Cala (Vn. Suối Tre). From NW of Ấp Suối Tre, flows NE into D. N'hap. cala, tre 'small bamboo'.

Daq Sindôc, Daq Nhrŭng (Vn. Suối Săng Đốc, Dar Yoa). From Gŭng Sindôc, flows NE into D. N'hap just above its confluence with D. Tambŭng. There was some confusion as to whether this should properly be called Nhrŭng, but that there is (or was) a Chrau name something like that is evidenced by the name Dar Yoa. The presyllable sin-san is lengthened to the full syllable săng, d → đ, plus sắc tone.

Daq Tamô Dar (Vn. Suối Đá Ban). Flows NE from Gŭng Sindôc into D. Sindôc. tamô dar, đá ban 'bedrock'.

Daq Tambŭng (Vn. Suối Tam Bung, Tầm Bung). Flows N from Bình Lộc, then E into D. N'hap. Vn. lacks ŭ, so ŭ → u. There is normal confusion in rendering the presyllable; tầm is closer than tam to the Chrau sound.

Daq Nhrung (Vn. Suối Gia Rung). The main stream Nhrung Mê rises in Gŭng Sindôc, flows N through Bình Lộc and Gia

Kiệm, then turns E into D. Tambŭng. A small tributary Nhrung
Con also rises in Gŭng Sindôc and joins it in Bình Lộc. Vn.
lacks nhr, so gia is substituted for nh.

Daq Jruc, Daq Juôc? (Vn. Suối Rúc). Flows S from Túc
Trứng into D. Nhrŭng. Lacking jr, Vn. drops the j.

Daq Con Chôc. Flows SE from 2 km. NE of Gia Tân into D.
Jruc.

Daq Tamô Dar. Small stream from S of Gia Tân flowing E
into D. Jruc.

(Vn. Suối Gur). From E of Gia Kiệm, flows N into D.
Nhrŭng. No Chrau name was obtained, but Gur is very likely
the Chrau name, as its form is neither Vn. nor French.

Daq Nlu Ndu, Daq Vôq Ndu (Vn. Suối Lou). From SE of Túc
Trứng, flows SE into D. N'hap paralleling the road. Lou is
a French spelling of Lu.

Daq Khlong, Daq Vôq Khlong (Vn. Suối Son). Flows E from
Gŭng Padôc into D. N'hap. ng is written as n in southern
Vn.; s is not so readily derivable from khl without assuming
that the transcriber wasn't paying very close attention. In
terms of historical language shifts khl →s would not be
surprising, but in terms of contemporary Chrau and Vietnamese
it is surprising.

Daq Jui, Daq Jui Vĭh Chŏh (Vn. Suối Dui). Flows E from
Gŭng Padôc into D. Nlê. vĭh chŏh 'snake bite' may commemo-
rate an encounter with a snake. j →d.

Daq Klăn (Vn. Suối Tràn). Flows E from Gŭng Klăn into D.
Nlê. Tràn is probably a printing error for Trăn. klăn,
trăn 'python'.

Daq Ndi. Unidentified, flows into D. Nlê above D. Njau.

Daq Njau, Njrao (Vn. Suối 30, Suối Bưng). From Gŭng Klăn,
flows N into D. Nlê. No apparent connection between any of
the names.

Daq Mlu. Unidentified, a small tributary of D. Njau.

Daq Chanding, Đinh, Daq Candeng. From Gŭng Paglơ? Tanlô
Viseng?, flows NW into D. Nlê.

Daq Chan'ha. Unidentified, above D. Nwa, flows into D.
Nlê.

Daq Nwa (Vn. Suối La-wa). From Tanlô Tamcoi near Gŭng
Paglơ (3 km. W of Núi Trần), from WNW into D. Nlê. n → l.

Daq Con Krang. Flows SW into D. Nwa.

Daq Gadayh (Vn. Suối Rách, Suối Cha Rung). Flows N from
Ấp Đồng Xoài (W of Túc Trưng), then W into D. Nlê. There
may possibly be a connection between dayh 'break' and rách
'rip'; otherwise all the names seem unconnected.

Daq Tamô (Vn. Suối Đá). Flows W from Gŭng Padôc into
D. Gadayh. tamô, đá 'stone'.

Daq Tiêq (Vn. Suối Tịa). Flows NW from the Túc Trưng
rubber processing plant into D. Tamô. Northern Vn. has glot-
talization in its nặng tone, making it a natural equivalent
for Chrau q; there are some northern Vietnamese in the area,
though Túc Trưng is mainly southern.

Daq Coq (Vn. Suối Cò, Suối Đốt). From 3 km. NW of Gŭng
Padôc, flows SW into D. Gadayh. coq, cò 'cattle egret'.

Daq Ndru (Vn. Suối Cha Rung, Suối Đá). From 4 km. NW of
Gŭng Padoc, flows W into D. Gadayh. There seems to be some
confusion in both the Chrau and Vietnamese names, with Ndru
also being applied to D. Tamô, and Cha Rung also being applied
to D. Gadayh and D. Padang.

Daq Vumdan. Flows S into D. Ndru, joining it near the
confluence with D. Gadayh.

Daq Hơp (Vn. Suối Con). Flows S into D. Ndru above D.
Vumdan.

Daq Unghiên. Flows S into D. Ndru above D. Hơp.

Daq Mongcaq. Flows N into D. Ndru above D. Unghiên.

Daq Padang, Daq Vôl Dang (Vn. Suối Chà Rang). From 3 km. W of Gŭng Klăn, flows WNW; then SW into D. Gadayh. Vôl Dang (vôl 'source') is probably the original Chrau name, with vôl shortened to a presyllable va- and then subjected to the p/v presyllable neutralization. If the Vn. name is actually connected to the Chrau, d became r, which is unusual. (Is the name Vumdan also confused with Padang?)

Daq Calê. A tributary of D. Padang, rising 1 km. N of it and flowing W into it.

Daq Ravum (Vn. Suối Con). A small unidentified tributary near the source of D. Gadayh, flowing into it from the S.

Daq Rao Ndu, Daq Gao Ndru. A small unidentified tributary of D. Gadayh, flowing into it from the N below D. Ravum. rao ndu 'wash people'. The g of gao may reflect the velar pronunciation of r around Túc Trưng.

Daq Glao (Vn. Suối Nứa). A small unidentified tributary of D. Gadayh, flowing into it from the S below D. Rao Ndu. glao, nứa 'large bamboo'.

Daq Chaq. Unidentified, probably a tributary of D. Ndru or D. Gadayh. chaq 'demon'.

Daq Sat (Vn. Suối Phèn). Unidentified, near Túc Trưng. sat 'sour'.

Daq Ranơm (Vn. Suối Bến Nôm). From W of Gia Kiệm, flows NW into D. Nlê. bến 'dock' is substituted for the presyllable, probably because its confluence with D. Nlê is a settled area. The ơ →ô shift is unexplained.

Daq Glao, Daq Canach (Vn. Suối Rừng, Suối Tăm Rong). From S of Gŭng Vam Vlôr, flows W into D. Ranơm in Palây Canach. glao 'large bamboo', canach 'puddle'.

Daq Palдôp. From E of Gŭng Vam Vlôr, flows NW, then SW into D. Glao.

Daq Jakim (Vn. Suối Gia Kiệm). From 3 km. NW of Gŭng Sindôc, flows N into D. Ranơm. ja- →gia is a close

phonological equivalence. Some southern Vn. dialects don't distinguish i from iê.

Daq Camvôq (Vn. Suối Con). Unidentified. camvôq 'head'.

Daq Nggang. Unidentified.

Daq Tanlô Pŭng. Unidentified. pŭng 'stomach'.

Daq Tanlô Nggŭc. Unidentified. nggŭc 'large snail'.

Daq Japhâng. Unidentified.

Daq Gachưr. Unidentified.

Daq Nsôm (Vn.Suối Bào Voi). Unidentified, probably near
Bến Nôm, in Palây Nsôm.

Daq Swai (Vn. Suối Đồng Xoài). Unidentified, possibly the
stream rising in Palây Swai (Vn. Gia Tân) and flowing NW into
D. Ranờm.

Daq Sâng (Vn. Suối Sâng). Unidentified.

Daq Talêi (Vn. Suối Ta Lê). Unidentified.

Daq Jêng Ba (Vn. Suối Giêng Ba). Unidentified. Possibly
the Chrau is derived from the Vn., as the Vn. has meaning
('third well') while the Chrau does not.

Daq Uq (Vn. Suối Sét). Unidentified. uq, sét 'clay'.

Daq Nho (Vn. Suối Nho). Unidentified.

Daq Ya (Vn. Suối Tranh). Unidentified. ya, tranh 'thatch'.

Daq Sikiêq (Vn. Suối Đất). Unidentified. sikiêq, đất
'earth'.

Daq Ca Ba (Vn. Suối Ca Ba). Unidentified.

Daq Lawe. Unidentified.

Daq Thăng (Vn. Suối Thăng). Unidentified.

Daq Laweng (Vn. Suối Xăng Quen). Unidentified. la →
xăng is unexplained; quen in many southern dialects of Vn.
is [weŋ].

Daq Ti Ca-ưp. Unidentified. ti 'hand', ca-ưp 'centipede'.

Daq Đŭh Jun. Unidentified. đŭh 'shove', jun 'deer'.

Daq Tanlô Meo (Vn. Suối Bàu Mèo). meo, mèo 'cat'.

PONDS AND PADDY AREAS

Mơ Trao. Paddy area S of Gŭng Sipiq, between the sources
of Daq Ramvăch Mê and D. Ramvăch Ntu.

Mơ Canduôr Mê. Paddy area between D. Canduôr Mê and the
source of Daq Ramvăch Mê, SW of Gŭng Sipiq.

Mơ Camvung. Paddy area between Daq Canduôr and D. Lawa,
2 km. S of D. Nlê. camvung 'muzzle'.

Tamăn Sikêch. Cleared area just E of the Canduôr-Nlê confluence.

Mơ Lawa. Large paddy area extending W from the lower part
of Daq Lawa.

Mơ Sat. Paddy area near Daq N'hap, 3 km. E of Mơ Canduôr
Mê. sat 'sour'.

Mơ Jri. Paddy area just W of Daq N'hap, 1 km. SW of Mơ
Sat. jri 'banyan'.

Tamăn Swai (Vn. Ruộng Đồng Xoài). Large paddy area SE of
Gia Tân. Named for Palây Swai on the other side of Highway 20.

Tamăn Con Chôc (Vn. Ruộng Chót). Large paddy area NW of
Gia Tân. Southern Vn. t [k] is equivalent to Chrau c.

Tanlô Viseng (Vn. Bàu Trưng). Pond between Gŭng Nwa and
Daq Nlê, 5 km. NW of Gŭng Klăn. Source of Daq Chanding?

Tanlô Tamcoi. Small pond near Gŭng Paglơ, source of Daq
Nwa.

Tamăn Joi. Large marshy area S of Daq Nwa.

Tamăn (Mơ) Cavêl. Unidentified.

Tamăn Trai (Vn. Ruộng Bàu Voi). Unidentified.

Tamăn Bu Đông (Vn. Ruộng Bù Đồn). Unidentified. The name could have been originally either Vn. or Chrau, but initial b is so rare in native Chrau words that I suspect a Vn. original here.

Tamăn Uây (Vn. Ruộng Lớn). uây, lớn 'large'.

Tanlô Tŭng (Vn. Bào Tung). Unidentified.

Tanlô Rach (Vn. Bào Dòi). Unidentified.

Tanlô Vôq Rawĕh (Vn. Bào Voi). Associated with Tamăn Trai? rawĕh, voi 'elephant'.

Tanlô Gachửr. Unidentified. The source of Daq Gachửr?

Tanlô Pŭng. Unidentified. The source of Daq Tanlô Pŭng?

Tanlô Nggŭc. Unidentified. The source of Daq Nggŭc?

Tanlô Japhâng. Unidentified. The source of Daq Japhâng?

Tanlô Jakim (Vn. Bao Gia Kiệm). Unidentified. The source of Daq Jakim (Vn. Gia Kiệm)?

Tanlô Ranơm (Vn. Bào Bến Nôm). Unidentified. The source of Daq Ranơm?

Tanlô Rông Gavơ. Unidentified.

Tanlô Ca (Vn. Bàu Cá). Near Bàu Cá. ca, cá 'fish'.

CONCLUDING REMARKS

A few observations may be drawn from the foregoing. A number of streams are called Suối Con 'small stream' or Suối Cát 'sand stream' in Vietnamese. Most of these nonspecific names will probably disappear as more careful naming and map-making progresses (perhaps with the official adoption of some of the Chrau names?).

A Vn. form that appears in many names is gia. In some cases it can be most simply derived from a ja presyllable, as in Jakim →Gia Kiệm, Jacắp →Gia Cấp. Less certain are proposed derivations from a ca or other presyllable, as in Cawêng →Gia Huynh, Calêu →Gia Lêu, Ca-ĭt →Gia Ích, Chaloq →Gia Ló, Sikwêch →Gia Quếch, Nhrung →Gia Rung; these have Chrau palatal or velar initials which could conceivably give rise to Vn. gia. In other cases, there is no presyllable at all from which to derive gia, as in Daq Rây → Suối Gia Ray and Daq Gũng →Suối Gia Gung; these possibly reflect a Cham ia 'water, river' (as in the first syllable of Nha Trang), which might have resulted from the early use of Cham guides or interpreters by Vietnamese in the Chrau area. Chrau daq →Vn. da →gia is also possible, but final q usually leaves a Vn. high tone. Other cases are unclear, as in Glao →Gia Lao, Conghwây →Gia Ôi, Glao Măng →Gia Măng, and Ndêt →Gia Hoét. It is significant that all names with Gia are of rivers, so that theories based on daq or ia account for all occurrences of gia, while the presyllable theory accounts (neatly) for only half. It is possible that all three factors were at work.

Considerable confusion is evident in the Vn. names transcribed as Bầu, Bàu, or Bao. Most of these names had been filtered through Chrau, French, or English speaking sources in oral or written form. The neutralization of the distinction between huyền and nang tones is characteristic of all three of these languages, and in some dialects of Vietnamese the distinction between bau and bâu is lost (cf. Hòa's dictionary). Further, the distinction between au and ao is weak in some Vn. dialects, and is totally lost on most French or English speakers. It is, therefore, probable that most of these Vn. names became corrupted in oral or written transmission from original bàu 'pond'.

Presyllables in Chrau tend to be short, open syllables
with low pitch. Vn. does not permit short, open syllables,
but does tend to retain the openness of such a syllable and low
pitch as a huyền tone: Tamŭm → Cà Mum, Jrang → Chà Rang,
Gavô → Trà Vô, Cabŏh → Tầm Bố, Simônh → Xà Môn, Tambung →
Tầm Bung, Padang → Chà Rang, and Vajiêng → Bà Giêng. Bà Rịa
could fit this pattern too.

Presyllable consonants in Chrau are often variable, as in
Tamŭm~Dimŭm~Camŭm, Cacat~Tacat, Dajao~Tijao, Tajô~Dijô, Caqwĕq~
Paqwĕq, so it is quite possible that the first syllable of
some Vn. names may have been derived from presyllable consonants other than those recorded here.

Final q (glottal stop) tends to be reflected in Vn. as a
high, rising (sắc) tone, as in Chaloq → Gia Ló, Dung Moq →
Giả Mó, Vôq Twaq → Thanh Tóa; but it is not totally consistent, as in Vluq → Lúp, Lút, and Sipiq → Sa Bi. The
rendering of final h varies, giving a mid tone in Nah Tung
Na Tung, sắc tone in Cabŏh → Tầm Bố, and hỏi tone in Tajăh →
Binh Giả.

Other sound shifts include r → n, as in Char → Chan,
Sigor → Sài Gòn; and j → d, gi as in Jui → Dui, Dijao →
Thời Giao, Vajiêng → Bà Giêng, Nji → Di, Pajăl → Cây Da,
Jŭm → Dình, Jêng Ba → Giêng Ba, Tajăh → Bình Giả, Jakim →
Gia Kiệm. Other sound shifts could be adduced, but these
seem to be the most significant ones.

NOTES

[1]This paper is based upon data gathered by the author while
residing in the Chrau area from 1959 to 1973. I am indebted
to many Chrau friends who were anxious to help preserve the
memory of the Chrau names for these geographical features.
Printed maps were also consulted.

[2]Forms in parentheses are usually alternate Chrau forms
unless preceded by 'Vn.' to indicate that they represent the
corresponding Vietnamese term.

REFERENCES

Bourotte, Bernard. 1955. "Essai d'Histoire des Populations
   Montagnards du Sud Indochinoises Jusqu'à 1945." *BSEI* 30:
   1-133.

Hòa, Nguyêh Dình. 1966. *Vietnamese-English Dictionary*.
   Rutland: Tuttle.

Thomas, David. 1971. *Chrau Grammar*. Honolulu: University
   of Hawaii Press.

SIL MUSEUM OF ANTHROPOLOGY PUBLICATIONS

1. Kelley, Patricia and Carolyn Orr. *Sarayacu Quichua Pottery*, 1976. (Also available in Spanish as *Cerámica Quichua de Sarayacu*.).......................$ 3.00

2. Mayers, Marvin K. *A Look at Latin American Lifestyles*, 1976..........$ 3.75

3. Neuenswander, Helen and Dean Arnold (eds.). *Cognitive Studies of Southern Mesoamerica*, 1977. (Also available in Spanish as *Estudios Cognitivos del Sur de Mesoamérica*.) $10.95

4. Branks, Judith and Juan Bautista Sánchez. *The Drama of Life: Guambiano Life Cycle Customs*, 1978...$ 5.00

5. Chenoweth, Vida. *The Usarufas and their Music*, 1979. ....$14.90

6. Gregerson, Marilyn and Dorothy Thomas (eds.). *Notes from Indochina: on ethnic minority cultures*, 1980.

TO APPEAR

Koop, Gordon and Sherwood G. Lingenfelter. *The Deni of Western Brazil: A Study of Socio-Political Organization and Community Development.* (Also available in Portuguese as *Os Dení do Brasil Ocidental—Um Estudo de Organização Sọcio-Política e Desenvolvimento Comunitário.*)

Mayers, Marvin K. *A Look at Filipino Lifestyles.*

Eakin, Lucille. *Nuevo Destino: The Life Story of a Shipibo Bilingual Educator.*

Powlison, Paul. *Epic Tendencies in a New World Mythology.*

Thomas, Dorothy M. and Carol Hinkle (eds.). *Tales from Indochina.*

Eakin, Lucille, Erwin Lauriault and Harry Boonstra. *An Ethnographic Sketch of the Shipibo-Conibo.*

These titles are available at

The SIL Museum of Anthropology
7500 W. Camp Wisdom Road
Dallas, TX   75236   U.S.A.

Residents of Texas add 5% Sales Tax.